Ned Wilson, as a young pilot in 1942.

FOR PILOTS' EYES ONLY

Confessions of a Pan Am Veteran

Ned Wilson

Paladwr Press

This book is dedicated to my children Kenneth, Alice, Scott, Nancy, and Joanne, who tolerated the sometimes unsettled life that resulted from my absence during much of the time when they were growing up.

Published 1993 by Paladwr Press,
1906 Wilson Lane, Apt. 101, McLean, Virginia
22102-1957

Manufactured in Hong Kong

Maps by R.E.G. Davies
Cartoons by Jerry Daly

Edited by R.E.G. Davies and John Wegg

Typesetting/Layout by Spot Color

Pre-press Production by The Drawing Board

ISBN 0-9626483-4-5

Second Printing 1996

Contents

Maps

by R.E.G. Davies

Cartoons

by Jerry Daly

Foreword

by John Wegg

I have read many biographies and autobiographies of and by airline pilots, from unashamed self-conferred heroics to turgid tales of non-events. Ned Wilson's book does not fall into either of these extreme categories. It is, as the shrewdly-chosen Mark Twain quotation that opens the book suggests, the unashamed story, warts and all, of a consummate aviator who thoroughly enjoyed his work for Pan American Airways, and retains his love of flying, with or without engines, in his retirement.

Ned started with DC-3s in Central America and Venezuela and finished flying jets flying around the world. He tells us what it was like to fly the Douglas, Boeing, Convair, and Lockheed piston-engined thoroughbreds which are now mostly museum pieces, and his beloved Old Man's Cadillac—the Boeing 747.

He tells us of his brushes with bureaucracy, and gives us his opinions of some of the regulations which have not met with his approval. He gives us an insight as to the personalities of his fellow crew members, characters who ranged from the deceptively casual, such as the pilot who navigated with a 'cigar-computer,' to those whose adherence to The Book was sometimes itself a hazard. He had much time for the ground crews who supported him, especially those in the Latin American countries where conditions were often less than ideal; but had little time for the prima donnas, either on the flight deck or in the passenger cabin.

One common element throughout the book is Ned's sense of humor that ranges from cynical commentaries on human foibles to racy anecdotes that never appeared in official debriefings. He tells stories against himself, revealing a characteristic confined to true humorists, and in pleasant contrast with that of his colleagues, some of whom apparently could do no wrong.

Above all, *For Pilots' Eyes Only*, is written in an easy, almost conversational, style, drawing on memories of the good things, tolerating the bad, and recalling the funny side of flying. Ned Wilson has produced a work that reflects the life of an airline pilot in a manner that carries the stamp of authenticity as well as the mark of authority born of experience. In so doing, he has concocted a treat for the reader, and made another valuable contribution to the annals of commercial aviation and of the late, great, Pan American Airways.

Ned Wilson, aged six, at the Wilson Ranch, with Ranger the pony, and Fluffy the dog.

Preface

"If I have seemed to love my subject it is no surprising thing, for I loved the profession far better than any I have followed since, and I took measureless pride in it. The reason is plain: A pilot, in those days, was the only unfettered and entirely independent human being that lived on the face of the earth."

Mark Twain

This book is intended to be one man's story of an airline career.

Most airline flights are routine and the job of an airline pilot is to ensure that the routine is maintained. This book, on the other hand, will relate some of the non-routine events that have stood out in my mind over the years. Some were exciting, some were humorous, all of them were memorable. I never kept a diary, nor other record, so this is written from memory, except for a few events that I can reconstruct from my logbooks. Some of the stories told may be remembered differently by other participants, but this will be an honest report as far as my memory serves.

I can hardly remember a time that I did not want to fly. Raised on a hardscrabble ranch in West Texas, I used to watch the occasional airplane pass over and wish that I could be up there in it. My older brother, John, was an oil well driller and when he and some other drillers bought a yellow Piper Cub, I thought that airplane in flight was the most beautiful thing I had ever seen. I still think that there is no prettier sight than one of those machines in a landing pattern. It was a J-2 Cub, but in later years my brother always said that he had learned to fly in a J-1 Cub. The only trouble with that is that Piper never produced a J-1.

Though my flying career started in 1939, and I had more than 39 years with Pan Am, I have never tired of flying and today, when I ride with some airline, I do so with my head 'hanging out the window'. I never tire of watching the earth go by below with its varied and always beautiful patterns.

I had thought I might call this book, 'All the Best of It', because I think that my flying years were at the heart of commercial aviation's formative years. Before the Piper Cub, and the classic Douglas DC-3 airliner, airplanes were not totally reliable; and after the Boeing 747 they would not be 'flown' by pilots, but rather be machines to be 'managed', electronically.

I have always enjoyed flying the airplanes, and still do. Even with the arrival of auto-pilots that could land a 747 without my help, I never liked to let them do it. I felt robbed of something that I wanted to do. Every flight, every take off, every landing, is a challenge; and there is always the desire to see how well it can be done.

Don't expect to read very many life-or-death sensational stories here, but if you wish to have an insight into what it was like to be an airline pilot and to share his day-to-day events, please read on. Some opinions expressed will be on such aspects as Air Traffic Control, flight physicals, approach minimums, and perhaps even a few on the proper way to fly an airplane. Please remember that these are my personal opinions, formed over many years of airline service.

I flew with many friends from whom I learned and who perhaps aided me in forming my opinions. I wish that I could name them all. Fred Knotts, Roger Sherron, Sam Enfield, Bill Saulsberry, H.B. 'Mutt' Fleming, 'Mike' Carmichael, Ed Swenson, Bill Monan, Ralph Wanless, Don Eno, and W.G. Stovall are a few who come most readily to mind. There were one or two with whom I would just as soon not have flown for one reason or another. Maybe I shall tell a few of those stories here, too.

Fasten your seat belts, and prepare for take off.

Acknowledgements

In compiling the stories told here I relied upon many fellow pilots who were kind enough to help my memory along at times, though I take full responsibility for errors or misrepresentations of any kind.

My most sincere thanks to R.E.G. Davies, who accepted the enormous challenge of editing my writings to make them presentable. Mr. Walter J. Boyne, author of excellent books about aviation, first gave me enough encouragement to make me continue the effort to see this in print.

Thanks also to many friends who reviewed parts of my manuscript and offered valuable advice. Kay Edwards of "The Write Stuff" did much typing and putting the edited version on computer disks. My wife Dolle was also a good proof-reader. Jennifer Sterling, of Spot Color, did the page composition and design, which included the selection of photographs, Jerry Daly's cartoons and Ron Davies's maps.

Your License Will Be in the Mail

In the fall of 1939 I was a student at the College of Mines and Metallurgy (now The University of Texas at El Paso). I was studying mining and mechanical engineering when I heard that there was to be a flying course. This program was called Civilian Pilot Training and was to be offered only to senior and junior classes. I applied, immediately, only to be told, of course, that I did not qualify because I was only in my second semester. The class had to have an even multiple of ten students with a maximum of thirty because there were to be three airplanes, and each could accommodate a class of ten students under one flight instructor.

At first the college received only about twenty applicants, and agreed to accept sophomore class members. With that they managed to reach twenty-nine. I had not stopped asking every day or so if I could join the class and finally they simply said, "You are number thirty." Persistence paid off.

Physical Palpitations

Now for the first hurdle—the flight physical. We were all sent to a C.A.A. medical examiner. I had to wait in the office while all the others went in and out, commenting on how tough the examination was. I heard how hard this doctor was on the eyes, the ears, the heart, etc. When my turn came, I was so nervous that my pulse rate was way up, and he would not pass me. But he suggested that I go home and come back the next day. The next day I either passed or he understood the reason for the high pulse rate and let me by.

This was a pattern to be repeated time and time again over the years. So often the doctor would say, "Lay there and relax, I'll be back in a few minutes." Knowing what the problem was made it hard to relax, but over the years most doctors understood and I kept on making the grade. My hiring physical with Pan Am was a case in point. After going through this routine a couple of times, the doctor finally said to me, "Well, stand up." His tone made me think that I had failed, so I was standing there thinking where I was going next to look for a job. He gave me a strange look and asked if I had just decided that he was not going to pass me. I said, "Yes, something like that." He said that my heart rate, which should have gone up when I stood, had, instead, gone down. Next he looked into my ears, telling me that he was looking for my brain. But he said not to worry, that because I was a pilot applicant it did not disqualify me if he couldn't find one! With or without a brain, he passed me. One doctor used to tell me that it would help if I had come in about half drunk! Alcohol should raise the rate, but he said that in my case it would probably relax me enough to help.

It is my belief that flight physicals, which cost the industry millions of dollars, have added little to the safety of flight. Doctors cannot forecast what will happen. There is at least one case on record of a pilot having just passed a physical with flying colors and dying in the doctor's office before he could put his clothes on.

Pilots with valid and current physicals have died during flight. In the airline world this has seldom caused a problem and the other crew members can handle the situation very easily.

Many of the examination techniques have been proved wrong. We used to have to line up two little sticks from about twenty feet away by pulling on strings. This was a check for depth perception, but it was later demonstrated that depth perception is of little use in landing airplanes and the test was discontinued. How many eager young pilots were lost to aviation before doctors realized that this test was invalid?

I doubt if safety would have been compromised to any degree if flight physicals consisted of about the same elements that are standard for driving licenses; eyes, hearing, etc. After all, between physicals, the pilot is made responsible for not flying if there is any health reason for not doing so.

Though I think physicals should be handled differently there have been many fine doctors who practiced preventative medicine and who worked to keep pilots flying. Dr Leeds, a Pan American doctor for many years, was one of these. I always preferred to go to examiners who were pilots themselves because I thought they understood the problems.

Bent Wire Gas Gauge

My flight training started on December 13, 1939. Was that a Friday? I don't know, but I have always considered 13 to be a lucky number. Like many others I had thought that flying would require fast reactions and events would seem as though they were happening very quickly. Not so. It all seemed to me to be very calm and even slow. I was fascinated by the Piper J-3 Cub. I liked the look of the gas gauge which was a simple piece of wire coming out through the top of the gas cap. It had a little bent-over end and was right in front of the windshield and could be used to help judge the angle of bank. A primitive but effective flight instrument.

The only other time I had been airborne was several years earlier when my Dad and I were in his old pick-up truck driving into the little oil boom town of Pyote, Texas. Just across from the railroad cattle pens, on a clear place in the mesquite and creosote brush where we often held cattle herds, was an airplane. My Dad arranged for me to take a ride. I was promptly and irrevocably hooked, and decided then and there that this was what I wanted to do for a career. That exact place was later to be the site of Rattlesnake Air Force Base, the home of Boeing B-29s. More than half-century later I learned that the pilot of that airplane was Jim Witt, who had punched cattle with my Dad. The year was 1936 and the airplane was a Travel Air, (registered N4322), a biplane with a water-cooled engine. Mr Witt told me—fifty years later—that the old engine was worn out at the time of that flight, and the airplane had been abandoned soon after that in some farmer's barn near Barstow, Texas. Yes, I looked for it.

Almost every pilot thinks his first instructor was the best, and I am no exception. Lavelle ('Val') S. Neher (License Number 35386) was only a year

A Travel Air 2000 biplane (4322), with water-cooled OX-5 engine, 1936. Travel Air of Wichita, Kansas, was formed in 1925 by Walter Innes Jr, Lloyd Stearman, Walter Beech, and Clyde V. Cessna, and built hundreds of Curtiss OX-powered Travel Airs.

or so older than I was. He was a pleasant, smiling guy, and in my minds eye I can still see his grin as I landed beside him on the day he let me solo, January 20, 1940. Maybe his smile was one of relief that I had made it safely around the field.

Early Tailspins

Today, many pilots, even flight instructors, have never spun an aircraft. We had to do that before we could solo, and I show only three hours in my log when I executed my first spin. Val was a big guy and in our J-3 he sat in front while the student flew from the rear seat. With only fifty horses up front and a field elevation of four thousand feet, any pilot can tell you that there was no excess of performance. We would take off and climb, with me trying to peek around his shoulders for a glimpse of the few instruments there were, until we were high enough to do a two-turn spin to the left and another two turns to the right. Then our time was up and we had to land.

I am glad that I learned to fly an under-powered airplane under such conditions. It taught me to feel the airplane, and not to depend on the engine to get out of trouble. The only better way is to learn to fly in a glider.

The Cubs we flew had swivel tail wheels but no brakes, a bad combination that made them hard to handle on the ground. Many years later, while telephoning Val and his wife, Sara, I mentioned that I was then flying Boeing 747s and she asked me if someone had to hold them by the wing tip to help turn them around in a high wind, something she had done many times for us, with our J-3 Cubs, at El Paso.

By the time I was ready to solo I became very impatient and after every landing I would look at Val's back and mutter under my breath, "Get out, get out!" When he did, I remember particularly the sudden expanse of space in front of me, with the control stick in the front seat (which I had never seen before) moving around as if on its own; and instruments that I had seldom seen before in flight.

A few days after this I was allowed to shoot landings by myself. We were using a pattern altitude of four hundred feet and I noticed that if I climbed much above that things begin to disappear, like the ground! I would ease back down and go ahead with my landings. I was flying with about a four hundred-foot cloud ceiling, which in those days was near the minimum for airline approaches.

I had several instructors before I finished this course; Robert French gave me more time than the rest. On May 23, 1940, I was ready for my check ride for a Private Pilot's License. The C.A.A. examiner who showed up was

(Left) Ned Wilson (on left) as a student pilot, with instructor Bob French, in 1940. (Right) Albert Meyers, tough flight inspector, who gave Ned Wilson his private pilot's flight examination and both his commercial and instructor's ratings.

Mr Albert Meyers. He had been there a month before to check the first ten students and had ridden with five of them and busted all five. The school withdrew the others. This time, I was to be the first. Nervous? You bet I was.

As we taxied out I looked at the back of his head with a flat top haircut, and watched him roll his own cigarette. Would the airplane burn up? Of course not, it wouldn't dare. He explained that he would not go up with me until he had seen two spins and watched me land three times. He got out and gave me instructions to take off and climb to three thousand feet; then, facing him, do a two-turn spin to the left and two turns to the right. Then I was to land beside him three times, making power-off approaches. If I touched down before I reached him I failed. Equally, if I landed more than two hundred feet beyond him, I had gone too far, and also failed.

The spins were no problem but I thought the landings were all a little too long. When I taxied up to him he asked me what I thought of the landings and I told him they were probably too long. He said, "Well, as long as you know." He climbed in with me and we went up together for the rest of the check. I do not remember it all, but he was known to be death on forced landings and gave me several. On one I saw only one place to go, where the city was leveling a site for a park. I did not even consider the wind. As we approached the ground he added power and asked why I came in down-wind. I knew I had to say something plausible, so I said, "Well, the only other choice I had was very short and I thought I had more relative distance here even if it was down-wind." I hadn't even seen any other place to land, but he accepted my explanation.

We landed and still he had not given me even a hint as to whether I had passed or not. In the office he gathered up the next candidate and as they started to the airplane he finally turned to me and said in the sweetest words I could have heard, "Your license will be in the mail." It was four days after my 19th birthday.

Red Fingernails

Now what does a pilot do as soon as he obtains a license? Carry a passenger, of course! My first one was a little blond girl from school. Her name? I don't have the foggiest recollection. I needed a passenger and she had enough nerve to go. All I remember is that she sat up front and never let go of the brace bars that formed a vee behind the windshield. I would not have been a bit surprised to see them squeezed down to the size of matchsticks. She had long, painted fingernails, and when we got out I was afraid she would bleed from where those nails had cut into her palms.

One of the early flights was to take my Dad to Sundown, Texas, where my brother was working as an oil well driller. We left Pecos, Texas, in a J-5 Cub, borrowed from Emmett Capps, on a nice morning flight. We had not gone far when little puffy white clouds began to form under us. I was soon afraid that we might be caught on top of those clouds. The airplane had no gauges for instrument flying and I would not have known how to use them if there were any, so I found a hole and descended below the clouds. It was only my Dad's second time in an airplane, the first having been when my instructor gave him a ride over the cattle stock pens in El Paso.

I did not wish to frighten him but found that to stay under the clouds I had to fly very low, just over the tops of the telephone wires along the road. We went along this way until we arrived at Hobbs, New Mexico, where I planned to refuel. When the weather improved we went on to Sundown and landed in a pasture where brother John was standing, pointing in the direction to land, there being no airport at Sundown. When we stopped I was horrified to find that the whole field was full of prairie dog holes, some big enough to flip us over if we had caught a wheel in them. John asked Dad how he liked the flight and he said that it was pretty dull at first, "But when Ned got down where I could see the pastures and the cattle, it was all right!"

The next morning we decided that my brother and his son, J.V., would go back with me and Dad would drive the car. We stuck sticks in the worst of the holes so that we could see to avoid them, and off we went.

A Pocket Full of Throttle

The J-5 was a three-place airplane with the pilot in front and a bench seat in the back for either one or two occupants. On the way we thought we should let John fly for a while so we worked out a way to maneuver him into the front seat. With about six inches room on each side of my seat, I was to go back on the left side while John would come forward on the right. J.V. would move over in the back from left to right. On cue we all started moving. As I started back I caught the throttle, located on the left side wall, with my pants pocket and at the same time J.V. pushed the rear stick over as he moved across. So there we were, three thousand feet in the air with the airplane on its right side and none of us with our seat belts on.

It was not as bad as it sounds. One of us reached the control stick and righted the airplane, I extracted the throttle out of my pocket, pushed it forward to regain engine power, and everything returned to normal.

After a while we reversed the process, but far more care-fully, and we went on to Pecos. I do not think we ever told Emmett Capps that story.

In the fall we started another 'Secondary' course. This one used a Waco UPF-7, a biplane with a radial engine. What more could this country boy ask? Real flying, open cockpits, wind humming in the flying wires, the sound and smell of a big radial engine, helmet and goggles (furnished by Martin Flying Service—one size fits all), lacking only a white silk scarf. And we learned to do rolls, loops, stalls, Immelmann turns, chandelles and maybe even invent a thing or two of our own.

This was only if Herbert Haas (License Number 6067), the instructor, was not along. It was said that he had learned to fly in World War I, and it certainly could have been true. The communication system, if it could be called that, consisted of a funnel into which he talked and the sound went into a rubber tube which ended in our ears. It was known as a 'Gosport'. There must have been a filter of some kind in that tube because it never seemed to transmit any kind words. Most of what came through was critical of my flying and sometimes of my ancestry as well.

Mr Haas possessed a quality that I later perceived in others: a change of personality when in the air. He could have nothing good to say during flight, but once on the ground, he would put his arm around your shoulders and tell you how good you were and suggest we have coffee together. He allowed me to fly solo in the Waco on my second flight. Then the next time we flew together he spent the whole time telling me that he doubted I could ever solo in it. After we landed I reminded him that I had already soloed the day before, and he just said, "Well, I guess you can fly solo tomorrow; let's go get coffee." One student came out of the cockpit, ready to start a fight, even before the airplane had come to a stop after landing. Herbert just laughed at him and in a few minutes both were in a good humor.

The hardest part of this course was landing at night. We landed on a dark field with only boundary lights around it, and no runway lights. The Waco had no landing lights. It was rather like feeling your way down a dark hall, wondering when you are going to bump into the door that you know is there somewhere, but where?

My flight check with an examiner was on January 20, 1941. The comments which he made in my logbook were, "Eager to learn", "Cooperative", "Punctual", "Relaxed", "Good control touch", "Good speed sense". I was walking on air!

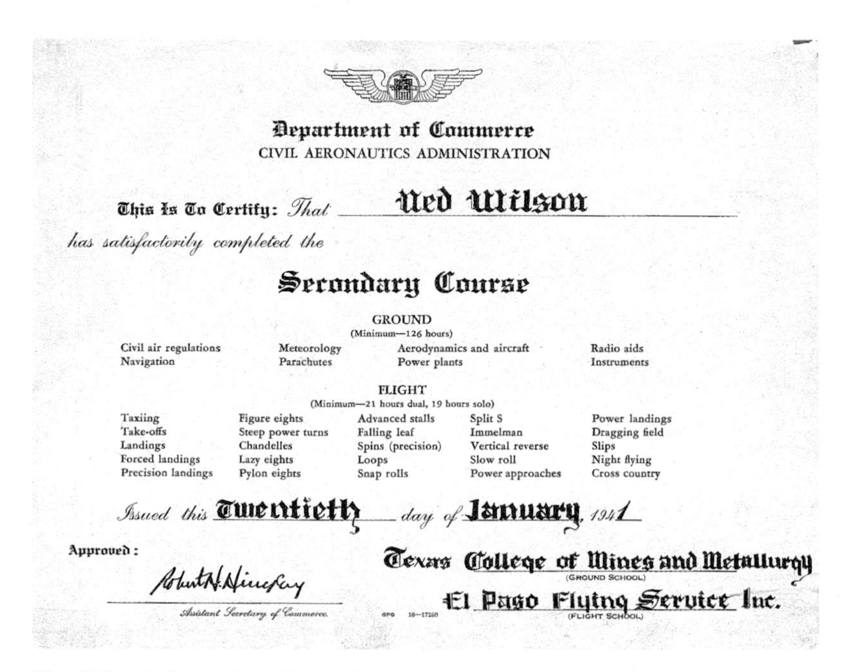

Department of Commerce
CIVIL AERONAUTICS ADMINISTRATION

This Is To Certify: That Ned Wilson
has satisfactorily completed the

Secondary Course

GROUND
(Minimum—126 hours)

Civil air regulations, Navigation, Meteorology, Parachutes, Aerodynamics and aircraft, Power plants, Radio aids, Instruments

FLIGHT
(Minimum—21 hours dual, 19 hours solo)

Taxiing	Figure eights	Advanced stalls	Split S	Power landings
Take-offs	Steep power turns	Falling leaf	Immelman	Dragging field
Landings	Chandelles	Spins (precision)	Vertical reverse	Slips
Forced landings	Lazy eights	Loops	Slow roll	Night flying
Precision landings	Pylon eights	Snap rolls	Power approaches	Cross country

Issued this Twentieth day of January, 1941

Approved:
Robert H. Hinckley
Assistant Secretary of Commerce.

Texas College of Mines and Metallurgy
(GROUND SCHOOL)

El Paso Flying Service Inc.
(FLIGHT SCHOOL)

GPO 16—17260

Ned Wilson's Secondary Course Certificate, for training in a Waco UPF-7 biplane.

Rookie Pilot

Having left college to continue flight training, I took a course at Big Spring Flying Service in February 1941. Called an Apprentice Instructor Course, the intent was to train an assistant instructor who would work under the direction of a fully certificated flight instructor. The whole idea was later abandoned and I never heard of it being used. We flew a Piper J-5 Cub and the work consisted of honing skills in teaching the maneuvers required to obtain a pilot's license.

Big Spring Flying Service was owned and operated by Art Wintheiser. My instructor in this course was J.M. (Robbie) Robinson. The Apprentice Instructor Course was followed by a Cross Country course, flying a Stinson Reliant. The instructor, Bill Edwards, who taught this course, was one of the few pilots whom I considered a real natural. He was a professional from head to toe and should have ended up as a top airline pilot. He did try to go to work for American Air-

Line-up of airplanes at Big Spring Flying Service, Texas, 1942.

lines but failed to pass its physical because he had a history of cancer, which had been removed from one knee. Many years later he died suddenly while flying a twin-engined Cessna from California to Big Spring. One of the passengers, who must have had at least some pilot training, landed the airplane.

Big Spring was subject to the strong and sudden winds which plague West Texas. It was not unusual for a student to be flying solo and to have a 30 or 40mph wind come up. All students had to be taught to land in the lee of the hangar if necessary, or to land on the wheels and keep the tail high into the air so as to keep the airplane from lifting off again, and on the ground, until help could arrive. Those who were not flying were always alert to run out and grab a landing aircraft and walk it to the hangar. Sometimes the wind was too strong for students to fly so the instructors would climb into a Cub, take it off and climb straight ahead, then slow up to less than the speed of the wind. The airplane would then be moving backward over the field. They could lower the nose and land, never having made a turn.

Finally I was assigned to a 'refresher' course with L.C. Jameson as instructor. He was a sheep rancher from the San Angelo area and we went back to the Waco UPF-7, brushing up on aerobatics, among other things. Mostly I flew and L.C. commented. He could say, "Shit!" into the 'Gosport' from the front cockpit and I could smell it in the back.

When Axes Fly

There was a farm house out in the country not too far from the airport. As we flew by a young lady would come out into the yard and wave to us. From about two hundred feet away and traveling at 100mph, she seemed very pretty when out, many of us managed to fly by rather often. Once I made the pilgrimage and found nobody at home. So I decided to go by a little lower, say between the house and the woodpile, just in case she had missed me. As I went by I suddenly discovered that her father certainly was at home. He was chopping wood and threw his axe at me. He could not have been a good bird hunter because he did not lead me enough. I sure would have had a hard time explaining an axe sticking from the fuselage when I landed. If he had been quick enough to hit the prop he might have made a kill.

Thank you Mr Meyers

Exactly two months before Pearl Harbor, on October 7, 1941, I renewed my acquaintance with Mr Albert Meyers, the C.A.A. flight examiner. I flew the Waco UPF-7 for a Commercial License and Flight Instructor Rating. The flight was much more relaxed than I remembered for my Private, though he left nothing out. He finally told me that I had passed and then wanted me to show him some aerobatics. We did a few rolls, loops, Immelmann turns, and he was satisfied.

After we flew he gathered all the students whom he had given certificates to that day and gave us a talk about how we were now professionals and should act and dress accordingly. He was one of the real gentlemen of the aviation scene. Every pilot I ever met who was licensed by Albert Meyers was proud of that fact.

Now that we were real flight instructors, what should we do? Vestus Pruitt, one of the new graduates, was the only one who had a car. Several of us went with him to some places around Fort Worth and Dallas. I know that we went and talked to enlistment officers of both the Army Air Force (USAAF) and the Navy. They would have been happy to have us, but would have started us as beginning students in primary flight instruction. Hey! We had just been qualified to teach that and were not about to start in as students again. Looking back I now understand their viewpoint, but I didn't then. And in my case I was still concerned about the physical. What if I busted it and they put me in the foot army?

We finally decided that the place to go was Coleman, Texas, where there was a contract school teaching Army Air Force Primary, and using civilian instructors. Four of us, Pruitt, John Hollingsworth, I.B. Hartzog, and myself, all piled into Vestus's car and headed for Coleman. After we checked in, we were assigned a flight instructor to show us the airplane they used, a Fairchild PT-19. It was a low-wing, open cockpit ship with an in-line engine. For some reason the other three had the same instructor but I had a different one.

Failed Flight Check

After one or maybe two flights I was assigned to take a check ride with one of two USAAF lieutenants stationed there to check instructors as well as students. I was the first one to be given this check ride. I do not know to this day if I was ready or not, or if they had already decided that I wouldn't do.

He put me in the front seat (the instructor's seat) but reversed the Gosport so that he could talk to me and I could not reply. He said that first he would fly the airplane for a while and that I should remember, in order, all the mistakes he made. When we landed, then I could tell him what they were. I did not think this was very fair. What I did not know was that he was going to fly for so long. He did climbs, turns, eights around a point, pylon eights, chandelles, stalls and on and on for more than half an hour. And I was supposed to remember everything. Then he let me fly for about forty-five minutes, including two landings which he thought were too far into the field.

After we taxied in and got out of the airplane he asked me to start at the beginning and tell him all the mistakes he had made. I should have just recited the mistakes that students could be expected to make. Such things as not holding the right rudder against the torque in the climb, not allowing for wind drift in his eights, poor recovery from stall, and so on. If he had made those errors I would be right and, if not, how could he argue with me?

But I was young, brash, and angry. I looked him in the eye and said, "Lieutenant, I think you flew that airplane as well as you were capable of flying it." Needless to say, that was not what he wanted to hear. I flunked.

I went immediately to the Civilian Flight Director and complained that I thought it was an unfair check. He agreed to ride with me himself at ten o'clock the next morning. If I satisfied him, he said he could persuade one of the military check pilots to ride with me again.

Too Young

At 0900 the next morning there was a general meeting for pilots and there we heard the news that the government had decided that it would not accept as a flight instructor any person who was under twenty-one. I lacked seven months. In all, nine of us were told that we could come back and try again when we were old enough. So I never knew if I could have made the grade or not. That is the only check ride in my entire career that I did not pass. I guess though, in retrospect, they did me a favor. I would probably have stayed there too long, as did others I knew. Some even ended up going into the service and having to start by taking the course that they had been teaching for years. Of the nine of us who left that day, at least one, other than myself, ended up with Pan Am.

Back to the ranch, and what to do? I had already ruled out the services, and the contract schools were not going to accept me until I was twenty-one. Then one day I went to the Pecos airport to fly an old Aeronca C-3 with a friend. While there a fellow came along and said that he and some others were starting an airport in Fort Worth and needed an instructor. A quick trip home to grab a bag, leave a note for my folks, and I was on the way to Fort Worth with him, flying the same J-5 which we had turned upon its side on the Sundown trip. He had bought that very same aircraft.

In Fort Worth I found myself working for Mr T.H. Black, a man about seventy years old. He ran a flying club and operated the airport which was an old farm. They called it the Mid-West Airport, and it has long since gone to developers. When I arrived, they were just grading the runways. We had the Cub and soon added a Taylorcraft and then an Aeronca Chief, which I flew back from Denton, Texas. It was the first airplane that I had flown without a check-out by some other pilot. After leaving Denton I flew for about fifteen minutes holding the wheel hard forward, to keep the nose down, while searching all over the cabin for the trim tab control. I finally found it on the ceiling.

Low Flight for a Farmer

At first there was not much to do and I could usually be found wearing coveralls and helping to convert an old barn to a hangar. Then one day a farmer came by and wanted an airplane ride, the kind that we advertised for $2.00. I shucked off my coveralls and rolled out the Aeronca. In checking it over I noticed that the main gas tank was empty, but I didn't worry about it because there was plenty of fuel for the flight in the auxiliary tank, located up behind the seat. So off we went to make a flight over the city of Fort Worth. I was just about high enough to clear the wires at the end of the field (it's not an airport unless it has wires at the end) when the engine quit. I lowered the nose to keep up flying speed and the engine recovered. Pull the nose up to climb and it would quit, let the nose down and it would start again. "Oh, yeah!", I thought, "The aux tank won't feed in a climb, should only be used in level flight!" Nothing for it but to circle the field very low, don't try to climb and plan to roll up to the gas pumps because the nose was raised on landing it was sure to quit again. I made the gas pumps and got out. The farmer stepped down and reached into his bib overalls to pay me. I tried my best to tell him that if he would only wait a minute for me to put fuel in the main tank that I'd give him a nice long flight over town, or over his farm, or anywhere he wanted to go. He said, "No thanks, I just wanted to be able to say I've been up in an 'airyplane', and I've been up." He insisted on giving me $2.00 and left. Scratch one convert to flying.

Oh, That New Aircraft Smell

One weekend when a rainstorm had left the field very wet, Mr Black decided that he wanted me to fly him to his ranch in the Texas panhandle. We started to take the Aeronca but he thought that if the runway dried up enough, some of the club members might want to fly it. We had five brand new Taylorcrafts out in the hangar, standing on their noses to conserve space. He told me to pick one out and gas it up while he wrote out a check for it and we would go in that. I was impressed. We flew to a point near Higgins, Texas, where we landed in a farmer's field and tied down the

Taylorcraft. That night a very big thunderstorm came up and I worried about that new airplane tied out on the farm. I awoke Mr Black and asked him to drive me out there and I spent the night in it. I tied the control wheels together with my belt to keep the ailerons from banging around, and tried to sleep—without much success. In the morning, when the storm had passed, Mr Black picked me up and we went to breakfast where he gave me an extra $10.00 for my concern about the airplane. My salary at the time was $125.00 per month.

In January I called Art Wintheiser to see if he could use another instructor at Big Spring Flying Service. He was glad I called because he was planning to use one of the students from his latest class but would rather have me because I had some experience. I asked who he was planning to use and he said, "Ray Plunkett." I told him that I would not come because Ray was a friend of mine and I did not wish to cut him out of a job. I already had one and would stay where I was. But Art said that if I would come he would use both of us. On that promise I agreed, and it was back to Big Spring, arriving on January 21.

My log shows that I flew in Fort Worth on the 20th and in Big Spring on the 22nd. On the day in between I drove my old 1936 Ford to Big Spring, burning out the engine on the way near Colorado City. A trucker took pity on me and tied my car behind him with a chain about twenty feet long. He drove about 60mph and my brakes were bad! When we arrived at about two or three in the morning, I was just glad to be alive. I felt safer flying with raw students than being towed behind that truck-driver.

Waco on the Nose

Ray Plunkett and I each had a class of secondary students. One day we were both practicing landings, using Waco UPF-7s, on the same runway. He had landed ahead of me and I told my student to roll past Ray's airplane as we landed. As we turned to taxi back I could see the Waco standing on its nose with gas running out of the tank in the top wing all over that hot engine. I told my student to continue taxiing while I started to take off my seat belt and parachute harness. I jumped out and ran to his airplane, where Ray was trying to wriggle out of his seat. Neither he nor his student was hurt, but it took some doing to extricate the student from the back seat as it was so far up in the air. They had rolled upon some boards covering a big hole intended for future drainage and the boards had caved in. There was no fire but the lower wing spar appeared to be broken. It was bent like a bow. But those Wacos were tough! In the hangar, mechanics cut away the fabric and the spar

A Stinson Reliant (NC18402) of the Big Spring Flying Service. Ned Wilson was flying one of these when a cylinder flew through the cowling.

wasn't even cracked. They recovered the wing and put the aircraft back in service.

How I wish I had been able to buy one of those Waco UPF-7s. They sure were fun to fly. The only thing better than learning to fly in them was instructing in them. They cost about $7,500 new. Today, in good shape will bring about $35,000 to $50,000, or even more.

Bang Goes a Cylinder

I was asked to teach a cross country course using the Stinson Reliant. We took three students at a time; one flew while the other two navigated. They had to prepare flight plans and work out problems in fuel usage, alternate airports, estimated times of arrival, and so on. On May 22, I had such a flight which was supposed to go to San Angelo, Abilene, and return. Between San Angelo and Abilene, we noticed that the engine did not sound right and once in a while it seemed to skip a beat. I decided that I would land at Sweetwater and have it checked. A mechanic ran the engine and found nothing wrong with it. He told me that he thought I had just let the carburetor ice up a little, and assured me that it was fine. So we took off for Big Spring, only about thirty minutes away.

Bang! Bang! Bang! Oil covering the windshield! Something making its way through the cowling in front of my face! The airplane was shaking and clattering all over. I throttled back, but did not shut the engine down because it was putting out a little power. I needed a place to set it down. We had recently experienced an unusually heavy rain and all the cotton fields were flooded. I was afraid that landing in one of them would flip us over on our back. A C.A.A. auxiliary field lay about ten miles ahead, if we could make it. We did, and I landed safely, to find that number nine cylinder had pushed itself off the block and was pounding its way through the cowling in front of me. So much for that mechanic's check. My students and I finished that trip in the back of a farmer's truck.

One other forced landing I had was funny and embarrassing at the same time. We had two J-5 Cubs and one of them had a starter on it. It was a weird arrangement with a handle that could be inserted into a hole on the instrument panel. Turning it would wind up some bungee cords and pushing it forward would release them to turn the prop over. It was a nuisance and we never used it, just throwing the handle into the baggage compartment behind the seats. We had plenty of student power to prop those airplanes. I was teaching stalls one day, when the engine quit and the prop stopped. We tried diving to make the airstream turn the prop over, but it wouldn't do it, so we landed in a cotton field. The student got out and hand-propped the engine and we came back home. When I explained what had happened, I was asked, "Why didn't you use the starter?" We had been flying the one with the starter and never even thought of it.

Parker Pen Time

My last class in Big Spring was a special one for pilots who already had some flying time and whom we were supposed to turn into flight instructors. Most of my students were considerably older than I was, and were required to have 130 hours when they started the course. When they finished, the C.A.A. came by to check them. All passed except one fellow, to whom the examiner said he would give a Commercial License but not an Instructor rating. But later in the day he asked that student back again and said he would give him another chance. The student, however, refused to fly again in spite of pleas from all of us. We told him that he was almost certain to pass because otherwise the examiner would not offer him another ride. But he would not go and, when pushed for an explanation, said, "I've got a Commercial License and I think that's enough today for a guy that only has 95 hours!" His 130 hours, at least part of it, consisted of what was known as 'fountain pen time'.

Fast Draw

I had two private students while teaching at Big Spring Flying Service. One was a girl who tried to teach me to jitterbug and I tried to teach her to fly. Neither of us learned anything. She never came back after she took a lesson from Ray Plunkett one day when I was not there. He flew once around the pattern with her, then got out and told her to go alone. She wouldn't do it and he told her either to solo or not come back. When I heard about it, I asked him what he would have done if she had tried to take off. He said, "Jump on the tail and hold it down!"

My other student was 'Mac' McCasland, a highway patrolman for the state of Texas. He was about thirty-nine years old and I was twenty. And he was the best natural pilot I have ever known. Just before he came out with enough time to solo, he had been sick with measles that he had caught from his kids and had not flown for about three weeks. I gave him a hard time, told him that he couldn't hold altitude, or make turns to the proper heading. Then I finally said, "Pull over and stop. I'm going to get out. I can't stand to fly with you any more." It was a wonder he didn't shoot me, but instead he made a perfect solo flight. Mac went on to obtain his Commercial License and for several years made his living shooting coyotes from a Cub for ranchers in west Texas. He tried carrying gunners for a while but was disgusted because they missed so often. He rigged a shotgun on the strut of the airplane in such a way that he could fly and shoot at the same time. They tell me he seldom missed, and never had an accident.

A bunch of us were standing around the ramp one day and Mac was in his uniform—pistol and all. One of the students said, "Mac, that gun wouldn't do you any good. Why, I can jump you and have your arms pinned before you could get that gun out of the holster." Mac said, "Well, jump."

The fellow lunged at him and Mac took one step back, pulled his revolver and fired it right between the student's feet. As 'the jumper' stood there shaking, Mac calmly said, "It would have been just as easy to put that bullet into your belt buckle." I have seen him roll a Coke can clear out of range, shooting two pistols alternately. He had enough medals to make a necklace for both his wife and daughter, and enough trophies to cover a kitchen table.

After I retired from Pan Am I ran into Mac and asked if he flew any more. He said he was only going to fly one more time. "You soloed me, and I want to make my last flight with you." And he did. He flew my Cessna 205 for about thirty minutes and did as great a job as ever.

Brownsville, Here I Come

In June 1942, I had finished a class and had a few days free but was at the airport anyway. I helped a man roll his airplane, a cabin Waco, out of the hangar. He said that he was going to Brownsville, Texas, to fly submarine watch for the Civil Air Patrol. Pan American Airways flew from Brownsville, and I was interested in the airline because of all the things I had heard about the company's standards: how it made pilots qualify not only as flyers but also as navigators and radio operators, and taught them something of mechanics, as well. I was interested, too, because the company flew to so many places overseas.

Ray Plunkett and I had agreed that if we could just be flight instructors for the rest of our lives at $200 per month that was all we could wish for. But it would not hurt to look, so I asked if I could go along. The man with the Waco said, "Sure," but that he could not wait for me to go to town to fetch a suitcase. So I just crawled in and away we went. In flight I learned that his name was Henry King, a well known movie director from Hollywood.

When we landed at Brownsville I saw a hangar with 'Pan American Airways System' painted on it and I wandered down the ramp into the hangar. I looked at all the airplanes and watched the work the mechanics were doing and finally asked where the offices were. Finding that they were in the terminal building, I started through the gate and was challenged by the guard who wanted to know where my badge was. "What badge?" I had a bit of a problem convincing him that I had come in off the ramp and did not know that badges were required.

I had enough sense to know that I should at least put on a clean shirt before I went to see the chief pilot. In the morning, with a new khaki shirt and black tie from J.C.Penney, I went to see Captain F.I.Jacobs, the chief pilot, who said that they could use me and would offer me employment. I told him that just as soon as I could return to Big Spring for my clothes I'd be back.

But when I arrived back in Big Spring a class of students was waiting for me, along with a hard luck story of not being able to find another instructor. I could not leave them in the lurch, so I stayed, and not until September did I call to ask if Pan American still wanted me. They still did. I asked if I could bring along a friend who I thought had about the same experience and they agreed. So Ray Plunkett and his wife accompanied me back to Brownsville. I went to the doctor to take my examination while Ray was interviewed. That night I found out that he was not accepted because he did not have any college training. We hadn't thought of that, but Pan American never went below a minimum requirement of two years, which was exactly what I had.

We sat up until the wee hours trying to decide if I should go with him to apply to American Airlines or stay where I was. Ray later became American's chief pilot at Dallas. I have nothing against American, but I never had any regrets for that decision. However, the delay from June until September did cost me untold amounts of money. About one hundred pilots had been hired in the interim. With a seniority one hundred numbers better, I would never have been demoted to copilot after having once checked out as captain. As it was, I went from captain to copilot and back to captain several times. I used to tell friends who were worried about checking out that there was nothing to it; I had done it five times.

With Pan American I made $200.00 per month as a student pilot. When I earned an instrument rating, my pay would go up to $220.00.

Milk Run to the Spanish Main

The command was crisp and clear: "Gear up!" I reached for the lever on the floor that would allow me to unlock the DC-3's gear (from its down position) and pulled the gear handle up. Looking out of my window I expected to see the wheel on my side retracting into the wheel well. It didn't move. The captain, Sam Miller, repeated: "Gear up!" Again I went through all the motions, and again the wheel didn't move.

Muttering something under his breath that had to do with copilots not being properly trained, he took over my job and tried to retract the gear himself. It remained stubbornly down.

"Pins!", he said, "Pins!"

Typical scene at Brownsville Airport in 1944, when the Douglas DC-3 was the standard main-line flagship of all the leading U.S. airlines, Pan American included. The DC-3A in the photo (NC25645) later served with AVENSA and subsequently became an executive aircraft. It was lost in a crash in the Caribbean in October 1971.

This plaque commemorates the historic role played by the border station in opening up air transport communications between the United States and Mexico.

Then it dawned on me. We had taken off from Mexico City without first being sure that the ground crew mechanics had removed the pins from the gear. These strong metal pins were inserted to prevent the gear from being retracted while the airplane was on the ground, but they had to be removed so that it could be retracted in flight.

I remembered how, on the ramp, Sam's head had been out of the cockpit window while he shouted, "If you don't get us out of here in two minutes, we will have to spend the night!" In their hurry to get us out the ground crew had not removed the pins, and we had not caught the mistake. So, here we were, in flight and nowhere to go. With the parasitic drag because the gear was down, the airplane would not fly fast enough to enable us to reach our destination, Tapachula, before night. At that time only daylight flights were allowed in Central America.

The date was December 18, 1942, and it was my first flight on an airline. I was twenty-one years old, had never traveled on any airline as a passenger, and here I was in the copilot's seat. We had left Brownsville, Texas, that morning on Pan American flight 501, and had stopped at Tampico, Mexico. After leaving Tampico, one of the generators had failed and we had been delayed in Mexico City to have it fixed. Our hurry to leave in time to reach Tapachula before dark had contributed to our being airborne with landing gear that could not be retracted.

I had been hired by Pan American Airways System on September 4, and had spent the time since then in its ground school, studying subjects such as instrument flying, navigation, powerplants, history of the company, and other aspects of the operation. Pan American was then considered to be the premier airline of the United States, if not the world. Since its beginning in 1927, it had not only pioneered the routes in Central and South America, but those across both the Pacific and Atlantic Oceans as well. In the process Pan Am had built its own facilities such as airfields, radio stations, and even hotels. It also developed the ocean navigation systems used around the world. The pilots were expected to be mechanics, radio operators, and navigators as well. When I went to work for Pan Am, some of these requirements had been dropped, but we were still expected to spend thirty days in the maintenance department. We spent several days each in such places as the propeller overhaul shop, the fabric shop, the radio shop, and ten days in engine overhaul. We were not required to obtain more than a radio telephone license, but we did have to learn to send and receive radio code.

During my ten days in engine overhaul, the place burned down. I do not think the cause of the fire was ever determined, and the fire department did not want our help, so many of us just sat on the nearby grass watching it burn.

During my time in the electrical shop I had noticed an attractive brunette who worked at putting Norden bomb sights into Lockheed Hudson airplanes, work completed under contract by Pan American for the Army Air Force. She and I sat together watching the fire and getting better acquainted; her name was Helen. She had wanted to join the armed services but her family had objected. So she came to Brownsville, and Pan American, to do her bit for the war effort. Her family agreed to that because a cousin was there to keep an eye on her. I bought her a Guatemalan jacket on my first trip, and we were married in her cousin's home the next March.

Flying Cabbie

I had been given my training on the Douglas DC-3. This amounted to a grand total of three take offs and landings, which was all that the Civil Aviation Authority required at the time for a copilot, in addition to a Commercial License with an instrument rating.

There was a story about three copilots in Miami being qualified. It seems there was a rough old captain who was to give them their 'bounces'. The three took a taxi to the airport together. When they arrived the taxi driver wanted to see the airplane and went on board with them. When the captain boarded he pointed to the cabbie and said, "You are first, get in the seat." Disciplinarian that he was, the captain allowed no protest, so the taxi driver got into the copilot's seat, and with a lot of help managed to make three circuits of the field. When the others had made their three, the captain told them to report to scheduling for assignments to their first trip. The cabbie said, "Great! Where is the personnel office? I'd like to get hired first!"

Fuel Dumping

Now, on my first flight, we were airborne with a gear that could not be raised. We had two choices. We could land 'overgross' or we could dump fuel down to a legal landing weight. This posed a severe dilemma for the crew. Landing overweight would be termed an emergency and would require written reports to the Civil Aviation Authority (the C.A.A. later became the Federal Aviation Agency, or the F.A.A.). On the other hand, we were not convinced about the safety of dumping fuel. Not too many years previously a Pan American airplane under the command of its first—and famous—chief pilot, Ed Musick, had exploded while dumping fuel near Pago Pago, Samoa.

Pilots do not like to write reports, so Captain Miller elected to dump the fuel, or at least to say that we had. He said to the radio officer and myself, "We have dumped fuel, OK?" We agreed, of course, then he said, "But the dump chute won't be down." The dump chute on a DC-3 was a tube under the rear of the fuselage and, once released to dump fuel, it could not be retracted. There would thus be evidence that we had never actually reduced our gross weight. So he decided that he had better dump some fuel. In those days, and especially on their first flights, copilots were seldom asked for their opinions. We dumped fuel, landed uneventfully, and spent the night in Mexico City. Another twenty years or so were to pass before the necessity of my dumping fuel occurred again, although it became much more common after we started flying jets.

Central America the Beautiful

The next morning at just about daylight we left Mexico City. We were behind schedule, of course, and needed to reach the Panama Canal Zone before night if we could. As we proceeded, beautiful and exciting wonders continued to unfold for me. First we passed by the snow-capped peaks of Popocatépetl (Popo) and its companion, Ixtacihuatl, known as 'The Sleeping Lady', both peaks almost 18,000 feet high. Then, over Puebla and by Orizaba, the highest mountain in Mexico or Central America—almost 19,000 feet—and over southern Mexico and the Gulf of Tehuantepec, where I had my first glimpse of the Pacific Ocean. I had never seen the Atlantic Ocean, either. We landed at Tapachula, on the border with Guatemala, on a runway located right in the middle of a banana plantation. From there we went on to Guatemala City, passing many volcanic peaks, some of which were active, and up to 13,000

Modes of transport in Guatemala City in 1942: (left) two-wheeled; (right) two-headed.

feet high. Lake Atitlán, in the highlands between Tapachula and Guatemala, was one of the most beautiful sights I had ever seen.

Entry into the valley, where the airport for Guatemala City lies, was alongside the active volcanoes of Agua and Fuego (Water and Fire) and over another beautiful lake, Amatitlán.

I was enthralled! I had never seen lands like this. They were so green, and so strange to a dry land boy from a Texas ranch. The jungles were full of colorful trees, and some of the cultivated fields looked as though they climbed the sides of the mountains at an angle too steep to walk up. I was not sure at this stage if Pan American was going to keep me, as I was on probation, and I kept thinking that if the worst happened, at least I would have had this one trip as an airline pilot over this strange and beautiful country. Little did I know that I would be flying over this same terrain for the next thirty-nine years.

I was not able to see Guatemala City that day because we continued on, trying to make up lost time, but when I did come to know it, I found it to be one of my very favorite places. People often ask me which is the place I would most like to go back to, and my answer is that it would have to be Guatemala, provided that I could go back in the 'Fifties. The old Palace Hotel where we stayed was the antithesis of the stereotype international hotel of today. It had a big lobby with leather-covered furniture, a very high ceiling, and a dining room where meals were served with all the charm of the Old World. My favorite foods were the *carne asada* with fried bananas, and avocado halves filled with a tomato and vinegar sauce. There were rooms of all kinds. Some were up half a floor or down half a floor from others; some were totally inside with no windows; and one, at least, on the very top floor, had windows on all sides. At 5,000 feet elevation, Guatemala was quite cool at night, and all the beds were covered with beautiful wool blankets made by the local Indians.

Every pilot bought blankets in Guatemala to take home and I still have several, to this day.

'Tee-Goose'—and other Friendly Fields.

San Salvador, on the edge of Lake Ilopango, was the next stop, and from there we went northeast to Tegucigalpa, Honduras. As we approached the city I could see nothing but rough canyons and rocks. Sam asked for partial flaps. I put them down, but I sure could not see any place to land. Then he wanted more flaps and asked for the gear down! I still could not see any place to land, but I was not about to question the captain—that just was not done, at least in those days. Then we made a turn around a low hill, Sam asked for full flaps, and in seconds we were on the ground at Tegucigalpa Airport. I found later that this was a normal approach to 'Tee-goose'. When they had a new copilot aboard they never explained it ahead of time, just to give him a thrill. And it did just that. The field was a dirt strip, as were many of the places at which we landed. It had a steep downhill slope, so that if you failed to touch down at the very beginning you often floated too far down the runway before landing, making it difficult to stop.

Managua, Nicaragua, on the shores of Lake Managua, was as far as we made it that night. There was No Room at the Inn for us, so the station

manager found beds for us in the barracks of the Nicaraguan military, and that is where we spent my second night as a Pan American pilot.

The first stop next morning was San José, Costa Rica. We reached there early in the morning and there was a low fog layer over the grass field where we were supposed to land. The only possible approach was downwind and downhill, not a good combination. Sam touched the wheels on the ground but decided that there was not enough field left to stop in, so he applied power and we took off again. We made it in on the second try, and I inflected that, previously, when I was a flight instructor, I had not wished to go to work for an airline because it was 'too dull'! In San José I bought a turned wooden apple with a top that came off to make a little box. It was the first purchase I made while with Pan Am, and it still has its place today on my bedside table.

Davíd, Panama, was next. It was known as the copilot's field because it was about 6,000 feet long and at least 800 feet wide. It was great for a copilot's ego; no matter what mistakes we made, that nice grass strip seemed to take care of it. Land while drifting sideways, or three feet in the air and you hardly noticed it. Every pilot knows how forgiving a nice grass field can be. Usually only the copilots landed here, but I did not make the landing this day. On the way back, however, Sam Miller let me make my first landing as an airline pilot in control.

Here, while I was at my job of checking on the fueling, a fellow walked up to Captain Miller in the terminal and asked about me. He had heard, he said, that I had gone to work for Pan American and he wanted to know how to find me. Sam told him to just step outside the door and holler! It was one of my students from my flight instructing days at Big Spring.

Report to Whom?

Albrook Field at Balboa, Canal Zone, was next. On the way there our radio operator handed up a message requesting to know "Is Ned Wilson aboard 501 today?" I couldn't imagine why anyone would want to know, but told him to reply, "Yes". In a few minutes came the message, "Have him report to the C.A.A. on landing." Oh, my! I had never even been to Panama, and this was my very first trip as an airline pilot, and already the authorities were after me! When we landed I made a dash for the shack which held the C.A.A. office, only to meet an old friend, Ray Dudley, a radio operator for the C.A.A. whom I had known when I had been a flight instructor at Big Spring. He had since been transferred to the Canal Zone, and had seen my name on the crew list.

Cover Up

On flights to the Canal Zone we were required to cover all the passenger cabin windows with pieces of cardboard, carried for the purpose, when we were forty-five minutes out. Supposedly this was to prevent spies from taking pictures of the Canal. Never mind that you could obtain all the diagrams that you wanted of the Canal by buying a copy of *Popular Mechanics* or *Life*. On one flight a lady passenger complained that she didn't like this as it gave her claustrophobia and made her feel sick. The pilot said, "Lady, I know it's bad, but how do you think we feel up front?"

We found out in Panama that our schedule had been changed. To put things back on schedule, our flight to Trinidad had been dispatched with another airplane and crew, and we were reassigned to the UMCA flight. This stood for Urubá, Medellín and Central Airways, which was actually owned by a Colombian general for whom Pan American operated route entirely on a contract basis, furnishing airplanes and crews. Our first landing was in Turbo, Colombia, where the airport was a dirt strip running along a curve in the beach. Here Sam gave me the take off, my first.

To reach Medellín from Turbo required a climb to 12,000 feet across a high plateau, then a circling descent to a narrow river valley. We then followed the river to the airport. There was no instrument approach; you had to be able to see the ground to find the airport.

Weather à la Carte

On one flight a pilot made it over the ridge and down to the river, where he encountered a heavy rainstorm. He called the field and asked what the weather was like at the airport. "Scattered clouds and a ten-mile visibility, captain." He believed from this report that the rain must stop before he reached the field, and he continued on, even though he could hardly see the ground. It rained harder, and again he asked about the weather and received the same reply, and on he went.

It was beginning to look dangerous now, because there was no safe retreat; but suddenly he saw the runway. Heavy rain was pouring down, and with only about a half-mile visibility, he landed. Hopping mad about the misleading reports, he jumped out of the airplane and grabbed the station manager by the collar. "What do you mean, 'scattered clouds and ten miles visibility'? Why, you can hardly see the runway from the terminal building!"

"But Cap-i-tán, if I would have told you what the weather was like, you would not have landed, and you are here!"

That was the kind of down-to-earth—literally—logic hard to argue with, but often done by some station managers who had passengers eager to get on the airplane. Dan Appling, at Tegucigalpa, would try to suck us in like that by telling us of, "A big hole to the southwest" or, "It's clear to the east, captain."

We ran out of daylight in Medellín and so spent the night again. Then we retraced our route to Brownsville, now flying flight 504, called the 'Sunray'. This schedule was supposed to include an overnight stop in Mexico City, but still behind schedule, we overnighted in Guatemala City instead. The next day we finished the trip, returning to Brownsville. We had started out on an eight-day schedule but had flown for only five days, spending not a single night at the proper place. But I was home for Christmas, which I had not expected. I guess you could say that it was a great break-in flight for an airline career.

Navigation 'por mano'

Flying through Central America at this time was, to say the least, different from airline flights as they are today. When we reported for a flight we first prepared our own flight plans with pencil and paper. We had no maps except those that we bought ourselves. There were no published instrument procedures, known as 'let-downs', for the airports and no published safe flight altitudes for the mountainous terrain. My only route manual was a small three by five inch notebook that I bought in the local book store and filled with information that I had gleaned from more experienced fellow pilots, and from what I had worked out for myself and considered important.

There was little help from navigational aids, only from a few non-directional radio beacons at the various airports. These were used by the radio operator taking bearings with a 'loop' antenna and reading directions to where the station appeared to be from the nose of the aircraft. It was up to the pilot to convert these 'relative' bearings to a compass direction. For instance, if the bearing was 90° (off the right wing) and the airplane was headed 270°, then the station was north of the airplane (90°+270°=360°). Interestingly, we made let-downs using these stations, together with a system called 'boxing the station', down to 300-foot or 400-foot ceilings and visibilities of one mile. Thirty years later, and with millions of dollars spent on fancy electronics, we were able to fly airplanes only to minimums of 200-foot ceilings and one-half mile visibility. I often wondered if the difference justified the expense. Seldom is a ceiling limited to a narrow band between 300 and 200 feet.

My little book contained comments such as:

San Vicente—church on north side of square, red roof W, cemetery E.—7 min. heading 320° to SJO airport.

Practically all of our flying was done by what is known as 'pilotage'; or flying by visual reference to the ground. Today, this is almost totally a lost art.

I continued to learn from the more experienced pilots. Some of the words of wisdom served me in good stead all my life. I learned never to trust just one check point. If you saw something on the ground that you thought you recognized, you always waited until you saw the next one (and you had better know in which direction and how far it should be) before you were sure that you knew where you were.

"It's not so important to know where you are as to know where you are not!" Especially in mountainous terrain.

"Never trust a bearing from a radio station unless you are also listening to the signal." If the signal was not clear the bearing was also in doubt.

Cigar Computer

Mike Carmichael had started his career in Mexico, carrying payrolls to the mines; had flown thousands of hours in Central America and probably knew it as well as anyone. Departing on instruments from Guatemala through a pass between two volcanoes, the one on the right 13,000 feet and the one on the left 11,000 feet, he was flying at 7,500 feet. A rather green copilot with him was nervously moving around in his seat. Mike asked, "Son, is something bothering you?"

"Well, I've never been so low through this pass before on instruments." Mike said, "Oh, well, I don't want to scare you, so I'll go up 500 feet!"

Mike was approaching sixty years of age when most of us were in our twenties, but he had wonderful distance vision.

Mike Carmichael, with his cigar—"tested and proved for thirty-five years"—and known to his friends as the Carmichael Computer. Mike knew how far he had flown by the length of the cigar stub still left unsmoked.

He would say to me, "Look out for that buzzard." At least a full minute would pass before the buzzard would come into my sight. On the other hand, his near sight was not so good and he did not like to wear his glasses. One day I was adjusting the azimuth (a rotating ring) around the Automatic Direction Finder to the compass heading and Mike said, "Son, if you are doing that for my benefit, you can stop it, because I can't see it."

Mike smoked one cigar right after the other. The first thing he did when he entered the cockpit was to spread out a big handkerchief over his lap so that ashes would not burn holes in his trousers. A flight attendant would come up and ask when we would be in Mexico City. He would pull the ever-present cigar from his mouth, measure it off with his fingers and say, "Oh, about right there." Copilots and captains shared hotel rooms and at bedtime Mike would put out his cigar in the ashtray, then turn out the light. When our wake-up call came in the morning, his routine would be: light on, cigar in mouth, light cigar, then get up.

Bells

With pleasure I remember so many of those early pilots, though some were real characters. At this time we were still following procedures taken from maritime practice. We marched to the airplane at the sound of one bell; then, at the sound of two bells the passengers would board. And the captain had to disembark first with the briefcase containing the papers—manifest and passenger list—before the passengers could follow. I never took home with me any company property, but I do regret that I never liberated one of those bells before they stopped using them. I think that every one of those bells disappeared within a week after that system was abandoned.

Pilots Will Be Pilots

One pilot, when he was in a playful mood, was known to put his head out the door, with all the passengers right behind him, and ask anyone near, "What place *is* this?"

Another pilot with whom I flew as copilot once showed me that he could go from San Salvador to Guatemala City (airport elevation at 4,850 feet) without ever rising above 5,000 feet. He did it by flying down all the valleys, with higher terrain on both sides. I wonder, today, what the passengers thought. He was later fired for buzzing his girlfriend's house in Guatemala just to show the tower operator (who wouldn't clear him to land because of the weather) that the weather was not all that bad.

When a copilot made a hard landing, his captain would customarily make him take the briefcase and leave the cockpit first. It once happened to Sam Miller when he was copilot. After his hard landing Sam shut the door behind him as he left and said, "The captain was so ashamed of that landing that he wouldn't face you." Sam later became vice president and operations manager of the Atlantic Division. He was a fast thinker.

Ralph Emory Wanless was one of my favorite captains. He was a patient, thoughtful instructor who taught me many useful things about flying airplanes. Once, with him, I was writing in my little notebook the times at which we left the blocks and were airborne, for later use when I would have to enter them in the ship's logbook. He wanted to know if I could not remember the times without writing them down. I said, "No." So he made me think back to our first departure and tell him the times off the blocks and in the air. Then, the times on the ground and at the blocks at the next stop. He made me do this all the way back to the beginning after each take off and landing. By the time we had made an eight-day trip with 34 stops, I could quote them all from start to finish.

Thunderbirds

In June 1943, I made a trip with Captain John Rowe. We had left the Canal Zone for Barranquilla, Colombia, and on the way ran into a very big thunderstorm. Though I later flew into thousands of thunderstorms, I can remember none worse than this one. In spite of all that John could do to keep it upright, the airplane made such violent pitches and rolls that all of our gyro-controlled flight instruments 'spilled' and were useless, leaving us on 'needle-ball and airspeed' (the most primitive of flight instruments). I remember seeing airspeed as low as 60 and as high as 180, but the panel was shaking so badly that it was hard to read anything. At times, I was not sure if we were right-side-up or not. Just at the worst, we became aware that there was someone between the two of us. It was an Army Air Force captain. He had one arm locked under the armrest of John's chair and one under mine. He said, "Do you need help?" John replied, "No! Get the hell out of here!"

We were flying an old DC-3 that had been used as a military transport and had not had normal seats installed, just bucket seats along the sidewalls. Our purser told us that this guy had unbuckled his seat belt and had fought his way up the aisle, sometimes on the floor and sometimes on the ceiling, to the cockpit. The Air Force guy told us later that he had thought we had been hit by lightning or had been knocked unconscious, and that the airplane was totally out of control. He was right on the money!

The airport terminal at Tapachula, on the Mexico-Guatemala frontier, in 1947.

The airport terminal at Guatemala City in 1942. The Douglas DC-2 was on a delivery flight to PANAGRA, based at Cristóbal, Canal Zone. This particular aircraft (NC14291) was later used in Uruguay and Argentina, and crashed in 1954.

The terminal building at Tegucigalpa ('Tee-goose'), Honduras, in 1947. The photograph was taken from the pilot's window of a DC-3.

The terminal building at Managua, Nicaragua, in 1947—another view from the pilot's window, indicating the close proximity of the arriving aircraft—a practice which is little different today.

The terminal at Davíd, Panama, in 1943.

The airport terminal at Balboa (Tocumen), Canal Zone.

When we passed through the storm we were so far out to sea that we could not see land and did not know exactly where we were. We were off all of our usual charts, and I had to retrieve an emergency chart that we carried and lay it out on the cockpit floor to compute radio bearings so we could find the course to Barranquilla.

We had no radar in those days, and it was a common experience to fly through thunderstorms. I do not think they come any bigger than those throughout Central America. Today we have pilots who have had the advantage of radar for their entire career and consequently have seldom—if ever—flown through a real thunderstorm. Bad as they are, many pilots that I flew with in later years had an exaggerated fear of thunderstorms.

On one occasion one of our flights had not reported its position for some time and was sent a message asking if the pilot could tell them where he was. He replied, "Affirmative, I'm right in the middle of the biggest thunderstorm in Central America!"

The first radar I saw was on our Douglas DC-6s. Once, going into Mexico City, with thunderstorms all around, an Eastern Air Lines crew, bound for the same destination, kept asking us, "Clipper, what does your radar show?" After they had made this request several times, we asked them if they had radar. The reply was, "If the SPAD didn't have it, we don't have it!" Eastern's president, Captain Eddie Rickenbacker, who had flown SPADs in World War I, was not known to go overboard in giving his pilots the latest in equipment.

On a DC-3 cargo flight through Central America, in a big thunderstorm, a Braniff crew once lost both wing tips and the ailerons (surfaces on the wing for lateral control) went with the wing tips. Miraculously, and with great skill, they were able to land safely. The pilot even had the nerve to stall the airplane at altitude so that he would know what speed he could safely use on the approach.

Though Pan American started flying through Central America as early as 1929, it never lost a passenger in this area. This was in spite of flying aircraft that could not climb high enough to clear the highest mountains, poor navigation facilities, inadequate airports, and weather that could be as hazardous as anywhere.

Some pilots have said that what they enjoyed most was making instrument landing system approaches to low levels, as commonly practiced in Europe. With proper training, any competent pilot can do that. I always thought it took more skill and judgment to fly where the conditions were always changing, where you could not depend on guidance by radar or electronic aids; where every decision depended upon your knowledge and understanding of conditions existing at the specific time and place. Success or failure rested on your skill and judgment. In later years, I was to hear many Pan Am pilots say that the best pilots seemed to be those who spent their early years in what was known as Pan Am's Western Division. I do know that I always felt more satisfaction when doing that kind of flying.

A Flush Beats a Straight

My second trip was not as pleasant as the first. I soon found that all captains were not the same, and that all were not as considerate of their copilots as Sam Miller. It was normal and usual for captains to share landings with their copilots on a more or less fifty-fifty basis, perhaps giving them the better airports or letting them land in better weather conditions. The fellow I was with on this second trip gave very few. The consensus seemed to be that he was not too confident in his own ability, and I found out later in my career that if a man was not sure of himself he was also very doubtful of anyone else.

We had flown for three days and had made seventeen stops. When we reached Trinidad, where we had a day off, he had not allowed me to make any landings or take offs. At Trinidad we stayed in what was known as 'the staff house,' which accommodated Pan American crews, plus crews ferrying airplanes to the war zones, Army Air Force pilots, British crews, and many others. A common pastime, as might be imagined, was poker. Some took it very seriously and played for big money, but many were like me and only played for pennies and for fun. We started a game that evening for very small stakes—I think it was a quarter ante with a three-raise limit game. We played until bedtime and someone suggested that we ante fifty cents and play one last hand, 'jacks or better'. Three hands were dealt, with nobody being able to open, and each time we put in the ante again. It was the biggest pot of the night when my captain, on my left, opened. Around the table of seven or so playing, none stayed in until it was my call. I had nothing in my hand but was not about to give him the pot when it only cost me fifty cents to draw some cards. I held one ace and drew four cards, and couldn't believe my eyes when I saw that I now held a flush!

I didn't know it, but the captain had opened with a straight in his hand. Naturally, he did not even consider that I, having drawn four cards, could beat it. After we reached the limit of three raises, he laid down his hand and reached out to gather in the pot.

I said that I had not played much poker, but that I thought that a flush beat a straight. This guy was furious and started to argue that I could not have the pot because you just don't play poker that way. I admitted that it was pretty stupid but was, nevertheless, legal. The rest of the players began to kid him, and one said to me, in his hearing, "Ned, you have really ripped your britches!

He will not let you make another landing all the way back to Brownsville." I replied, "Well, if I did make one it would be one more than I made on the way down."

Without speaking to me, my captain stomped off to bed. The first stop on our flight the next day was Maturin, Venezuela, and he told me that it was my landing. Oh, how I would like to be able to say that I really greased one on and showed him up. The truth is that I bounced it so high that it seemed to me we could have gone over the hangar, but it was probably about three or four feet in the air. He grabbed the controls and made the recovery, and that was the last chance I had for a landing on that trip. Even at Davíd, 'the copilot's field', he did not offer me another landing. To my relief, I never had to fly with him again and, in fact, within a few years he was no longer with Pan American.

A Three-Pilot Reliant

My logbook shows that I had made six trips on Central American routes when I was asked to become a flight instructor, giving instrument ratings to those pilots who had been hired but who did not yet have one. As I had just become married to the girl I had met when going through shop training, this suited me fine. The airplane we were using for training was a Stinson Reliant, a type with which I had given instruction before I came to Pan American. This beautiful airplane carried either four or five people and had a 300hp radial engine. However, the one Pan American was using was unique, in that the airline had installed another set of controls and a separate instrument panel in the back seat, so that the airplane seated four—and three of the seats were pilots' seats.

The student sat in the back with a curtain pulled around his position. There was no chance that he could see out and he was thereby forced to fly on instruments. When instructing, I used the left front seat and a second student sat on the right and acted as safety lookout for other airplanes until his own turn came. It was a wonderful set-up. I wish I knew what happened to those airplanes. I think Pan Am had three of them in various locations. They would be worth a mint today. My guess is that they were sold to someone who took all the extra equipment out and converted them back to normal.

He Flew Them all

Some of the instructors were 'line' pilots and some were hired only to be flight instructors and did not fly the line. One of these was a fellow by the name of Bill Daniels. He was the type who, to hear him tell it, had flown every airplane ever built. If you mentioned Consolidated B-24s, he had helped test them; or he had flown P-51 Mustangs to Africa, or whatever. One day some of the students made up a fictitious airplane. They gave it a designation that nobody had ever heard of and made up all kinds of performance figures for it. It went faster, flew higher, and did things that no other aircraft had ever done.

Then they went over to the corner, within his hearing, and started discussing 'their' airplane. One would mention how high it would go, and another how fast. In about two minutes Bill joined the group and, sure enough, he had helped flight test that one, too!

I did flight instruction for several months using the Stinson, as well as the twin-engined Cessna T-50 Bobcat, known as the 'Bamboo Bomber.' We also had a Lockheed 10, but my logbook does not show any time in that.

He Couldn't Hear the Horn

B.B. (Bernie) Wilson was being groomed to instruct in the Lockheed and was sent up alone to practice single-engine landings. As the propellers would not 'feather', the procedure was to pull one throttle back and make the approach. Because of excessive air resistance with the gear down, and with the propeller windmilling, the gear was left up until the last minute on final approach, then put down. Of course, with the gear up and one throttle pulled back, the gear warning horn was continually sounding off, making it difficult to hear the radio. When Bernie complained of this, the captain in charge of training showed him a circuit-breaker in the airplane that would stop the warning horn from sounding off. Before take off, he was cautioned to make sure to put the gear down, as he would no longer have a warning. What he did not know was that the circuit-breaker killed the entire gear system, which operated electrically and, when he put the gear switch in the 'down' position, the gear stayed up. Unfortunately, the wheels were not visible from the cockpit even when down.

Bernie said that he thought that was going to be the best landing he had ever made, until it dawned on him that he was so low that there could not possibly be any wheels down there! He started to add power, but too late: the props were already ticking away on the pavement. He slid it in on its belly, jumped out, and ran away from it, afraid of fire. When he saw that it was not going to burn, he went back and put his headset on. A young lady in the tower was saying, "Lockheed, will you please taxi off the runway? There is an aircraft on final." Bernie replied, "I'd sure like to taxi off, but it doesn't roll very good with no wheels under it!"

The one who had told Bernie to take the circuit-breaker out was the head of training, Captain Stone, who had flown the line until Pan Am replaced the Ford Tri-Motors with Douglas DC-2s. He said that airplanes were becoming too complicated, and that men were never meant to fly anything bigger than the Fords. So he took over the training department and did a good job.

Buoys—and Cowboys

About this time I was offered an opportunity to transfer from the Western Division to the Pacific Division in San Francisco. I would have been on the flying boats there, including the famous Boeing 314; but they had a very large complement of crews, and I would have been a very junior officer and (so I had heard) such people did little actual flying, sometimes only one or two landings in a year. They were mostly used for in-flight relief and to stand in the bow to catch the buoy when docking. At the time, Pan American did not recognize system seniority, but used base seniority for advancement. I could see that if I stayed where I was, I had a good chance to become a captain within a short time, even before I would be a first officer in the Pacific. So I turned down the offer.

It was the right decision for my career but, in retrospect and in later years, I wished I had gone to San Francisco, just to have that experience and to be able to say, today, that I flew the flying boats. I had only one opportunity to fly one, when I was in Miami for some training. They were using a Sikorsky S-38 for navigator instruction, and I went along just to see the operation. The captain gladly let me sit in his seat and fly for about two hours.

Had I been on the boats, I might have been like a cowboy type from a western ranch, who was put on the bow and told to tie up to the buoy when they came to it. The normal procedure was to pass the buoy going downwind and then to turn and approach it going into the wind. Instead, as they went by it the first time, this guy made himself a lariat loop and lassoed the buoy. Of course, everything came to a sudden halt as they came to the end of the rope.

Chocks Away and Doors Ajar

In October 1943 I was sent to New Orleans. Pan American had begun scheduling flights to Guatemala and Panama, using a Boeing 307 Stratoliner. This was an unusual airplane, the biggest successful 'tail dragger' ever built in the United States. I only heard that term many years later, but at that time it was considered to be a normal landing gear, whereas those airplanes that had a nose wheel were the exception, and were called 'tri-gears' or 'tri-cycle' airplanes.

We trained at night because that was when the airplane was available, as it was not on an assigned schedule. My first flight in it was on October 10, with a fellow trainee, H.B. (Mutt) Fleming, who was coming in to be the local chief pilot. I was staying with my wife, Helen, at the St Charles Hotel whenever we could. There was a five-day limit there and sometimes we had to stay elsewhere or find a rented room in town. When I came back from the flight I told her that I was sorry that I had come to New Orleans because I was sure that I could never get along with the new chief. He was red-headed, had bloodshot eyes most of the time, and I could tell that he had a temper. I just did not think I could work for him.

I thought that I was generally pretty good in judging people, but this time I was very, very wrong. My association with Mutt turned out to be one of the best that I found in the company. Later he would joke that his eyes were bloodshot only when he was sober, and he said that his eyes cleared up when he had a hangover. We were good friends for many years, until his death in 1951.

I took my check ride for a rating on the Boeing 307 a few days later. I remember that one of the landings was not what it should have been and the examiner asked me who had taught me to land the airplane. What was I to say, with the flight instructor sitting right there with us? I just said, "Well, nobody taught me to land it like that!" I passed, and received my rating.

Only ten Stratoliners were built. One was destroyed (spun in) when Boeing was demonstrating it to the Dutch airline, K.L.M., and five were delivered to T.W.A. One went to Howard Hughes as his personal airplane, while

Boeing 307 Stratoliner Clipper Flying Cloud, *one of the Pan American fleet which, after post-war operations in Haiti as a VIP transport for 'Papa Doc' Duvalier, finally came to rest in Arizona, where it is awaiting restoration by the Smithsonian Institution's National Air and Space Museum.*

three were delivered to Pan American. Of them all, the only complete one still in existence is the one I took my rating on, NC19903, *Clipper Flying Cloud.* It will eventually be restored and find its final home in the National Air and Space Museum in Washington, D.C.

At the time, I was making $220.00 per month. One of Mutt Fleming's first official acts was to transfer the copilots to Guatemala so that he could pay them $70.00 per month foreign allowance. As this was a 'paper' transfer, we were not allowed to move any household items. As I recall, I was the only married copilot, so the rest of the guys just lived in hotels on both ends. I was the only one who actually moved to Guatemala, my wife and I moving into an apartment, Mansion San Francisco, on Seventh Avenue, just a few blocks away from the main Plaza. We lived on the second floor and had a small balcony where we could eat breakfast and look across at a flock of buzzards which always sat on the roof of a building on the other side of the street.

On my overnights in New Orleans I stayed in a hotel where the company had one big room with about eight beds in it. It was not the best of resting places, with people coming and going at all times of the night. But at least we did not have to worry about any females being present. Pan American, at the time, used only male pursers, and flight stewards.

I have just read a book by a female flight attendant with a domestic airline who said that, some years back, boys had started taking over their jobs in the airlines. At Pan American it was the other way around, as they started with and used men in all jobs for many years. The places we went to and the layover facilities were considered unsuitable for women.

Five Cent Carrots

Grocery store food in Guatemala was expensive, but the local market was not too far away, and things there were cheap. We could buy three large avocados for five cents. However, my young wife had not learned to bargain as was the local custom. If you did not bargain, you were not playing the game and they would simply keep raising the price until you played the game, too. I went with Helen one day and I told her that no matter what they asked, she was to offer exactly half. She priced some carrots—a big bunch—and was told, "Eight cents."

The dining room of the Palace Hotel in Guatemala City, in 1944. This was a favorite haunt of the Pan American crews at the most important staging point on the Central American route during the early years.

An aerial view, at noon, of the Hotel Tivoli Canal Zone, another 'home-away-from-home' for Pan Am crews during the pioneer years.

She looked at me, and at the vendor, but couldn't quite get herself to say "Four". Very timidly, she said, "Five?" He said, "Va!" (OK) and I had a trader! She could haggle with the best of them after that. But I don't think she ever became used to the sight of live iguanas at her feet, or the smell in the meat areas.

Guatemala City was a lovely place to live in at that time. The streets were swept by hand each morning at about daylight, and each cart driver—and there were many carts—was required to have a shovel and pail to clean up after his animal. And it was safe, both on the streets and in the home. Justice was often swift and sure. It was said that a thief, if caught, often just 'disappeared' somewhere down a nearby back alley. We stood on our balcony at one time and saw shells being fired across town during one of the many revolutions that took place, but we were never troubled at all. The climate there is one of the best, for at 5,000 feet altitude, the city is seldom too hot and the air is clean and pure. In the rainy season there is usually an afternoon shower to cool things down, sometimes developing into a thunderstorm. This used to give us trouble in trying to land, but on the ground it was of little consequence, and the air smelled so wonderful afterward.

Backwards Career

One of our pilots at this time was H.C. 'Chip' West. I later loved to tell his story to copilots who thought they had been waiting too many years to check out as captain. Advancement was slow in Pan Am and it was not unusual for some crew members to fly twenty years as copilot. So I would tell them about the man who went to work as a captain and retired as a second officer.

Chip had gone through Army Air Corps flying school in the same class as General Curtis LeMay. He later worked for United Air Lines for some years and then decided to leave them and go into business for himself. When the war started he wanted to return to flying and went to work, as a captain, for Pan American Air Ferries, which was set up to fly aircraft for the government to Africa and Europe. These pilots were later absorbed into Pan Am proper and retained their rank, but their seniority date was set at the date of the merger. That meant that they were flying as captain with copilots who were actually senior to them. I was one of those and I flew many trips as copilot to Chip, yet later he was to fly some flights as my copilot. After some years Pan American experienced an economic slowdown which required Chip to go back to copilot ranking and at a seniority level which meant that he could not check out again. Then, in about 1960, we began to fly Douglas DC-8 jets in Houston, Texas, and we had only three complete crews. Chip could not hold a spot as first officer, but did not want to transfer elsewhere, so he remained as second officer, and took retirement with that rank. So went the story of the man with a backward career.

No Flaps, No Lights, No Radio

I had a trip with him in late November. We were to fly from Guatemala to Mérida on the Yucatán peninsula and then on to New Orleans.

On the way to Mérida, one of our generators stopped working. The airplane had four engines, but only two generators to furnish electrical power to operate the landing gear and flaps. The gear could be put down manually as well, but the flaps could not be put down without electric power.

In Mérida they worked on the generator but our flight engineer, Buddy Beard, reported that he did not think it would continue to function. Chip elected to take off, a decision that surprised me, and sure enough, only a few minutes out the generator failed again. It was a dark night and I fully expected to return immediately to Mérida, but Chip determined to press on. In about the middle of the Gulf of Mexico the other generator decided to go on strike in sympathy with the first. It was dark, there was no moon, and we had no lights either in or on the airplane. The radios did not work. Now it was six of one and half a dozen of the other which way we might go, so on we went. We found New Orleans without radio aid, but, of course, we had made no position reports (or any other reports) because we had no radio. We did not know it, but because we were unreported the airways had been closed for two hours flight time in both directions from New Orleans.

I asked Chip which runway he intended to use. He said that we would land to the southeast, as that was the normal wind direction, and that if we were wrong, he thought that the people on the ground would have enough sense to turn off the runway lights. Buddy went into the bowels of the airplane to crank the gear down, then returned for the landing. There was no way to activate the flaps, and none of us had ever *seen* a no-flap landing on this plane, much less *made* one. I was holding a flashlight on the instruments to read out to Chip the airspeed and altitude.

Because of having no flaps, Chip was still too fast on the first approach and the runway was too short to take a chance, so he applied the power to make a missed approach. All engines sputtered and backfired. In the excitement we had not adjusted the mixture controls into the rich position for landing. Buddy and I nearly broke each other's hands making the adjustment. The second approach was perfect; we landed and taxied to the ramp. By the time I got off the airplane, 'Mutt' Fleming the chief pilot, was at the bottom of the stairs. He handed me a passenger ticket, and said, "This is for Eastern Air Lines parked right there. They are holding the flight for you and you are to go home. Your Dad has had a heart attack." He had somehow cleared me through customs. I asked how long I could be gone and he said, simply, "When you get there, you let me know when you can come back."

It was then I knew why we had continued when, normally, I think Chip would not have pushed ahead like that - he had been told by the southbound crew about my Dad.

Let me say right here that in those days, at least in the places where I was stationed, Pan American was a good company to work for. If you gave them your best you were always treated generously. I always felt as if I was working among friends and for friends.

Some years later a flight was approaching Mérida where, at that time, our airplanes landed three days a week only. On the alternate days, flights overflew and went directly to New Orleans. The pilot was on the public address system, telling the passengers: "Ladies and gentlemen, on the left, as we leave the coast of Yucatán, you can see the beautiful city of Mérida—Oh, hell! I'm supposed to land there today!"

He must have been flying something other than the Boeing 307; as I recall, the 307 had no P.A. system.

Vertigo

The only time I ever experienced vertigo in flight was also on the Boeing 307. On a night flight over the Gulf of Mexico, we had been in steady rain for a long time, and I was flying in the right seat. I guess, without realizing it, I had let the airplane bank a little to the right. The instruments indicated that we were in a right bank, so I rolled to the left a little. In my head, though, we were now in a left bank, and as soon as I looked away for a moment I would unconsciously bank again to the right. I would have to make a correction when I looked back at the instruments. Each time I went through this sequence I would seem to be leaning further over to the left. Apparently I was flying the airplane correctly, because the captain had not noticed anything. But by now I felt as though I was lying on my side, and when I looked over to the captain it seemed that I was looking straight down. It was a strange feeling, and I finally had to give up and ask him to take over, explaining that I had vertigo.

He said "Well, get up and walk around and it will go away." I told him I was afraid to unfasten my seat belt, for fear I would fall right down on top of him. However, I did get up and, as soon as I did, the sensation was gone. That is the one and only time I can remember having vertigo.

Pressurization My Foot

The Boeing 307 was a great old airplane, and I'm glad that I was able to fly it before it went out of service. The cockpit seemed large enough to hold a volleyball game in. It was a dream to land, though it bounced often enough to keep you humble. It was sometimes known as 'Boeing's three-engined wonder' because only too often one of its four engines would quit, and all four of them seemed to throw out more oil on the airplane than they kept inside. It was the first airliner to be pressurized for passenger comfort. But that too was minimal and often did not work at all. Angie Eno, the wife of Captain Don Eno, told me of a time when she was a stewardess on the 307 between San Juan and New York. She sat in the rear on the jumpseat, with her foot holding the main door ajar so that it gave a little relief from the heat; neither the pressurization nor the air conditioner was working. All in all, great fun!

Filet of Iguana

My education in flying Douglas DC-3s continued. I was flying with people who were doing this job because they liked to fly airplanes. To most of us it was not just a job, it was a challenge, and the one and only thing we wanted to do.

Sam Enfield was the first captain to allow me to fly from the left (captain's) seat. There was no rule, then, that said the captain had to fly from the left, but it was the seat of 'command.' When a captain let you use his seat it meant that he had confidence in you and that he liked your flying. There was never any doubt that the captain was in command nor that he was responsible, no matter what happened. I had early on made a rule for myself: I would never touch the controls when the captain was flying unless I thought it was so necessary that I would be willing to sacrifice my job for doing so. I would do it to prevent an accident if I thought that I, or anyone else, might get hurt, but not until then.

The captain was next to God. What he said went. In those days—the 1940s—he was in complete command of all aspects of the flight. He did not, for example, have to accept an airplane if he thought it needed any maintenance. He did not have to depart unless he was satisfied with the weather. I never found it to be any other way for as long as I worked for Pan Am. I never knew a pilot to be censured for holding a flight to have something repaired, or for delaying a flight due to weather. Some few occasionally abused this authority. One pilot delayed a flight until the ground crew changed the seat cover on his seat, which he thought was too dirty. There were white canvas covers on our seats, and the control wheels were wrapped with twine in nautical style.

I once saw a logbook in which was written, "Flight 502 delayed leaving Panama because captain was unable to obtain breakfast. Furthermore, the captain was unable to obtain breakfast until he had broken three plates upon the dining room floor." It was said of this person that if service was slow he would hold out a plate from the table and drop it, and continue this activity until he was served.

Most pilots, though, made every effort to make schedule, in spite of thunderstorms and other severe weather in mountainous terrain, with very little radio aids, and questionable and inaccurate weather information.

No Sailor

During those early days in Brownsville, with another copilot, Bob Morley, I bought a half-interest in a sailboat. It was only fourteen feet long and had only one sail, but an old sailor who lived in Port Isabelle built it for us. I quickly found out that there was a lot to be learned about sailing. I wanted to take Helen out in the boat, but she did not care for that much water. But on one nice day when there was a light breeze (too light) I persuaded her to come with me.

We sailed off about two miles downwind from the docks, and I could not tack back against the wind. I assured Helen that someone would realize our plight and bring a power boat from the docks to rescue us. Sure enough, someone came for us, but in a sailboat. They began to tow us to the dock, and I explained to Helen that they could do this because they had a bigger boat with more sails. Then one of them asked to change places with me in my boat. He sailed my boat so well that he cast off the towline and sailed it on in to the dock.

Full Credit Work

In May 1944, I started to train for my Airline Transport Pilot rating, in preparation for check-out as captain. The training was given by line pilots, much of it by Jimmy Maxwell who at the time was the chief pilot in Brownsville. My logbooks show about twelve hours of training in Brownsville, after which I was sent to Miami, Florida, where I added a couple of hours more, and on June 22 took my flight test for the rating. Having passed it, I could now log one hundred percent of my flight time—then copilots could log only half of the time they flew.

Fly By Wire

In July I was sent on a check trip with Check Captain Walter Fitch, to determine whether I could make captain. The first trip was not to his liking. He reported that my landings were not good enough. Some of them, "Bordering on dangerous," he said, one coming too close to the runway end in Tegucigalpa. He attributed that to my having only recently returned to the DC 3 from the Boeing 307. He also said that he did not wish to check me out because we had not encountered enough bad weather on that trip.

I was given a couple of practice periods to improve my landings and left with him again on July 17 for a trip to Panama and back. His report shows that he thought my landings, "much better, now satisfactory," that he found the weather on this trip to be worse than normal, and he considered that I had handled it very well. So he recommended that I be made a captain.

Only one hurdle remained: before any pilot could be released as a captain he must have a 'pre-command' check given by the chief pilot. This check could not be designated to anyone else, and he was away on a trip to hire more pilots. Mutt Fleming was now the assistant chief pilot in Brownsville, so he sent a wire to Captain Maxwell, saying that I was ready for command, but first needed a pre-command check. A wire came back, "Pre-command check complete, put him on schedule." As far as I know, I'm the only pilot who obtained his pre-command by wire.

Captain Ned

Mutt called me into the office before they scheduled my first captain trip, and I have never forgotten what he said. He told me that I now represented Pan American, and that if I ever got into trouble he would back me to the hilt if what I was doing was safe, even if I had broken a rule or two. But, he said, if I flew in an unsafe manner he would be the first one to hang me up by the heels, even if what I had done was totally in accordance with all the rules.

My first trip as captain was to Guatemala and back, starting on August 4, 1944. My pay now had risen to $604.00 per month. I never did find out how they arrived at that number, but it was very much appreciated, as by that time I had a wife and child to support. My copilot on the way back from Guatemala was a fellow who had been a supervisory pilot at Coleman, Texas, when I had been released for not being twenty-one years old.

This was really a great time in my life, I was twenty-three years old. Our firstborn, Kenneth, arrived on July 12, and now I was a captain. I must admit that I always felt like a captain even when I was flying copilot. If I was permitted to fly a leg, I did it as I thought it should be done without looking to the left to see what 'he' wanted. So I had no fear at all of taking command. I have been asked many times if I felt a great responsibility for my passengers. The answer is that I had a big concern for their well-being, but that the old cliché was applicable, "If I got there safely, so would they." The pilot is always the first one at the scene of an accident.

Twenty-three was then, and still is, the minimum age for holding an Airline Transport Pilot's license. I received mine one month and four days after my twenty-third birthday, whereas some of my contemporaries had to wait until they were old enough to check out. One of these was Johnny Greenacre, who flew in command of cargo flights for several months until he was licensed to fly passengers. He looked very young and once I was his copilot on a trip.

He was glad to see me because he was never called 'captain' by anyone on the ground. In those days we neither wore stripes on our sleeves nor any insignia to designate the rank of captain, exçept the difference in the wings. He thought that I looked young enough so that he would be recognized as the captain. Our first landing was at Tampico, Mexico, and the station manager came up and said to me, "Captain, here is your manifest." Johnny took his hat off and threw it on the floor, shouting, "Damn it, I'M THE CAPTAIN!"

On one of my early trips in command, leaving Guatemala for Mexico, the station manager brought a passenger to me, saying that he would not travel unless he could ride in the cockpit with the crew. He was chief pilot for PANAGRA, in Peru, and thought I looked too young to be the captain. I said that he was welcome to the jumpseat in the cockpit and that is where he sat until we were about half-way to Mexico City. Then he went back to his seat in the cabin, having decided either that I could do the job, or that the jumpseat was too uncomfortable.

We're Not Here Yet

On one of my trips into Panama we were flying down the coastline, keeping low because of cloud cover, and were just abeam a military installation called Rio Hato, where fighter crews trained and operated. We received a message that Albrook Field, our destination, was closed because a Navy plane had crashed there and was burning. They suggested that we should land at Rio Hato and wait until the situation cleared. We had no time to notify our purser, Martín Galvan. We had just enough time to contact Rio Hato tower, then turned in and landed. Because of the special cardboard inserts that were required in Panama to cover the cabin windows, Martín had no idea that we had not landed, as usual, at Albrook Field. He made the normal landing announcement to the passengers that we were arriving in the Panama Canal Zone.

Imagine his surprise when he opened the cabin door to find hundreds of soldiers, with guns, surrounding the airplane, and that we were at a place that he had never seen before. I opened the door of the cockpit just in time to see him pull the cabin door shut and, with great presence of mind, say to the passengers, "Everybody sit down. We're not here yet!"

Most of these stewards/pursers were fine young men and extremely competent, even overqualified for the job. One of our pilots said that using them for stewards was a waste –over-kill—like using a sledge hammer to drive a tack.

When we were flying DC-4s, our purser on one flight, Blackie Herman, had a man try to board in Mexico City carrying a huge suitcase. Blackie told him that he could not bring it into the cabin because we had a full load and there was no place to put the suitcase. The man wanted to know who was going to stop him from bringing it on board, at which Blackie replied "If it comes to that, I'll stop you. Why don't you just let me have it checked for you?" The man was irate and said, "Just take this whole damned airplane and shove it up your rear end!"

Blackie calmly said, "Sir if you can do that with the suitcase, you can bring it on board."

Mutt's Minimums

About three months after I was checked out I had an early morning flight out of Mexico City. Our destination was Brownsville and the weather reports showed it to be zero/zero, as was our alternate, Tampico. The rules said that I either had to have a series of weather reports showing a trend that indicated the weather would be above minimums at arrival time, or a forecast showing that it would be operational. No forecast had arrived in Mexico City. I was holding the flight, waiting for better weather, or for the forecast to arrive, when the chief pilot, my friend 'Mutt' Fleming, showed up. He was a passenger on my flight and had a guest with him, the chief pilot of Mexicana, the Mexican national airline. Naturally, he did not want the flight to be delayed and encouraged me to go, saying, "Ned, you know it's just morning fog and it will burn off by the time we get there."

Later, when I had more time in command, I would have had no problem with this. I would have simply pushed the clearance over in front of him and told him to sign the space for the captain's signature, and I'd be glad to go as his copilot. I did not do that and, in fact, I had an idea in the back of my mind that he might be trying to see if he could pressure me into doing something illegal. So I refused to go. This went on for two or three hours, and he was getting more upset with me all the time. Finally, he went out to the airplane to see if he could hear a forecast over the on-board radio. While he was there, a weather report came in for Tampico showing it above minimums, so I cleared for Tampico with the understanding that if Brownsville's weather improved before we arrived there we would reclear and go on without landing in Tampico.

When I reached the airplane, Mutt asked me what my intentions were. When I told him, he said, "That's not a damn bit better than what I wanted you to do three hours ago." By now I, too, was angry and I told him. "I wouldn't fly the trip the way you wanted me to if you were not here, and I'm sure not going to fly it that way just because you are a passenger!"

After we were in the air I received a message that Brownsville was forecast to be open by the time we arrived, so I recleared. Then I went back to tell Mutt and to apologize. I thought I was probably on my last trip in command of a Pan American airplane. But he said, “No, it was your trip and I didn’t have any business interfering.” I think maybe each of us learned to respect the other a little more at this time. When we finally arrived in Brownsville it was still below minimums and we had to hold for about thirty minutes before we could land.

Snooze Factor

Certain questions always come up when people ask about those early days. Did we ever sleep in flight? Of course we did. In fact on long night flights I used to set up a sleep schedule with the copilot—thirty minutes for me, then the same for him. I thought then, and think now, that it is much better to grab a few winks in the seat and arrive, more refreshed, at your destination where you may have a difficult approach to make. Otherwise, both pilots are tired at the very time when alertness is most required. I guarantee that a pilot asleep in his seat will come wide awake at the first strange sound or unusual movement.

I continued this practice throughout my career except when, on larger aircraft and on longer flights, we had multiple crews. Then we could switch off and take turns sleeping in a passenger seat, or, in some of the Boeing 747s, on bunks in the cockpit.

Of course you did not have to go to the extreme lengths to which one DC-4 pilot once did. In flight, with an F.A.A. inspector sitting in the jumpseat, he plastered the windshield with newspapers, slid back his seat, and went to sleep. That one cost him a fine of $1,000.00. You needed to be sensible, not stupid.

Strobed Prop

Without radar, we had to penetrate weather fronts and thunderstorms as best we could. There were theories. Some pilots liked to hit them low, some high, some in the darkest place, some where the lightning would let you see through. Nothing worked all the time. Once on a night flight out of Brownsville I was maintaining three thousand feet because an inbound flight was at four. We entered a cold front and the lightning was severe. We were flying with all the cockpit lights up bright to keep from being temporarily blinded by lightning, but strangely enough the flight was pretty smooth. I looked out my window just as a big lightning bolt let loose, and by that light was shocked to see the propeller stopped! I could read the Hamilton Standard decal on it. For a second, I just knew that the engine had quit; then it dawned on me that the strobe effect of the lightning had simply created the illusion that the propeller was stopped.

Just then, the northbound flight called. Frank Skillern wanted to know how rough it was in the front. I told him that there was more lightning than I had experienced before, but that the turbulence was not too bad. A few days later our paths crossed and he bawled me out for that report. He said that it was so rough that he thought the engines were going to come out of the mounts, or that he would lose the wings. The difference was either because we were of different levels, or because he might have been a mile or so from where I was.

One day a stewardess spilled coffee all over Frank's uniform shirt and trousers. His suitcase was in the baggage compartment just behind him, so he took it out and was preparing to make a change. Down to his drawers, he felt a draft of air and looked back to find the cockpit door open. Twenty-one passengers' heads were out in the aisle, looking at him.

The standard procedure for a DC-3 in turbulence was to put the landing gear down to make the aircraft more stable. One dark night we could see heavy lightning ahead, and thought that we were going to hit it at any moment, so we put the gear down to be ready. After flying along for ten minutes or so without mishap, we decided it was further away than we had thought, and retracted the gear. We did this exercise about three times before we actually entered the thunderstorm. When we first saw it, it must have been thirty minutes away—seventy-five miles or so—but the lightning was so intense that we thought it was right in front of us.

Help From The Friendly Skies

Leaving Guatemala one night in rain, we tried to make a position report when only about thirty miles out, but even that close we had already lost radio contact with Guatemala. After several tries, a female voice came in with perfect clarity, saying, "Clipper 502, this is United Air Lines in Salt Lake City. I read you loud and clear; would you like me to relay your position to Guatemala?" Radio skip could do that to you on the frequencies we used in those days.

I do not want to make it sound as though all our flights were that tough. Many days and nights were simply beautiful. One night after dinner at the Palace Hotel several of us were taking a stroll around the Plaza for exercise. It was a beautiful night with a full moon, and one of the fellows asked, "What does that moon make you think of?" A copilot, certainly more serious-minded than most, replied, "Well, it sure would be a good night for a flight to Mérida!"

Most flights were routine. I always made an effort to arrive at any terminal as near to the exact scheduled time as I could. I always held the view that people meeting someone at the airport would be less likely to call the flight by its assigned number, such as "Flight 518", than to say, "I'm meeting someone on Pan American's three-thirty flight." If, therefore, that flight rolled up to the terminal at exactly three-thirty, they were impressed; and so I would put on a little extra power or, if necessary, slow up a little so as to come in right on time.

Quick Check List

We were not normally too involved with passengers except on board the airplane. However, one day when I was having lunch at the Palace Hotel in Guatemala, a man came up to say that he had missed a flight and really needed to leave. I called the terminal, took a cab with him to the airport, and put him on the next flight out. He wrote a letter to the company to report that he had asked me why I, a pilot, had gone to so much trouble, and that my reply had been, "I am only protecting my job." That is the way I felt as long as Pan Am was paying my salary.

At lunch one day a lady from the next table leaned over and asked what pilots are doing when, after taxiing out to the runway, they stopped for a while before taking off. As I was trying to think how to tell her about running the checklist and checking the engines, a colleague with a quicker mind replied, "Oh, we do a quick check on the engines, sing two verses of 'Into the Wild Blue Yonder', have two minutes of silent prayer, then we take off." She thanked him very seriously and turned away. I would have liked to hear her story at the bridge club.

Cross Wind Take Off

Though most flights were routine, I guess there were two flights that I should admit did not fit that description. We had landed at Davíd (the copilot's field, remember?) in a very strong crosswind, at least thirty-five or forty knots. When we were ready to go we were sitting at the terminal on a little concrete pad just large enough to hold the airplane. I had wondered how we were going to take off without doing a ground loop, with the wind blowing straight across the field which was about 800 feet wide. I decided that, with all that wind, the DC-3, which needed only about 60mph to become airborne, could probably do so crossways on that field. When we were ready to taxi I told the copilot to tell the tower we were ready for take off. They didn't understand, of course, and cleared us for taxiing. I said, "No, we want clearance to take off." They were bewildered, but gave us the word to go, and take off we did—from the terminal straight across the width of the field. I was right, the DC-3 flew, but I could probably have been fired for taking that risk. On the other hand, had we tried to take off normally, we might have ground looped and damaged the aircraft.

Education for a Sailor

On a flight from the Canal Zone to Brownsville we had a ship's captain on board for two days. It was the first time he had flown and, as we became better acquainted, we began to compare our jobs. He understood our navigation, our power plants, and systems, but he was convinced of one thing: the airplane would not fly on one engine. He was in the cockpit with us and claimed that we told passengers, just to keep them happy, that we could fly on one engine; but that he knew better.

As we talked, I slowly pulled back the throttle on the left engine, cut the mixture and pushed the button to feather the propeller. I trimmed it up to fly on one engine, and he had no idea what I had done. Then I told the copilot to fly it for a minute or so. I slid my seat back and asked the captain to look over my shoulder at the left engine. There it sat, dead as a doornail, with the propeller stopped. He just calmly looked at it and said, "Well, what do you know! It *will* fly on one engine!" We restarted the engine and went on with the flight. None of the other passengers commented.

Four-legged Chickens

Our meals at the time were box lunches, and I thought they were pretty good. They usually comprised of a piece of meat such as a chicken breast, a sandwich, an apple, and a piece of cake. One day I wandered into the commissary in Mexico City where these box lunches were prepared. I asked what they did with the rest of the chicken. "What do you mean, 'the rest of the chicken'?" I said that we always seemed to get the breast, boneless, and that I knew chickens had such things as wings and drumsticks. The cook began to laugh until I thought he would cry. Then he explained that what I (and our passengers) had been eating was not chicken—it was iguana!

No Argument

In November 1946, I was asked by Mutt Fleming, who had taken over as chief pilot in Brownsville, to be a check pilot. I had to be approved by the C.A.A.

for this job and that required a flight with an inspector. Before I tell you about that flight, let me first discuss the DC-3.

The Douglas DC-3 has many admirers who think it was—and still is—one of the best airplanes ever built. I am a member of that fan club. Yet it never met the requirements of 'Transport Category' aircraft. When the C.A.A. came out with those rules, an airplane was supposed to reach a certain speed and, if an engine failed, at that point either be able to stop on what was left of the runway or to take off with one engine. The DC-3 would fly at about 60mph, but would not fly on one engine until it reached 80/85mph. So there was a short period when you could not afford to lose an engine unless there was plenty of runway in front of you. And runways were not often very long on Pan American's DC-3 routes in the 1940s.

On this flight the instructor pilot was C.D. (Tex) Barry. I was flying from the lefthand seat, of course, but Tex allowed the C.A.A. inspector to occupy the right seat. Tex was standing in the aisle between and behind us. On the first take off, just as I asked for the gear up, Mr C.A.A. cut the mixture on the left engine. This was against Pan Am procedure. We had a rule that engine failures below 1,000 feet were simulated by 15 inches of manifold pressure and 1,500rpm. We actually stopped engines only above 1,000 feet.

Tex told him to put the mixture back in and to simulate failure, but he refused to do so, saying that I could feather the propeller (stop the rotation) if I wanted to. I started to do that, but Tex grabbed my hand, saying that we could not feather the prop below 1,000 feet. I now had the worst of both worlds. I had the failed engine along with the tremendous drag of the 'windmilling' propeller. The airplane was barely flying. I could not make it fly high enough to start a turn back to the field with safety, and between the two of them they would not allow me to regain enough power nor to stop the propeller rotation.

We continued straight ahead for several miles, flying just above stalling speed, and the argument went on. Finally, Tex gave in and told me to go ahead and feather the prop. With that I was able to gain a little speed and altitude and return for a single-engine landing. On the ground we restarted the engine and the C.A.A. man began to discuss what we were going to do next, but Tex cut him short, telling him that we were through with that flight. We taxied in and went straight to the chief pilot's office, where a long discussion ensued. The outcome was a rule that Pan American adopted throughout the system, whereby no C.A.A. personnel were permitted to sit at, or touch, any control on our aircraft during a flight check. From then on, they gave check rides from the jumpseat, and only through our own check pilots.

Check Captain

The flight that followed the next day was such an anti-climax that I cannot remember any of the details. However, I was designated as a company check captain, a job that, also at a later date, I did on several other aircraft.

At this time a check pilot had several duties. He gave evaluation flights to new hires, six-month checks to regular pilots, instruction to pilots being upgraded to captain, and routine checks. Every six months each airline pilot requires a check on his flying ability and observation of his ability to fly the route. The latter was usually boring, just sitting in the jumpseat watching people who were very competent at their jobs.

I had one unfortunate experience not long after I started checking. We kept hearing negative things about one of the pilots: that he would fly off the normal routes at night over terrain too high to sustain flight should he lose an engine; or that he pushed too far in trying to land in bad weather; or that he would make a take off with less than take off power just to see how much runway he used. Copilots were beginning to avoid flights with him if they could, but it was not considered good policy to discipline a captain merely on the reports of copilots.

One day I was called into the office and told by an assistant chief pilot that I was being assigned a check trip with this man, all the way to Panama and back, and that I was to 'bust' him. In the room with us was his boss and mine, Mutt Fleming, and I just turned to him and said, "Mutt, if those are your orders, I will turn in my resignation as check pilot now." He told me to forget that idea; to ride with this guy and write up whatever I thought was right.

It was an awkward trip. The pilot knew he was 'under the gun' and I think he fully expected me to fail him. But he could fly the airplane very well and, of course, he pulled none of his tricks while I was in the copilot's seat, so I tried to find out if he knew how to stay safe over our routes. For instance, instrument flying was not allowed in or out of Tegucigalpa because of terrain, but we all knew that it was possible to be caught with deteriorating visibility on a departure and, if that happened, you needed to know where to turn to stay off the mountains. So, leaving 'Tee-goose', I put the hood up to simulate his being on instruments, to see if he would take the best direction. He just pulled down the hood and told me that it was not legal to make an instrument departure from that station, so he could not use instruments. I could not argue with that.

In the end I had no choice but to pass him, though reluctantly. The issue was not his flying ability, but his judgment, which is extremely hard to determine. I worried about that decision, but luckily not for long. He landed at San

José, Costa Rica, on a wet grass field and, I really think, through little fault of his own, slid off the field and through a fence.

I was present when he was told that he was being fired for that. He was also plainly told that no other pilot at the base would have been fired under the same circumstances, but that he was being dismissed for all of those other things that we knew he had done but had not been able to prove. At last they could hang one on him, and so they did.

Tough Steaks

One of the new hires for whom I gave an evaluation was M.O. Haskins. He was a good pilot, but marched to a different drummer. He came into the office once and said he wanted to resign and, when pressed for a reason, said that he wanted to beat the hell out of one of our captains, and did not want to be fired for it. We had a captain who was very unpopular and 'Mo' was not the first to have problems with him; so he was told just to be sure it did not happen during a trip or on company property. I think they did have some fisticuffs.

The next time he came in to quit was for a different reason. He said that he was now earning $320.00 per month and that he was soon due for a raise to $370.00. He figured that if he ever made that much money he could not afford to quit, so he wanted to do it while he could afford it. He was not to be talked out of it, so he left. Some time later my wife and I had dinner at a restaurant which Mo had opened, where he advertised on a big sign out front, "Guaranteed the toughest steaks in town."

My logs show the names of some of the pilots to whom I gave normal route checks: Roger Sherron, Johnny Musser, Kenny Floro, Lew Deweese, Ed Noyes, all excellent pilots with whom I would ride anywhere in the world. Trying to determine if a pilot was a safe one or not was very hard to do. There were different approaches and, just because a man did not do something exactly as I would do it, this did not mean that his way was unsafe.

Once, after retirement, I was asked by a fellow pilot to give my recollections of a flight on which I had checked him, and on which there had been some disagreement. I told my story and then he told me his. There were such discrepancies between his version and mine that you would have thought we were talking about two different flights.

In recent years the F.A.A. has addressed this problem by requiring every pilot to do everything exactly the same. They call it 'standardization'. To my mind it has only lowered the standards to the minimum level. Mediocrity is a good name for it.

Non Pilot Error

In those days we were staying in the Canal Zone at the old Tivoli Hotel, a wonderful wooden building dating from the heyday of the Canal operation. It had no air conditioning, and in that hot, humid climate it would have been unbearable except that the walls of the individual rooms had been built partition-like to within only two feet of the ceilings. That helped to cool things down but did not make for privacy or sound-proofing.

The hotel was very formal—ties and jackets required in the dining room; waiters in white coats with linen towels draped over their arms, and silverware arrayed out to a foot on either side of the plate. The management fixed up a less formal place on a side porch where flight crews could eat if they did not wish to put on a coat and tie. Maybe they were just trying to keep us out of sight.

There was a wonderful veranda with rocking chairs lined up all along the length of it. You could often find crew members here on their days off, rocking away and discussing all those things that crews talked about: sex, salary and seniority and, of course, accidents. One day a bunch of us were doing just that. There had been a spate of airline accidents that year and we were hearing way too much 'pilot error' from the press to suit us. Everyone was in defensive agreement that it should not be called pilot error. But one of our captains said, "You know, I think maybe we *have* to call it pilot error, because if it's *not* pilot error, then it can happen to you and me!"

It was an interesting viewpoint which I never forgot. Most pilots are egotists and think they would never make the mistakes that others make. Such egotism stems from the self-confidence, born of years of self-discipline, that is necessary to make a good pilot. I know that there have been several accidents that I do not think would have happened to me. But if they were caused by some equipment failure—not pilot error—then they could have happened to me, too.

The Fist...

Our crews still included radio operators whose job it was to send and receive messages by Morse Code. They were a strange lot. They could carry on a conversation in the cockpit on any subject while carrying on another entirely different conversation on the radio with their key or 'bug'. Radio operators can recognize each other's style of transmittal just as easily as they identify a voice or handwriting. They called it 'the fist'. The time came when they were phased out and we went to voice communications, and on one of my trips into San José my radio operator decided that he would disguise his 'fist' by sending with his left hand. The ground operator took him to be a student and sent back the message very fast, "Go get the regular operator—you stink." Switching to his right hand, my radio operator sent, at an even faster rate, "You don't smell like a red rose yourself!"

...and the Foot

Radio operators were positioned just behind the captain's seat; this set up an opportunity for a little fun with new pilots. On the DC-3 the yoke did not come up between the pilot's legs but rather on the side next to the cockpit sidewall. The captain would give a new pilot the chance to fly and, by prearrangement, the radio operator would put his foot up alongside the left side of the airplane and gently push forward on the yoke. The airplane would nose down a little and the pilot would trim it to fly level and then the radio operator would let the pressure off and up would come the nose. This could be repeated again and again; meanwhile the captain would say, "I thought you knew how to fly! Keep this thing level." The captain would take over and, of course, it would go along nice and smooth, until he gave it back to the copilot, and the whole thing would start all over again. It could drive you crazy until you caught on.

On the flying boats at one time there was a crew member who liked to put his foot on the control pedestal between the pilots. It annoyed a certain captain and he determined to put a stop to it. He brought aboard an old uniform shoe of his own and when the foot appeared on the pedestal he grabbed it and pulled off the fellow's shoe. Quickly switching shoes, he dropped the good one down beside his seat out of sight and, opening his side window, threw the old shoe out. The crew member looked at the one shoe he had left and said, "Well, I have no use for just one shoe," and before he could be stopped he threw it out, too!

Down the Hole

And so it went. Back and forth, up and down Central America, finding our way over and under, through and around thunderstorms, and in and out of mountain valleys, between volcanic peaks and over beautiful lakes. Coming into Tegucigalpa, we knew we were in the canyon that would lead to the airport by observing a certain cave in the canyon wall.

Approaches to airports were made any way that seemed practicable, sometimes by established let-down procedures, but often by some improvised method. If we could find a hole in the clouds anywhere in the vicinity we could go down, and, knowing the terrain, find our way to the airport underneath. At

San Salvador the runways were just on the edge of Lake Ilopango which would often be clear when the airport was covered with clouds. I have gone down over the Lake until I was as low as the runway, and if I could see the runway from there, never mind the ceiling, I could make my approach at runway level and land. If we were concerned with being legal (and that is not synonymous with being safe) we could always suggest to the guy on the ground that it looked as though the ceiling was four hundred feet instead of the two hundred that he reported. He would always agree.

Hitchhiker

On one trip out of San José, the pilot thought the controls felt very odd after take off, making the airplane difficult to fly. He returned to the field only to find that there was a man lying on the horizontal stabilizer. He had his arms hooked over the leading edge and had kicked holes into the fabric-covered elevator to put his feet into. What a ride he must have had! Nor was he our only hitchhiker. At least two others tried to take a free ride in this way. They were on other aircraft types, and I shall tell about them later.

Bottle to Throttle

Now is the time, perhaps, to answer that other burning question in your mind. Was there drinking? Yep. Not as much perhaps as that stereotyped picture of hard-drinking, carousing airline pilots that you have heard about. We had some teetotalers and, at the other extreme, a few who drank more than a little, but the majority were typically average social drinkers. At the time the only C.A.A. rule was that you were not supposed to operate an airplane while under the influence of alcohol. The eight-hour rule (from bottle to throttle) came much, much later. Pan American had its own, stricter, rule: no liquor within twelve hours of flight. Seldom was this custom abused, and I personally saw this happen only twice. Once was as a new copilot at Guatemala when it seemed to me that my captain had indulged too much the night before and entirely too close to flight time. As we went to the airport I decided that I would board the airplane only because I was going to be sitting at a set of controls. Feeling as I did, I would not have ridden his airplane as a passenger. Actually, it amounted to nothing. As we went into the cockpit he turned to me and said, "I don't feel too good, would you like to fly today?" I flew the entire flight, or at least until, after several hours, he 'felt better' and maybe flew a leg or so. The other time was years later, on a different airplane.

At the end of a long day it was usual for the crew to gather for a 'debriefing'. Had I taped some of those crew gatherings I would not have to write this book from memory. Maybe I would be rich—for truth is stranger than fiction—but more likely I would have been sued down to my toenails by some of the participants.

One-Piece Swimsuit

Stewardesses were doomed to bear the same exaggerated reputations as did the pilots. Some of the very finest young ladies I ever met were cabin crew, but a few were some of the trashiest. I was asked many times if I would allow my own daughter to be a stewardess and my answer was "Of course." Her character and her conduct would not change by reason of becoming a stewardess.

I have a fond memory of a flight out of Tapachula. One day our stewardess, Virginia Royce, came to the cockpit and asked me to come back to the cabin in exactly five minutes. I wondered why the wait of five minutes, but I agreed. When I opened the cockpit door, all twenty-one passengers were singing "Happy Birthday!" And every one had a gift for me. Some, wrapped in toilet paper, were as small as a 'chicklet' (chewing gum) that was a staple on Pan American in those days. But everyone had something, and I was forced to walk down the aisle, hat in hand, gathering up all those presents. They don't do that on Boeing 747s today.

Another girl was at the hotel pool at Caracas wearing a two-piece bathing suit. An attendant told her that the hotel rules required a one-piece suit. Her reply was, "Fine, which piece do you want me to take off?" These were the days before bikinis and well before the topless style came into vogue.

On a flight from Medellín to Panama we were flying in stratus-type clouds, very smooth. The copilot went to the back and the stewardess came forward and sat down in his seat for a minute or two. She began to ask questions about how the airplane flew, and how the instruments worked. I explained the artificial horizon and the directional gyro. Then, making sure that she knew which way to move the yoke, and that she knew to move it very gently, I gave her the controls. There was nothing dangerous about it. I was in my seat ready to correct anything that she might do and, in fact, she had little to do. The DC-3, being very stable, will just go along in level flight very nicely, almost by itself. If a wing dropped a little low, as indicated by the small airplane on the face of the artificial horizon, I would prompt her to level it by a little pressure to turn the wheel until it showed to be level again. Or if the nose dropped, to pull back slightly. We went along for ten or fifteen minutes like this, with her keeping the airplane level and on heading, until the copilot came back to take his seat. Nobody in the back ever noticed.

The rest of this story came some thirty or more years later, when I was fully repaid for that harmless and innocent deviation from the rules. I was president of a chapter of *Amigos de las Americas,* an organization to train high school students to perform simple medical procedures for people in remote areas in Central and South America. The mother of one of our students approached me and asked if I was Ned Wilson. When I admitted to it, she told me that I had given her the greatest thrill of her life; I had allowed her to fly a DC-3.

Penitentiary

One of our recreations on days off in Panama was to go swimming in one of the military clubhouse pools. Two of us were on our way to the Albrook clubhouse for that purpose and we had to catch a bus in front of the Ancón Police Station, where a beautifully-kept lawn had a fence around it consisting of cement posts with a chain looped through them. My friend was standing on the chain between two posts.

I thought it would be fun to throw him off, so I took a run and jumped on the taut chain between the next two posts. But instead of throwing him off, the corner post broke right off flush with the ground. A bus pulled up about then, but there was no chance of boarding it. A police officer came through the door and shouted, "Stop, in the name of the law!"—the first and only time I actually ever heard that term used in real life.

He grabbed us by the arm and took us into the station and said, "Sergeant, book these boys!" "Yes sir, what charge, sir?" "Deliberate and malicious destruction of police property!"

When the officer left the room, the sergeant's manner became a little less grim, and he said that he didn't know what to do with us, but he would call the penitentiary. "PENITENTIARY!""Yes," he said, "They make the posts. I'll have to see what they cost." He told us to go on swimming and to stop by on our way back to the hotel. The post cost us two dollars.

Three on a String

I cannot leave the DC-3 without repeating a story told by a friend on another airline. They had a jokester flying a 'Three' and, when he needed to leave the cockpit, he would tie a piece of string to a convenient place in the cockpit. Then, backing out of the cockpit, keeping the string tight, he would make his way all the way down the aisle to the back. Looking around for a likely passenger, he would say, "Sir, would you mind flying the airplane while I go to the bathroom? Just hold this string, and if the nose starts to go down, pull back on it a little. If the nose gets too high, let off on the pressure a little."

After a few minutes in the 'can', he would come out and very politely say, "Thank you very much, sir, you did very well." Then, winding up his string as he went, he would go back into the cockpit.

If you were one of those passengers who 'flew' a DC-3 with a piece of string, now you know.

"Sir, would you mind flying the airplane while I go to the bathroom?"

Rain in Las Piedras

In September 1947 Pan American suffered some staff reductions that resulted in fewer crews at Brownsville. Along with others, I was due for demotion to copilot. But four of us were given the chance to go to Venezuela to fly as captains for a Pan American subsidiary called Aerovías Venezolanas, known as AVENSA. We would fly the line in Venezuela and at the same time train Venezuelan pilots.

In those days, the company was known as the Pan American Airways System, and the 'system' had meaning. Pan American had subsidiaries in many countries, including about a dozen nations of Central and South America. It owned varying percentages of shares in each company which it used as local feeder systems to the main trunk route of the parent company, which usually stopped only in capitals or major cities.

It was a good system. It was good for Pan Am and good for the U.S.A. Juan Trippe's well-known desire to have a 'Chosen Instrument' international airline for the United States made a lot of sense. Other countries have their flag carriers, sometimes government-subsidized, but the United States chose not only to compete against these, but also to have its own airlines competing against each other. Trippe offered to form the Chosen Instrument from a consortium of all U.S. airlines. It would not have been Pan Am alone, but he could never sell this idea.

As a fallout of this policy and with growing economic independence in Latin America, some years later Pan Am was forced to divest itself of all those subsidiaries. But in 1947 I was able to fly for AVENSA as others had done for AVIANCA (Colombia), Aviateca (Guatemala), SAHSA (Honduras), LANICA (Nicaragua) and many others.

Four of us, B.B. Wilson, Matt Clasper, Earl Johnson, and myself arrived in Venezuela about the middle of September. We met with the chief pilot, Guillermo Ochoa Tucker. His father was Venezuelan and his mother a U.S. citizen, which explains the 'Tucker'. In Latin countries men often append their mother's maiden name as a suffix. My Venezuelan pilot's license has my name recorded as Ned Wilson Vickers. Tucker was usually called 'Ochoa', and that is how I will refer to him. He was an unusual and very smart man. He did not speak English very well at the time, and one of our first meetings with him was amusing.

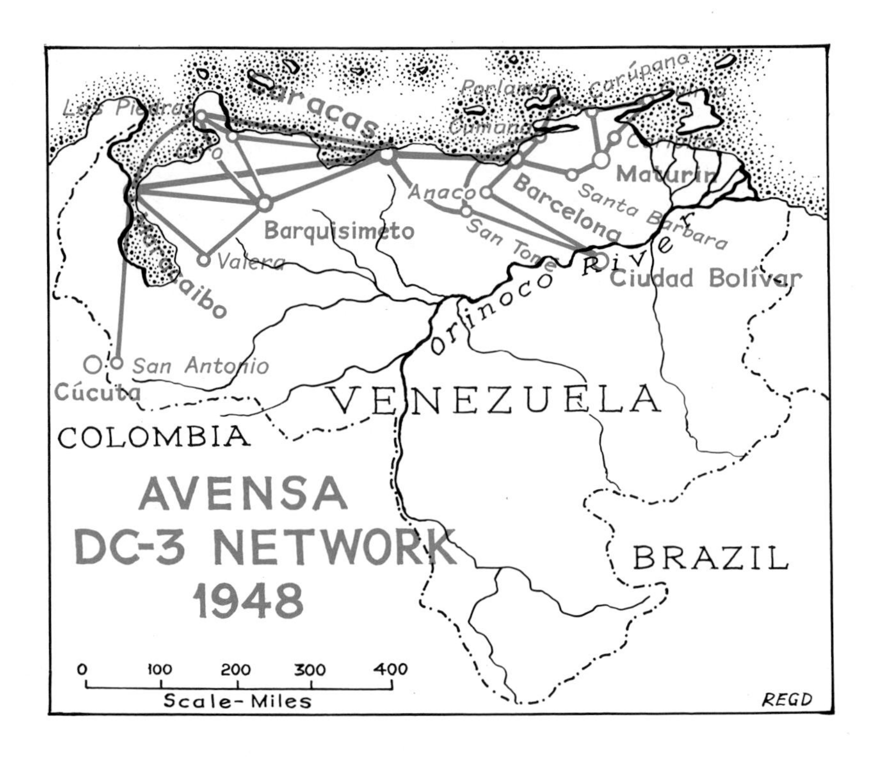

Captain Guillermo Ochoa Tucker ('Ochoa'), AVENSA's chief pilot & operations manager during the 1940s and a master of his trade. The aircraft is a Lockheed 10 Electra.

You Can See the Next Airport from Here.

He handed each of us an oil company road map marked with red 'X's at the places where there were airports that AVENSA served, and began to tell us, "All the roads in Venezuela are good." I did not understand why we cared very much about the roads, as I thought we would be flying. It finally became clear that when he said 'roads' he meant 'routes.' He also told us that when we were on trips that we should not drink the water as it might make us sick. We were to drink beer provided on the airplane. We found that Coca Cola was also provided, and we usually subsisted on that.

I made the mistake of asking about weather information. "Weather information?"

"Yes, sir. Does AVENSA have its own meteorologists, or does the Venezuelan government have a weather service? Just where do we find out what the weather is like?"

He looked as if I were a fool and said, "Cap-i-tán, from thees airport choo are seeing the naxt one." We found out that was true because most of our flights were only fifteen or twenty minutes long. If you wondered what the weather was like at the next airport, you just looked over there.

300 Kilos in the Back

We were used to a very complicated system that Pan Am had to determine the 'CG' (center of gravity, or balance) of the airplane. Again I asked who was responsible for loading and balance of the airplane. Ochoa told me to put 300 kilos in the rear baggage compartment. No matter how I asked the question that was the only answer I could get, "Put 300 kilos in the rear baggage compartment."

The next day or so I went to Pan Am and borrowed a slide rule that they used for weight and balance. I ran every problem that I could think of and I found out that no matter how a DC-3 was loaded, if you had 300 kilos in the rear compartment it was within limits. If you had an empty airplane, with only 300 kilos in the rear compartment, it was nose-heavy but within acceptable limits. If the airplane cabin was full and you had 300 kilos in the rear compartment, it was tail-heavy but also within acceptable limits. Pan Am could throw away its 'slip sticks'.

As a matter of fact, in the mornings when we left we would be given the total weight of the airplane and nothing else. If we wanted to keep track of the weight during the day, we had to subtract what came off at any station and add what went on. It finally got to where I just made sure there was at least 300 kilos in the rear baggage compartment. We could seat 28 passengers in the

DC-3 and if they were all there, you knew you were heavy, and that was that. Some of our flights had as many as seventeen take offs and landings in one day.

Ice Water in the Ears

Before we got our Venezuelan licenses we had to take another physical. This one was a doozy. It took three different doctors. The one who was responsible for eyes and ears had a new wrinkle. He would fill our ears with ice water and then have us stand on one foot with our eyes closed. We guessed that this was to see if we still had balance with the ear canals frozen. Matt Clasper was going to quit and return to Pan Am rather than submit to ice water in his ears, but we finally convinced him that it would not do any permanent damage.

Que Dices, Cap-i-tán?

The physical took three days, the flight test for the license took about ten minutes. Then we were ready to start flying the line. Ochoa had said that for our first trip he would try to find a copilot who could speak a little English. The night before my first trip I thought about the DC-3 to visualize what there was in the cockpit that I could not handle alone. I figured that the only control that I could not reach was that for the cowl flaps. This was on the sidewall to the right of the copilot and had three positions: open for taxi, closed in flight, and 'trail' (floating) for take off. I consulted my Spanish/English dictionary and studied how I would give the command to trail the cowl flaps.

The next morning when I got ready to start the take off I grandly said, "*Pongese los aletas del motor en el position trail.*" All I got back was, "*Que dices,* Capitán?" (What did you say?). Repeating, again I got a blank look of non-under-standing. Nearly in flight by now, I resorted to English and said, "Damn it, trail the cowl flaps!" "Oh, sí, Capitán." And trail they did. It turns out that all the Venezuelan pilots had been trained to use the cockpit commands in English and did so, even when flying with each other. "Gear up, gear down, half flaps, props low pitch," etc, and they might not speak a word of conversational English. My Spanish was pretty meager at the time, but when you have a Spanish-speaking crew, and you overnight in towns where no English is spoken, you will learn fairly fast, especially if you want to eat.

Caracas, the capital, was only about ten miles south of the coast where the airport of Maiquetía was located, but in 1947 it was about an hour and a half drive over a road that had some three hundred turns up and down the mountain. On our first ride up the mountain the driver kept cutting to the inside of curves, over on the left side of the road. When we complained, he said that it was a one way road, all up on one road and down on the other. Just as we relaxed, after hearing this, we met a truck coming downhill on our road. He said that it was a government truck and that it could go either way it wanted to go.

Home, Sweet Home!

Places to live were very scarce and hard to find. Bernie Wilson and I finally found a house on the beach at a little village called Catia del Mar, about seven miles west of Maiquetía. We rented it and sent word to our wives to come on down, as we intended to share the house. My wife and I and Ken, our four-year-old, took the bedroom on one end of the house, and Bernie and his wife took the other bedroom on the far end of the house. Between us was a big living room and a kitchen. The house was all open—wooden shutters instead of glass windows which were not required in that climate. It had a large veranda on the beach side. The yard was full of coconut trees; so many that I was afraid one would fall on Ken's head while he was playing in the yard.

The beach was almost too close. Our bedclothes stayed damp from the spray. The beach was also strange. One day it would be a nice, sandy beach, but we would get up one morning to find a vee-shaped wedge that would consist of big, round stones, no sand. That would grow, day by day, until there was no sand at all, and the entire beach would be covered in stones. Then, in a few days, a vee of sand would appear, and grow daily, until the whole beach was once again sand. It was good for swimming and we could catch lobsters—the clawless kind—by swimming along the rocks and just reaching into holes and pulling them out.

Thievery was rampant, and we had a case or two of someone trying to break in, so one night Bernie and I spent the whole night in the rocks along the beach, watching the house to see if we could catch someone. No luck, just a sleepless night.

Trimmed Approach

AVENSA's copilots had started with the company when they had a total of thirty-five hours flight time in a Piper Cub. In about a year some of them were flying as captains, and very successfully so. But I sometimes wondered how the passengers withstood some of the landings. Often we would hit hard and bounce many feet into the air. I would have to grab the wheel and a handful of throttles and nurse the aircraft back to the ground before it stalled. After one of these, a copilot said to me, "Cap-i-tán, choo are flying thees airplane at se-exty miles per hour!" As far as he knew, that was below the stalling speed, and he was close to being right.

Captain Rivas, at the helm of one of AVENSA's Douglas DC-3s.

One of the fellows who flew with me was a fine young man by the name of Pelucarte. He was very small and weighed next to nothing. I was always concerned that he might not be able to hold the rudder if we lost an engine, but he never got into trouble. He would overuse the trim tab on final approach (maybe we should not call it 'final'—we sure hoped it would not be our final approach). With the power reduced, that would have been all right, but if power was applied to go around I did not think he could hold it as the nose would pitch up strongly. I warned him, but he kept saying that he could handle it.

So one day I let him roll the trim all the way back and then I added full throttle on both engines. It took both his hands to keep the nose from coming up and he could not get a hand free to roll the stabilizer trim forward, nor even to pull the throttles back. Finally I relieved him by reducing the power, and said, "Now Peluca, what do you think?" He allowed as how he did not need to use the stabilizer all that much on approach. The last time I saw him, many years later, he was flying DC-10s on flights to Spain, and had previously flown the Boeing 747, as well. He preferred the 747.

Self Service

Many, if not most, of AVENSA's flights were fifteen or twenty minutes from airport to airport. One flight from Maturín to Cachipo took less than five minutes. Gear up, turn on course, gear down, and land. Cachipo had no buildings of any kind on the airstrip, just a big tree alongside the runway. There were no personnel. When we left Maturín two men went with us, a ticket-seller and a baggage handler. They rode standing in the baggage compartment behind us. When we landed they opened the service door in the cockpit, dropped out to the ground, and ran around to open the cabin door. There was a small kitchen table under a tree, and they would pull it out and sell tickets, load the baggage, and away we would go to Guiria, leaving them behind. As they snoozed under the tree, we would go to Guiria and come back. Then they would stand in the baggage compartment again on the trip back to Maturín.

Champion Chickens

AVENSA maintained good schedules, was seldom late, and gave pretty good service. Enrique Boulton, who was the major stockholder and president, tried hard to make it a modern airline. One thing he did not like was for us to carry fighting cocks—'chickens', he would call them—in the cabin. It was a hard rule to follow because we often had men aboard who participated in that sport, and they thought as much, if not more, of their feathered friends as they did of their families. Usually, they had the 'chickens' in cloth sacks that hung over their knees.

On a flight into San Tomé I had such a man with four fighting cocks in sacks over his knees. As luck would have it, Mr Boulton was on the ground there and, as we stood talking, those cocks crowed. He said, "Captain, are you carrying chickens in the cabin?" When I said that I was, he told me to make the man put them in the baggage compartment. I had already tried that, and I knew the man would not do it, but I tried again. The man was destined to the island of Margarita, off the shore from Barcelona, and we would be there in less than an hour. But, to keep from parting with his 'chickens', he got off in San Tomé where he would catch a bus to Barcelona and from there, a boat to Margarita. He probably arrived there the next day.

Palm Tree and Derrick-Hopping

San Tomé was an oil company camp in beautiful savannah country with occasional palm trees to relieve the flat land. We had an early-morning flight from Ciudad Bolivar, on the Orinoco River, and at certain times of the year there would usually be a low cloud cover at Ciudad Bolivar and over the route to San Tomé. There were no let-down facilities at San Tomé, so if we wanted to land, there was only one thing to do. We would take off and stay under the clouds, sometimes not over one hundred, or maybe two hundred feet high. For twenty minutes or so we would fly along, dodging around palm trees and the occasional oil derrick. Passengers never seemed to mind in the least. I have looked back through the cockpit door (which was always open) and seen them sitting there relaxed and reading their morning paper as if we were at a cruising altitude of 10,000 feet.

Engine Out Performance

At Ciudad Bolivar I saw proof of the fact that a DC-3 will not fly on one engine until it has acquired enough speed. An Aéropostal (government airline) crew got into an argument about it after arriving one evening. The captain maintained that he could continue a take off on one engine if he lost one before he left the ground. The copilot did not think so.

The next morning as they were rolling on take off, and after the tail came up, the left propeller was suddenly feathered. The airplane continued the attempt to take off. It rose to about twenty feet, stalled, and crashed on its nose. Nothing at all was left of the cockpit area. When I walked up to the wreckage, the first thing I could put my hand on was the throttle quadrant. All else had simply been ground off. We had no proof that the engine had been deliberately shut down, but it sure looked suspicious. In any case, the take off

The airstrip (on the left of the picture) at Valera, Venezuela, in 1947. In this part of Venezuela, a piece of level ground was a luxury.

should have been discontinued after the engine quit. But it certainly resolved the argument.

Hors-d'Oeuvres

Flights to Porlamar, on the island of Margarita, were always a pleasure. The water between the coast and the island was so clear that we could see groups of whales that were usually in the area. Sailboats moored off the coast looked as if they were sitting on the bottom. There was an old lady at the airport who cooked 'empanadas' using the top of an old oil drum for a stove. These were pieces of tortilla wrapped around a small piece of cheese and fried on the top of the oil drum. We would usually buy a paper bag full of these things and eat them for several legs. Dee-licious! Better than popcorn.

Another treat was to be found at Carúpano, a town on the coast where we spent the night on some flights. The first time I stayed there I was puzzled, for no sooner had we checked into the hotel, the stewardess was handed a bucket. She went straight to the beach and came back with this bucket full of small clams that she had scooped up on the beach. With a tray of lime slices, we sat on the veranda opening those little clams. A squirt of lime juice and you had a tender morsel. Our hors d'oeuvres before dinner.

Rats and Goats

The places where we stayed at overnight stations were, to say the least, anything but luxurious. At Ciudad Bolivar we stayed in a private home. It was a nice home, considering everything, and I was put in a big room. The ceiling was made of reeds woven into a pattern, and there was a kind of shelf all around the room about six inches under the ceiling. The bed was right in the middle of the room and over it was a mosquito net. I hate sleeping under those things and, anyway, had not seen any mosquitos. I asked why it was there and was told that 'the pilots' made them put it there. I elected not to use it and left it pulled up above the bed. After I turned out the light and was just about to go to sleep, I felt something run across my feet. Thinking I must be mistaken, I drifted off again, only to be awakened by something on my bed. I turned on the light and saw that the room was full of rats! Then I knew why the mosquito net was there. The rodents were using that shelf as a highway, and would jump down and run across my bed. I pulled that mosquito net down, tucked it under the mattress and slept right in the middle of the bed.

Guiria had no hotel and we stayed in a building owned by the station manager of our competitor, TACA. Two rows of rooms were separated by a narrow patio, not of nice green grass, rather a pile of beer cans about four feet high. The toilet and a shower of sorts were way out back. My room had no window, only a small slit high up on the outside wall. The only furniture was a cot with a straw mattress and the only light was a bare 15-watt bulb too weak to read by. The crowning touch, though, was the room across the patio. There they kept a goat and a pile of corn. I tried sleeping on the beach one night, but the sand fleas ran me back to the room.

The best hotel was not in Venezuela at all, but in Colombia. We used to land in a little town called San Antonio on the border with Colombia and crossed the border to stay in Cúcuta where there was a very satisfactory hotel run by Germans. Cúcuta was important to us for another reason, too. Meat and fresh vegetables were hard to find in Venezuela, but Cúcuta had a nice public market where meat was always available. We could also buy eggs and tomatoes. We would go to the market early in the morning and buy a whole tenderloin of beef, or a beef tongue, or a leg of lamb. In fact, we brought back so much meat that AVENSA was forced to build trays to fit into the baggage compartments on these flights to prevent the meat juices from corroding the metal floors.

Border Crossing Know-how

At one time a small revolution in Venezuela had closed the border; crews could not go to Cúcuta and were forced to spend the night in the airplane, or drive ten or fifteen miles to another, rather poor, hotel on the Venezuelan side of the border. I was flying with a copilot named 'Eduardo', and on the way I asked him if he wanted to sleep in the airplane or go to this other hotel. Eduardo was a burly sort of a guy and in the Venezuelan National Guard he held some rank. He said that he would rather go to Cúcuta. I agreed, but told him it was impossible. He said that he would get us there. When we arrived he had the driver take us to the border and, of course, found it barred. The guard told Eduardo that the officer in charge, a certain general, was in town. Eduardo insisted that we be taken to see him. I went along just to see what would happen. When we found the general, Eduardo told him that we had special permission from the general in charge at the Maiquetía airport to cross the border. I knew of no such permission, but Eduardo produced a piece of paper with the signature of the general on it, and I wanted to laugh. What he was waving around under this guy's nose was a pass that all of us had been given to get through the guards at Maiquetía. I had one just like it, and it had nothing to do with crossing the border. But it did have a general's signature on it, and Eduardo never gave him a chance to really look at it. The local general jumped on the running board, took us to the border, and ordered the guards to lift the bars for us. We were the only crew in nearly a month who spent the night in Cúcuta.

Bootblack

At one small town hotel they had a huge register for us to sign in on. It required name, age, birthdate, citizenship, place of birth, address, employer, occupation, and perhaps more. They wanted us to fill out every bit of that each time we arrived. Never mind that we came in every few days in uniform and they surely knew who we were. So one day, in a funny mood, I put down 'Bootblack' for my occupation and never gave it a second thought. That is, until about three weeks later I was called into the chief pilot's office. It seems that some government bureaucracy or other had picked up the register and they wanted to arrest and fine me for 'falsifying hotel records'.

I thought it was a joke, but Ochoa convinced me that they were serious about the whole thing. I tried to tell him that I really was a bootblack, that nobody else did my shoes, but this was one time that he, too, was serious and told me that I had better not do this again. I did see a grin on his face, though, as I left his office.

We had agreed to come with AVENSA for a four-month assignment but, as the time approached to go back to Pan American, Ochoa asked if we would stay longer. I was reluctant because Helen was carrying our second child who was due in April. When I told him this, his reply was characteristic of him. "Two millions babies are born every year in Venezuela." I agreed to stay.

Tarzán

Our stay was not easy on Helen. She had a four-year-old child to take care of and was expecting another. We found another house about two blocks off the beach, and rented it from an American who taught at the Naval Academy in Maiquetía. it was typical for the area—tile floors, no hot water, a kerosene stove on which Helen learned to bake cakes and pies that were as good as those cooked on any other type. But the best thing about the house was that it came with a dog. When I went to look at the house, I found, lying on the porch, a big dog with a muzzle on. If I even set a foot on the walk to the house he was on his feet; hairs on his neck stood erect and he growled as though he would eat me. I did not go up to the house, muzzle or no muzzle.

The next day I saw the owner, Mr Kirkland, and he asked me how I liked the house. I told him I had not seen it because of the dog. "Oh, yes," he said, "That is Tarzán. I'll take you over tomorrow and introduce you." And he did, just as you would introduce humans. "Tarzán, this is Mr Wilson. Mr Wilson, this is Tarzán." When we moved in, the first thing I did was to remove the muzzle. He was almost as big as a St Bernard, and spotted brown and white. He was four-year-old Ken's constant companion, would not let him out of his sight. Ken would put a dishtowel around his neck and pretend to be Superman. Then he and the dog would roam the neighborhood. I never needed to worry about anybody hurting Ken. That dog would have torn them up, but he never offered to hurt any child that Ken was playing with. When our next child, Alice, came along, it presented Tarzán with a problem. He solved it by going with Ken to wherever he was playing and as soon as he got settled, Tarzan would come back and check on the baby, going back to Ken every few minutes.

During the time we were there, every house in our neighborhood was robbed except ours and the one next door. Tarzán would not leave the house at night, but he would go out into the street and bark in the direction of a break-in. We would walk down the street the next morning asking who got broken into last night. He always knew.

Down the street was a house occupied by two single men. They said that a thief could not break into their house because it had good bars on the windows and solid wooden doors. One morning they woke up to find that someone had drilled holes into their kitchen door until a piece could be pushed out and it was possible to reach and turn the lock. The two men rigged a machete with a nail through the hole in its handle, and with some rubber tire tubes for power, so that when a trigger was touched the machete would come down over the hole in the door. They said they would pick up a hand off the kitchen floor and take it to the police station, saying, "Just find whoever fits this and you will have your thief."

We worried that they would be the ones who got into trouble, but actually their trap stayed there for weeks and nobody ever bothered it. We figured that every thief in the area knew what awaited them.

Dragon

On my way to the beach to go swimming one day I passed the house of one of our friends and heard the wildest screaming that I had ever heard. Thinking that someone was being murdered, at least, I ran over to the house. I found the wife's mother, who had just come to visit from the States, standing on the porch facing a big iguana and unable to move. The iguana had crawled out on a tree limb which had grown under the porch roof and the two of them were eye to eye. I think she thought she had encountered a dragon which, to be fair, it did resemble.

Maria Alicia

One thing that Helen did like in Venezuela was having the baby there. Her doctor, Dr Hedrick, was a German and the hospital was modern and very nice. The doctor did not believe in women getting up too soon after giving birth and kept her there for at least a week. The hospital rooms were all furnished with two beds and a family member was expected to stay with the patient. The nurses all thought that I was a cruel monster because I did not spend the time there with her.

I was so sure that we were going to have another boy that I thought they had made a mistake when they brought our daughter out to me. We named her Mary Alice, but of course the name on her Venezuelan birth certificate is Maria Alicia. By Venezuelan law, she had to have her own passport when we prepared to leave the country. Venezuela recognizes dual citizenship, but the U.S. does not, so at the age of eighteen she had to choose to be a U.S. citizen; Venezuela still recognizes her citizenship there.

The bad thing was having to go up and down the mountain to the hospital in Caracas. Those three hundred curves always made Helen sick and I do not think we ever made it without stopping to let her throw up once or twice. Even then they were talking about putting in a tunnel (later done) and I asked Captain Ochoa how big he thought the tunnel would be. He said that he didn't know, that it would, "Depend on how big they make the hole."

We were doing lots of flying. I averaged more than one hundred hours per month the first sixteen months, flying as many as one hundred twenty-seven hours in some months. And this at fifteen and twenty minutes per flight. We were probably making more money than Pan American pilots on the top equipment, at that time Boeing 377 Stratocruisers. We were being paid $1,100 per month for the first 80 hours and overtime for anything over that. We could live on the overtime and Pan American deposited the rest in our bank. Venezuela had a two percent tax on money paid in the country.

Shoe Importer

Life in Venezuela could be frustrating. Ken's grandmother sent him a pair of shoes. I received a postcard in the mail telling us that a package had arrived on such and such a ship. Did we accept or reject it? Of course we accepted and sent the card back. About three weeks later I opened a large manila envelope stuffed with papers and instructions to take them to Caracas for processing. So up the hill we went again. This particular office was open only two days a week from 3 pm to 5 pm. When I arrived I stood in line for more than an hour to reach to the first window. Once there a clerk stamped all the papers with a wild flurry and, taking one paper, told me to go to the next line. I could not make it through all the lines that day so had to come back again. This time I made it through all the lines, paid a tax amounting to three times the value of the shoes, and ended up with one piece of paper.

I asked when I could collect the shoes. Guess what? I could not have the shoes because I did not have a permit to import shoes into Venezuela. Tax refund? Don't be silly, I had accepted the package, I had to pay the tax. But I could not have the shoes.

I have been told that I have a stubborn nature. I guess it's true because I applied for a permit to import shoes into the country. It took about three more weeks of my spare (?) time, but I ended up with a permit to import shoes (plural) into Venezuela. I could have opened a shoe store if I had a mind to. I reclaimed Ken's shoes and requested our families not to send us anything else while we were there.

Do it Yourself Traffic Control

Our flights were mostly straightforward, nearly all during daylight, and generally in good weather. We did have a few places, however, such as Valera, that were in mountainous terrain and, with summer thunderstorms, could make us earn our pay.

Barquisimeto was one stop that did quite often require instrument approaches, but it had no radio facilities designed for that. We used a broadcast station in the town and took care of our own traffic control. Nearing the airport we would radio, "AVENSA, ten miles out at eight thousand for approach." Then you might hear, "TACA on approach leaving seven for six." "Aéropostal out of five." "TACA, leaving six for five." Listening, you knew where everyone else was and you broadcast what you were doing. It worked fine and I have seen as many as seven airplanes making approaches there at one time, all without any traffic control from the ground. And very safely.

Rain at Las Piedras

At Las Piedras (The Rocks), a stop on a peninsula jutting out into the Caribbean north of Coro, I remember several incidents. The average annual rainfall there was less than two inches. But one day I arrived there in the midst of a heavy thunderstorm. When I landed there were about five or six inches of water on the runway. The runway was not cambered, but was low in the center. Whoever built it thought it did not rain enough to justify building up the center so that it would drain.

Douglas DC-3s have been in service all over the world on wheels, floats, and skis. This one, piloted—if that is the word—is aquaplaning on about three inches of flood water after a cloudburst at Las Piedras (where, according to Ochoa, "it never rains").

As I landed, the water pushed forward from the wheels made a big 'rooster-tail' that went up in front of the wings and clear over the top of the aircraft's tail. There was so much pressure from that wall of water, going in under the wings, as well as rooster-tailing, that it broke or bent the push rods that activated the flaps. We continued the flight, just making no-flap landings at the rest of our stops.

The next day I made a trip to Captain Ochoa's office to discuss this with him. I felt really bad, as this was the first (and last) time that an airplane I was flying had been scratched in any way that could be attributed to me. As I walked down the hall, I could see him in his office and, when he saw me, he started laughing like a hyena. When I entered his office, he said, "You are lucky, I have lived here all my life and I never saw it rain in Las Piedras. You got to see it rain in Las Piedras!"

I told him that I sure did see it rain in Las Piedras and, "Did you know that I broke the flaps on the airplane?" He said, "Oh, yes, I know that, they are fixing it in the shop now, but you got to see it rain in Las Piedras, ha, ha, ha!" And that was the end of that. No report, no investigation, nothing.

Hole at Las Piedras

A few weeks later I was taxiing out at Las Piedras. The runway was paved, one of the few so graced in Venezuela, but the taxiway was dirt. Thousands of aircraft must have taxied over the same spot, but on that day it gave away under me. All I knew was that the airplane ended up on one wing tip and the propeller was bent when it hit the ground. I shut the other engine down and walked back through the cabin where people wanted to know what had happened. I told them that the gear must have collapsed on the right side. Well, not quite. The ground had simply fallen in. A cave in the limestone was under the taxiway and the top had finally broken in. The gear was hanging down in the hole. I think it took about two days to get that DC-3 out of the hole. I reported it, but did not discuss it with Ochoa because I thought he would think it was funny.

Many years later, after I retired, I told this story to a friend in Texas. He said, "Oh, yes, I remember that." His father had worked in an oil refinery at Las Piedras and had taken him, at the age of twelve, to see the airplane in the hole. Small world.

Curse of Las Piedras

Another time, en route to Las Piedras at one thousand feet altitude, I heard the left engine go rough and cough. I felt sure that it had swallowed a valve, so I quickly pulled the throttle back and feathered the propeller. Maybe too quickly, as the copilot asked me why I had done that. He had not heard a thing, and argued that there was nothing wrong with the engine and that we should start it up again. I told him we would do that after we were on the ground, and I did. It sounded like a washing machine tearing itself apart. He was convinced. It had swallowed a valve.

One airplane was lost while we were with AVENSA. Several of us had been asked about a certain copilot, whether or not we thought he was ready to fly as captain. In this case, we said, "No," explaining that we thought he lacked experience. Ochoa decided to put him on as captain on cargo only and allow him time to gain experience. In his first month he left Las Piedras for Maracaibo, one of the few AVENSA flights we had that lasted as long as forty-five minutes. The flight was over water almost all the way. A few minutes after he departed, one message came over the radio, "All stations stand by, I have an emergency." Nothing else was ever heard from him. Whatever the emergency was, it must have been catastrophic, because no sign of the aircraft was ever found.

Guard Duty

As few, if any, of the pilots had telephones and, in any case, most of them lived in Caracas, two hours away, AVENSA used a system called 'Guard Pilots'. Every day one pilot was assigned to come to the field, in uniform, and just sit there. If any pilot was not there for any reason five minutes before the flight was supposed to depart, the guard pilot took it. Then the next pilot arriving from a trip was automatically the new 'guard'.

All of us Pan American pilots loved to draw guard duty because we knew that the chances of our taking a trip out of it were very much in our favor. Because we had to be there anyway, we wanted to make all the money we could, and those trips paid well. Captain Ochoa liked to have us, too, because he knew he could depend on us to be there. Occasionally the local pilots did not show up simply because they did not want to fly, or they had something else to do.

On one of my flights I came back feeling as sick as a horse. I guess I had the flu, but all I knew was that I ached all over, even behind my eyes, and felt awful. As I left the airplane, the chief mechanic saw me and asked what was wrong. When I explained, he told me to go into his office. His desk was cluttered, with grease over everything. He told me to pull down my pants and lean over the desk. I felt so miserable that I did not argue with him, and then he pulled out a syringe from one of those filthy desk drawers and gave me a shot in the butt. I suppose it was penicillin, but I was too sick to care what it was. I just went on home to bed, and soon recovered.

Call Me Captain

Venezuelan pilots were, for the most part, very rank-conscious. A new captain on his very first flight stormed into the chief pilot's office about ten minutes before he was due to depart and demanded a different copilot. His story was that this copilot had gone out to measure the amount of gasoline aboard, as was his job, but had come back to report, "Sanchez (not his real name), we have three hundred and twenty gallons." The captain wanted another copilot because this one had failed to address him as *Captain* Sanchez. I don't think Captain Ochoa accommodated him.

Also, you had to be careful of the way you criticized their flying. When I was a flight instructor in the U.S.A. and a student bounced a landing, I might say, "Dummy, you didn't flare!" But here you would say, "Pablo, that was a very nice approach and your speed was just right, but perhaps if you had flared just a bit more we would not have hit so hard."

One Way Ticket to Bogotá

It happened on AVIANCA in Colombia, but it could just as easily have happened with AVENSA. After the flight landed, as the captain walked through the airplane he noticed that one passenger was still strapped in his seat and appeared to be asleep. He gently shook the passenger to waken him but he was, in fact, dead. He informed the station manager and told him to take care of the situation. Envisioning a lengthy hassle with the local authorities and much bureaucratic action, he went into the coffee shop to get a cup. After about fifteen minutes the station manager came in to tell him that the airplane was ready to go. "Have you taken care of that dead man?" "Yes, sir."

So the captain boarded and, to his great surprise, found the dead passenger still sitting in his seat. He hurried back out to ask the station manager why the dead man was still on the airplane.

"But Cap-i-tán, we can't take him off, he has a ticket for Bogotá!"

Maintenance En Route

AVENSA had a pretty good maintenance program. Sometimes they ran over the normal time limits for replacing parts, but it was usually kept within reasonable bounds. Mr Boulton had sold a large interest in the airline to his brother, who owned a trucking business. This Mr Boulton was keenly interested in his new investment, and walked through the hangar where the mechanics were changing an engine. Boulton asked what was wrong with it, and was told that it had simply reached its time limit. He said, "You mean that engine didn't quit running? Put it back on the airplane! We never change a *truck* engine until it quits running." It took some explaining to convince him that that is not the way it is done on an airline.

Pan American's major maintenance was done either in Miami or Brownsville, and we ferried the airplanes to these places when they were scheduled for major repairs. Bernie Wilson had one of these flights. His first stop was in Port-au-Prince, Haiti. Before he arrived there, the left engine quit and he landed, only to find that the right engine was almost out of oil and could have run only a very few minutes more when it, too, would have quit.

On investigation, he found that AVENSA maintenance in Maiquetía had a leaky oil cooler that they could not fix and, instead of just throwing it into the baggage compartment to send it to Miami, they had installed it on the right engine of his airplane so it, too, would be fixed when the major overhaul was done. They had not told him because they knew he would not have accepted it.

Customs Non-Check

Helen made a trip on one of these flights to visit in Brownsville. This trip was manned by a Venezuelan crew and when they left Miami they filled the airplane with all sorts of things such as TV sets, radios, and appliances that were very expensive in Venezuela. She told me that after they left Miami they pulled up the floorboards and put a bunch of stuff under the floor.

Their trick was to arrive in Maiquetía about ten minutes before Customs closed for the day. Customs would then seal the door of the airplane so they could check it out the next morning. But they did not know that a DC-3 has an emergency exit just above the pilots' seats, on the very top side of the fuselage. So, just before the crew left the cockpit, these guys would unlatch that emergency hatch. One guess as to how much stuff was left in the airplane for customs to find when it made the inspection the next morning.

Heart Maintenance

All in all, AVENSA was not bad duty. Good flying, good money, and, in spite of some of the inconveniences, a pretty good place to live. The climate was fair and it was a nice place for the children. I would probably have stayed longer, but at about this time two events took place that convinced me to go home.

One was my old bug-a-boo, the flight physical. When I took the one in late 1948, the heart doctor said that he found a discrepancy in my EKG. He did not take me off flight duty, but he did continue to have me come in for periodic EKGs. He took them after a period of fasting, after meals, after exercise, and even took some EKGs during induced sleep. Finally he told me I was okay, but that I had some sort of freak read-out and that he was going to write it up in medical journals; he charged me $600. But he had me frightened. And I did all the wrong things. I would not exercise; I would even walk very slowly so that I would not put any strain on my heart. I was only twenty seven years old, but I was convinced that I could have a heart attack any day. When I flew I would size up my copilot very carefully, to see if I thought he could handle it if I died during the flight. I was not comfortable with it.

When I did return to Brownsville, the first thing I did was to go to a heart specialist and give him the whole story. He gave me the most complete physical that I have ever had, and said that he could not find a thing wrong. He intimated that the doctor in Venezuela had just wanted that $600.

Rough Justice

Then on Christmas Day I had an early morning flight and was driving to the airport, a distance of about seven miles. The road was narrow, and alternated between cuts into the hillsides and earthen fills between the hills. On one of these fills I met a car coming very fast, and on my side of the road. I could not escape to the right because the slope down the fill was about forty-five degrees—too steep. I slowed down and began to honk my horn to get his attention, but it did not seem to change anything. That car just kept coming, and did not look as if it was slowing at all. I thought that it would surely hit me head-on.

That was when I made the decision to try to go around him on the left. It may have been a foolish thing to do, but on the other hand, it may have saved my life. As I made the turn, so did the other car, trying to get back to his own side. He hit me in the right front door, and my car rolled several times, going down the slope on the left side of the road.

Miraculously, my car came to rest on its wheels. Equally miraculously, I was not hurt except for a scratch where my knee hit the ignition key. Every door was jammed shut except mine on the driver side. My car had fallen so far down in the ditch that I could not see the other vehicle. I climbed up the slope and found that nobody else was hurt, either. They were so concerned with the damage to their car (which was bent so that the right front wheel was touching the left rear wheel), that they had not even looked over the side to see what had happened to me. That made me mad.

The driver had obviously been drinking, and I think that his intent was to play 'chicken' with me. As we stood there arguing, he hit me across the face with a strip of chrome trim from my own car. He literally cut my ear in half, I grabbed him, and was on top of him trying to bump his head on the pavement when someone pulled us apart, and the police arrived. And a good thing, too, because this guy was running to his car to get a gun. He said he was going to kill me.

They took us both into Maiquetía and put us in jail. I was not permitted to call anyone, and even if I could we did not have a telephone. This was a civil jail, and I wanted out while the other fellow still showed signs of being drunk. I thought the traffic police needed to see that. But I could not get out. A doctor was called in to sew up my ear. They kept showing me papers written in Spanish, and though by this time I spoke fairly good Spanish, I could not understand those papers. I did understand that if I signed them they would let me go. So I finally told them to prepare another set of papers with the other driver's name where mine was and my name in place of his. If he would sign that set I would sign the other set.

They humored me and did what I asked; but what I did not know was that those papers had nothing to do with the accident, they were about the fight afterward. His assault with a weapon was a serious offense and these papers said that I agreed not to pursue that charge. The chief steward of AVENSA arrived at about the time I was released, and he drove me home. It was about three in the afternoon, and Helen did not know anything about the accident. When she saw me get out of the car with my bloody shirt and my ear all bandaged, she instinctively thought I had been in an airplane accident. She raced to the car saying, "Oh, my God! Was anybody killed?"

Anyone who has lived in a Latin American country knows what I was up against as a result of this incident. Justice is doubtful at best, and depends more upon who you are and who you know rather than upon the circumstances. I found out that the man who hit me was a colonel in the Venezuelan Air Force and had a mean reputation. It was said that he had killed a man with a pistol only two years before, and that he had run over a little girl with his car within the previous twelve months. I held no illusions that I could emerge from the case without being held responsible for the accident.

Venezuela had some tough laws regarding auto accidents, too. The responsible party was required to pay not only all the damages, but also to pay a fixed amount per day to the non-responsible party while his car was in the shop. It was rumored that some cars stayed in the shop for years, while the owner and the mechanic split those daily fees. Also, I could not leave the country while I had any judgment against me.

The accident occurred on a Saturday and I had to be in court on Monday morning. The only person I told my story to was my next-door neighbor who was a refugee from Cuba and who had a menial job with a cargo forwarding company. He told me he would take care of it, but I put no faith in that.

On Monday, Captain Ochoa went with me to court after telling me that I was sure to be blamed, but that he would do what he could to help me avoid the costs. On the way to court we met the colonel on the street. Ochoa told him that I was not going to pay for his damages because he (Ochoa) knew where the colonel had been, where he was going, and who was with him in the car. He said that if I were ordered to pay the damages he would see that it cost the colonel his job as chief pilot for a cargo company. The colonel did not agree to this, and said we would wait and see what the judge had to say about it. The position that Ochoa had taken was very strongly in support of a foreigner against one of his own countrymen, and I appreciated that.

When we appeared in court the judge asked for our driving licenses and, when we surrendered them, he turned to the colonel and began to question him. "How fast were you driving?" "Oh, about sixty kilometers per hour."

The judge said, "Don't you know that the speed limit on that road is fifty-five km/h?" "Oh, I guess I was going only about fifty km/h." He thought he was going to get away with that. The judge replied, "The evidence is that you were traveling in excess of one hundred km/h, but you admitted to sixty km/h, so that will be a fifty Bolivar fine for exceeding the speed limit."

Next, he asked the colonel if he had been drinking; he denied that he had had even one drink. The judge declared, "The evidence is that you were drunk, and that will be a fifty Bolivar fine for driving drunk."

Then the judge inquired which side of the road he had been driving on, and of course he answered that he had been driving on his own side. The judge once more said, "The evidence is that you were within one-half meter of the lefthand side of the road, and that will also be a fifty Bolivar fine for driving on the wrong side. You are responsible for the accident and you will pay all damages."

None of us knew what this 'evidence' was or where it came from, for there was no testimony from anyone present in the courtroom. The judge turned to me and said, "Here is your driver's license, Mr Wilson. Thank you for coming to court." I had been asked no questions at all.

As we left the courtroom Captain Ochoa said, "Ned, I don't know how you did that, but for the rest of the time you're in Venezuela, don't walk around any dark corners because that man will kill you."

I did not know how I had done it, either. Only when I talked to my neighbor did it become clear. He had gone, on Sunday, to the site of the accident and taken with him a policeman who worked with his company. Then he took this policeman to his boss and asked him to explain the facts of the situation. His boss (still on Sunday!) secured an appointment for the policeman with the governor of the state. After listening to the policeman, the governor called the judge and said, "You have a traffic case in the morning, and I want the person who was responsible for it to get the blame in your court." No names mentioned.

Talk about the luck of the Irish! The colonel had been beaten by his own system. I was never able to collect any damages, as I was unable to find a lawyer who would take him on. I had lost my car, a ten-year-old Studebaker, but I felt very lucky, and very grateful to my neighbor.

Dress Code

I stayed a few more months, but I was not comfortable there any more, and decided to give notice. Before we left Venezuela, we wanted to spend a day shopping in Caracas. Ken did not like being dragged around all day in the city heat, and I promised him that we would go to the movies in the afternoon. All day I kept him going with that promise. When the time came, we arrived at the movie house only to be told that I would not be admitted because I was not wearing a coat. I was wearing a pair of nice slacks and a clean, shortsleeve sport shirt. But the rule—as I was told—required a coat.

As we were arguing about it with the attendant, a tramp came up. He wore a greasy, once-white waiter's jacket but had no shirt, and no shoes. He was promptly sold a ticket and in he went. I knew then it was time to go home.

Flying for AVENSA was one of those experiences that I would not take a million dollars for, but I would not give ten dollars to do it again.

Lluvia en el DC-Tres

I am often asked, "What is your favorite airplane?" Like most pilots, I came to like almost every airplane I flew, or, to paraphrase Will Rogers, "I never knew a 'plane I didn't like." Each had its own per–sonality and after working with each one for a while they all seemed like old friends; like friends, each one needed to be treated differently. Let us start with the Douglas DC-3.

It has been said that if you could *taxi* a DC-3 you could *fly* it. With a fully swiveling tail wheel instead of a nose wheel, it could dart in any direction at any time, almost like an excited puppy straining at the leash.

The pilots who taught me would neither allow me to use the brakes while taxiing nor lock the tail wheel to hold it straight until in position for take off. Careful use of power and full use of every flight control was essential to make the DC-3 go where you wanted it to go while it was still on the ground.

Pan American's procedure for landing was to come in as slow as possible, with the tail low. A three-point landing was acceptable but it was considered preferable to have the tail wheel just a few inches off the ground at touchdown. Even a mildly hard touchdown was a perfect set-up for a bounce. We used this approach because it was best for short and rough runways, and we had plenty of those. A fast landing on the main wheels with the tail high was very much frowned upon, and we often laughed at the Air Force pilots who landed them in just that way.

Leaks

I am amused today when I hear people speak of their flights on a 'small' airplane, usually meaning a twin-engined type about the same size or even bigger than a DC-3. When I first flew it I thought it was huge. It was the first airplane in my experience that was roomy enough to walk around in. It could seat twenty-one (sometimes twenty-eight) passengers, had a flight attendant, and even had a galley and a toilet. The side cockpit windows could be slid back, and we often flew that way in hot weather, which was most of the time in our assigned areas. With the windows open, any paper dropped in the cockpit would promptly sail out the window, and I have seen flight plans,

The famous 'Gooney Bird', the Douglas DC-3, known for its forgiving handling qualities and ability to land in any reasonable field. More than 10,600 of the type, and its variants, were built in the United States, nearly 500 in Japan, and more than 6,000 (as Lisunov Li-2s) in the Soviet Union.

maps, and other documents lost in that way. On my first flight in command we were crossing the ridges into the valley of Mexico City, and were flying in and out of rain and thunderstorms, cruising at 12,000 feet. Suddenly I caught a glimpse of a small town and, as the windows were largely fogged over, I jerked open the side window to take a better look. My oxygen mask sailed right off my face and out the window.

One characteristic of the otherwise beloved DC-3 is well-known. The windshield leaked water right into your lap in any kind of rain, and most pilots carried a raincoat or poncho to put over their legs. One pilot wrote in the log-book, "Light rain outside, heavy rain inside."

Wobble Pump On

The airplane was hard pressed to climb much above 12,000 feet with a load and, in any case, that was as high as we were supposed to go with a passenger load because we had no provision for oxygen in the passenger cabin. I have seen it taken to 15,000 feet when necessary, to be sure that we were not going to hit a mountain.

We could (and did) fly the DC-3 through almost any weather. It would roll and pitch and was slow to respond in very rough air, but it would stay right-side-up and you did not have to worry much about anything coming off. Sometimes in heavy rain the engines would cough, spit, and misfire, but I never knew one to drown out and quit.

When I first flew the 'Gooney Bird' there were no flight instruments on the copilot's panel, just engine instruments and other gauges. The copilot was expected to look across the cockpit to the instruments on the captain's panel. One of the copilot's duties was to operate the manual wobble pump to supply fuel to an engine in case the engine-driven pump failed. The pumphandle was located on a bulkhead to his left and below his hand. This was later changed and electric pumps were installed with switches in the overhead or 'eyebrow' panel. During one dark night over the Yucatán an engine quit because there was no fuel pressure. The captain called for "wobble pump on". After a while

"Light rain outside, heavy rain inside." (DC-3)

he looked around to see why the pressure was not coming up, and found the copilot out of his seat and down in the aisle, fumbling around on his hands and knees. When asked what in the hell he was doing down there, he replied, "I'm trying to find the wobble pump!"

DC-3 Tail Wheel Retraction

They used to ask a new stewardess to check and see if the tail wheel was retracted after take off. It did not retract, of course, but there was a panel in the rear of the toilet which could be opened, and you could see into the rear baggage compartment. After take off the captain would ask her to open this panel and be sure that the tail wheel was up into the rear compartment. One smart girl caught on and got back at the cockpit crew. Several minutes after being sent on this wild goose chase, she came up front and told the captain that she could not find the tail wheel, but that the passengers were all complaining that

The captain's panel in a Douglas DC-3. More than a hundred thousand pilots have sat in this 'left-hand seat', have collectively made millions of take offs and landings, and flown more than a billion hours.

they were unable to get out of their seats. When he asked her why, she said, "Because I've taken all the baggage out and put it into the aisle, trying to find the tail wheel." The captain hurried back to the cabin to apologize to the passengers to find that the joke was on him.

The DC-3's main gear did retract, but did not come all the way into the wheel wells behind the engines, remaining just a little below the engine cowling. Two pilots were doing some practice landings at Brownsville, and somehow landed with the gear retracted. The captain stomped into the office declaring, "Well, the manual is right. You can still use the brakes with the gear up!" He had just proved it. The only damage to the ship was a couple of bent propellers; it was soon flying again.

Brownsville was known to be one of the best DC-3 maintenance bases in the world. The ground engineers and crew did excellent work and not only kept Pan American's airplanes in good shape, but repaired and rebuilt them for others. Once a hurricane damaged a privately-owned DC-3 in Houston, and the owners tried without success to locate someone to repair it. A Pan Am mechanic looked at it and told them that if they would put it on a barge and ship it to Brownsville, it could be made flyable for a cost of around $10,000. The owners were skeptical of this estimate, as it was about 50% less than others they had obtained, and they had their doubts about the credibility of this bid from a common mechanic. He suggested they call the head of the maintenance department; they did so and were told that if this man had said it could be done, it would go on contract and be guaranteed. The pilot who flew the repaired aircraft told me that it flew better than before.

The 'Three' has carried children to school, fish to market, delivered newspapers, taken sightseers over the Grand Canyon, flown hunters into remote areas, acted as a gunship in Viet Nam, pulled gliders in World War II, and has been put to hundreds of other uses—from carrying kings to collecting garbage. It has flown on wheels, skis, and pontoons. It will probably be put to some other uses that have yet to be thought of.

The Douglas DC-3 may not have been the best airplane I ever flew, but it surely stands very high in my regard. You had to fly it every minute and every landing was a challenge. There was no autopilot, although it did have a wing-leveler; no radar, very little radio, and nothing was automatic. It did not meet modern requirements for Transport Category aircraft, and yet it was one of the safest airplanes ever built. As far as I know, it has never been grounded for a mechanical or other defect, in any country in the world. Pan American flew it for untold thousands of hours throughout Central and South America, in areas where it had to go around rather than over the mountains, and in all kinds of weather, without losing one passenger. I would like to fly it just once more, if only to hear that familiar chant before landing, "Gear down, locked, green light, pressure, and I have a wheel."

Crack-shot Caretaker

It was supposed to be our day off in Panama, but Roger Sherron and I had volunteered for a special assignment: we were to fly a load of diesel fuel out to the San Blas Islands off the Caribbean coast of Panama.

Early in the morning when we arrived at Albrook Field in the Canal Zone, we found that several drums of fuel had been loaded and tied down in the cabin of the DC-3. After a quick check of the airplane and of the weather, we were on our way.

The trip was very brief. A former World War II military strip, it was already being covered by the fast-growing jungle, always quick to swallow up anything not guarded daily. The concrete of the runway was cracked and broken, and grass was growing tall out of the cracks. After we landed, we walked down a road that was now reduced to a mere track; we passed buildings that not too long before had housed soldiers. The structures were rotting and would soon be reclaimed by the jungle.

San Blas Island, off the coast of Panama. The entire surface is occupied by houses.

We walked until we reached a dilapidated pier jutting out into the bay, and met the person who needed the fuel we had brought. He was the caretaker for Pan Am's radio station there, what we then called an aerophare, but what is now known as a non-directional beacon (NDB). Pilots took bearings on these radio signals for finding their position or to 'home in' to. This man lived in a very remote spot with the San Blas Indians for the sole purpose of keeping our radio on the air. The fuel we had brought would keep his generators running to produce the electric power necessary for the radio.

The caretaker directed some Indians to unload the barrels, then took us in his boat to the nearby islands where the Indians lived in an extremely densely populated village; their grass-thatched huts stood with less than an arm's length between them. They chose to live on this island—about a mile offshore from the beach—to escape the mosquitoes and other insects which made life nearly impossible on the mainland. The men commuted by boat each day to the mainland to tend crops of bananas, coconuts, and sweet potatoes, returning to the village each evening. The women made shirts and skirts using a reverse appliqué method of sewing which was very attractive. They used anything for a pattern for the appliqués—there were shapes of bats, birds, and iguanas. They even beat Andy Warhol to the idea of pictures of tomato cans. Samples of their work, known as 'Molas', were available in the tourist shops of nearly all the hotels in Panama City.

We had also brought the caretaker a simple single-shot point two-two rifle, which he had requested for killing rats that were infesting his radio shack. As we got into the boat, Roger very carefully demonstrated, with his usual attention to detail, how to load, cock, and fire it. The fellow listened respectfully and attentively, nodding his head at each of Roger's wordy admonitions.

When Roger had finished his lecture and surrendered the gun, we were thirty yards to sea and bouncing up and down in the waves. The caretaker quickly inserted a bullet, casually raised the rifle and took a quick shot at one of the metal cleats on the distant dock. Ping! It hit dead on, then he repeated it, ping!

While we were having lunch in the old barrack that served as his home, we learned that before he had given up the rat-race to come here, live simply with the Indians, and care for our life-line radio, he had been a policeman in a mid-Western state. He had obviously been an expert marksman, possibly related to Wyatt Earp.

After lunch we flew back to the Canal Zone. A short flight in miles, but an incalculable distance between lifestyles. It was certainly a better way to spend the day than sitting at the hotel playing cards.

Convair's Hot Rod

When I returned from Venezuela to the U.S. in the early summer of 1949 I was back where I had started. After nearly seven years with Pan American, I was again a DC-3 copilot. Because I had flown with a Venezuelan pilot's license for the past eighteen months, I had to requalify as a Pan Am copilot. Jimmy Maxwell, who had given me my original three take offs and landings, had to do it all over again to satisfy F.A.A. and company policy. The years that I had been flying the airplane in command did not count because it was for AVENSA and not Pan American. So I was assigned to fly out of Brownsville again, often with some of the same captains whom I had checked in earlier times. This was never a problem for me, as they were all fine pilots and I worked well with them. Most of them let me fly from the left seat, anyway, but I always made it clear to them that I knew who was the P.I.C. (pilot in command). The best crew in an airplane are two competent people who work harmoniously together. But while my pride was not hurt, my pocketbook was.

That July, however, we received a new airplane, the Convair 240, a modern airplane in all respects. A twin-engined aircraft with reverse thrust (the propeller blade angles could be changed to produce a rearward pull), auto-feathering propellers, air-conditioning, and a good pressurization system that allowed us to fly above 20,000 feet, and thus above all the mountain tops in Central America.

During our training on the 240 I first heard of the F.A.A.'s 'V' speeds. There were many of these (I just counted 31 in a pilot's handbook) set up by the F.A.A. They defined speeds for many conditions, but only two or three were of real interest to us at the time. V_1 was the lowest speed at which we could continue take off with a failed engine, and V_2 the speed to climb with a failed engine. I liked the remark by an American Airlines friend of mine, who said that V_1 and V_2 were okay, but he liked V_3 or V_4 better. Speed of air over the wing is what keeps an airplane flying and these minimum speeds set up by the F.A.A. were not always in great favor by the pilots.

Elevator Going Down

The Convair 240 was great fun to fly because we could do things we could not do before. We could descend at several thousand feet per minute, in contrast

The Convair-Liner Model 240 was to be Pan American's standard airliner for its feeder routes when the venerable DC-3 became outmoded.

to unpressurized ships in which we had to restrict descents to 300ft/min to avoid damage to the ear. On one flight an air traffic controller asked that we report each thousand feet on the descent. He was thinking of about three minutes between each report. We started down at about 6,000ft/min and I just opened up the mike and gave him: "Clipper 502 out of one six thousand" and continued each ten seconds until we were down to about 12,000 feet, without ever letting up on the microphone switch. Then I heard, "Never mind, just report level at ten thousand."

Reverse thrust was new to us. One night when leaving Brownsville, we were cleared to hold on a taxiway that was across the main runway from where we were positioned. We first turned facing down the take off runway and the tower said, "I asked you to cross the runway and hold on the other side." The captain replied, "Wait just a second." He pulled the throttles into reverse thrust and backed around the corner into the taxiway.

The auto-feathering feature, designed to feather the propeller automatically when an engine failed, sometimes caused us embarrassment. We would land and pull the throttles into full reverse for a quick stop and both props would feather. So there we would be, sitting on the runway with both engines dead.

The Convair-Liner also used water injection into the engines for more power on take offs. The water would cool the engines so that they did not overheat at high power. But at high altitudes such as Mexico City, the water injection would not always cut in, and because the take off weight had to be restricted unless we had water, we would taxi back and leave some passengers behind. Deadhead crews would be taken off first, of course, and this often happened to me. On some flights we would deadhead to Guatemala on one day, fly to Panama and back on a DC-3, then deadhead home again on a 240. A drop-off in Mexico just came out of your own time, and in those days we were not paid for deadhead flights. On too many occasions, I arrived home on one day and had to leave again on another trip the next day.

The airplane performed so well, especially on take off, that we could climb away from the fields at an angle that was steep enough to look spectacular. The government airline in Venezuela, LAV, was flying the Martin 202 aircraft which looked very similar to the Convair 240 but which could not match its performance. The government passed a local rule that no airplane could climb above one thousand feet until it was ten miles from the field. This was supposed to have been in the interests of traffic control, but the obvious reason was to prevent us from showing up their airplanes.

Loyal Passenger

I remember one flight in the Convair 240 when Brownsville was socked in with fog, and we could not land there. After holding as long as our fuel would permit, we flew northwest to McAllen, Texas, and landed. Our dispatch service said that Brownsville was expected to be below minimums for at least a day, and maybe more, so they wanted us to discharge all our passengers, who would be put on a bus to Brownsville. We would then initiate a flight back to Mexico City and pick up a schedule south from there.

But we had one passenger on that flight who did not want to get off. He said he had bought a ticket on Pan Am and he wanted to ride Pan Am. We explained that we now did not intend to stop in Brownsville, but were instead going on to Mexico. He said, "But you will come back to Brownsville some time, won't you?" He insisted on staying with us, so we took off for Mexico. About thirty miles north of Brownsville the dispatcher called us to tell us that the weather was at the bare minimum for landing. We promptly ducked in and were the only airplane to land there in about three days. We were able to go home, and another crew was called out to go south, and our loyal and persistent passenger was the only one to arrive in Brownsville by air during that time.

Respect for Pan Am

During a revolution that was taking place in Guatemala, there had been some strange attacks by an unknown aircraft, flights over the city, strafing of buildings, bombing a water tower; but no deaths. One morning on take off from Managua, Nicaragua, as we were climbing out in a Convair-Liner, an unidentified voice came over our headphones, "Clipper, what is your position, and what altitude are you climbing to?" We gave our location and intentions. The voice replied, "Okay, I'll stay out of your way." No identification was ever given.

On our arrival at Guatemala we had to land downwind to the north because we were advised that one of those mysterious raids was going on over the city. I was glad to know that the local *revolucionarios* treated Pan Am with proper respect.

By the standards of the day—it was introduced in 1948—the Convair-Liner was considered a hot rod, like a small sports car. Unfortunately, because of Pan American's system of pilot seniority, I was always in the righthand seat, officially, that is. I wish that I had had the opportunity to fly it in command. It was a fine airliner.

Nobody Hurt in the Back End

I began training on the Douglas DC-4 in February 1950. It had four engines and was a sturdy workhorse. I do not remember the name of my instructor, but he was a 'line' pilot as opposed to one of the instructor pilots who did not fly the line. And he was good.

There was an argument making the rounds at that time as to the correct procedure when making a 'go-around' after failing to land on an approach. Some thought that the gear should be retracted first, and some thought that bringing up the flaps first was better. This instructor told me to fly at approach speed with gear and flaps full down, and then had me retract the gear while holding altitude. The result was a small gain in speed of about five to ten miles per hour. Putting the gear back down, we repeated the maneuver but retracted the flaps first. We gained speed so rapidly that we had to pull the throttles back to avoid exceeding the limiting speed with the gear down. After that practical test, there was never a doubt in my mind. Landing flaps cause more drag, by far, and should always be brought up first.

My instructor then covered the airspeed gauge and told me to take off, fly around the field and land without having the benefit of seeing that instrument. When I did so, a student who was watching my flight commented that I was never off more than 10mph from the speed I should have had at any time. When that student flew it, the results were the same. One other thing he asked us to do was to land the airplane as close to the end of the runway as we could, and then using maximum braking without blowing any tires, to see how quickly we could stop. When we looked back to see how little runway we had used, we were amazed.

These maneuvers were not part of the normal curriculum, but they gave us great confidence in the airplane and in our ability to make it perform for the best results.

Pan American had many great people flying for them. There were doctors, lawyers, teachers, accountants, preachers, farmers, and people of almost every profession—an untold pool of talent. Most were there simply because

Though unpressurized, and not so elegant as the Lockheed Constellation, the Douglas DC-4, which began life as the military C-54 Skymaster, gave most of the world's leading airlines, including Pan American, their introduction to landplane trans-ocean and long-distance flying after the end of World War II.

they preferred to fly, and the majority was real pleasure to work with. Occasionally, though, there would be one who made the job less enjoyable.

'Baby' Smokes

I encountered one of these on the DC-4. (I will call him 'Terry', because I never knew a pilot by that name.) This man had a strange sense of humor. He thought it was funny to catch another crew member in the confined space of the toilet and to squirt a can of bug spray through the louvered door. Once when he and I spent the night in a hotel in Mérida, Mexico, our room contained some finely-etched drinking glasses. At departure time I packed my bags and went to the lobby to await pick-up. Having forgotten something, I returned to the room and opened my bag, to find that he had put a full dozen of those glasses into my suitcase. The point of that was just to see my embarrassment when customs checked my suitcase at New Orleans.

He smoked big, black cigars costing at least a dollar each, and he laughed at me and called me 'Baby' because I wouldn't take one when offered. One day I accepted, and lit up. The DC-4 had a little tray that ran along and under the windshield to collect water that leaked around the edges. A small tube ran from there through the side of the airplane and, by the resulting suction, pulled this water outside. When he wasn't looking, I pulled this tube loose and applied it to the end of the cigar. The suction caused the cigar to burn very quickly and to become so hot that I could hardly hold it. Then, when he was looking, I would put the cigar in my mouth and puff just a little. He kept waiting for me to feel sick, but I burned up my cigar long before he had finished his. Then I snuffed out the short butt into the ash tray and said, "Say, Terry, those are pretty good cigars; do you have another?" The only reply was, "Oh, go to hell!" I had the satisfaction of telling him 'the rest of the story' many years later at a retirement party. He had never guessed how I had 'smoked' that cigar.

The DC-4 had two sets of throttles; the ones on the captain's side were several inches longer than the ones for the copilot. This gave the captain more leverage so that he could overcome any movement of the copilot's throttles. Terry also liked to use these long throttles to pull back suddenly just as the copilot started his landing flare. The sudden loss of power, as well as the greatly increased drag that resulted, caused the airplane to sink very rapidly. If the pilot making the landing corrected quickly enough and pulled back the control wheel rapidly, he could save the landing and make a reasonably good touch-down. Terry would laugh his head off at this stunt. I never thought it was funny.

Once I decided to set him up. At Mérida on a hot afternoon when the air was rough, I made a long, low approach with more than normal power and the nose held high. Sure enough, as I crossed the runway threshold he jerked all the power off. Instead of trying to save it, I just turned the wheel loose, and before he could react and grab the wheel we hit hard—like a ton of bricks. For a second I thought I had made a very serious mistake, because I half-expected to see the wheel struts coming up through the wings. He said, "Goddam, Ned! Why didn't you hold it off?" I told him that when he reached for the throttles I thought he wanted to take control of the airplane, so I gave it to him. He never tried that one on me again.

Hard landings were supposed to be recorded in the logbook, but there was no definition of a 'hard' landing. It was up to each individual's judgment. Once when I was in command of a DC-6 I made a landing that surely was on the verge of whatever was considered hard. I turned to the flight engineer and asked him, "Did you consider that a hard landing?" He had his head down between his knees and glanced up to say, "I don't know, sir, I'm still looking for my tie clasp."

I was with Terry on another flight out of Guatemala City and, over the jungle, he descended to about a thousand feet. He said he was looking for Mayan ruins. Several times I suggested that we should instead hunt for smoother air, as it was mealtime and our cabin crew were trying to serve passengers. But we continued to bounce and bump along in the rough air. Finally, thoroughly disgusted, I excused myself and went back into the passenger cabin. As I went down the aisle the steward was coming forward with two meal trays. About that time we hit a bump that caused some of the food to bounce off the tray and land on the floor. The steward raised both trays to the height of his head, turned them upside-down and slammed them to the floor. Then he headed for the cockpit. The stewardess shouted to me, "Get back to the cockpit, he will hit the captain!" I said, "I sure hope so, and don't worry, I'll get up there in time to fly the airplane." I did go back to the cockpit, but words are all that flew.

"Clean it up, Slim"

Slim Eckstrom was flying a DC-4 during one of the flight checks that each of us had to take twice a year. Slim was one of Pan American's very early pilots, and he stuttered. During the check the instructor pilot simulated a lost engine on take off by pulling the power off on number one engine. Slim made no comment, but simply flew the airplane around the pattern and landed it.

"That won't do, Slim, we will have to repeat that maneuver", the instructor told him. So on another take off he again shut down the number one engine. Again Slim made no comment but just kept flying without asking for the gear up or the engine to be feathered or an engine-out check list. The instructor thought he would bring things to a head and shut down the number two engine. Now there was no chance to make it around the pattern unless the airplane was cleaned up i.e. by reducing the drag by feathering the propellers or retracting the gear. Still Slim made no comment.

Finally, as the airplane slowed and was approaching an airspeed where it would stall, the instructor said, "Slim, SAY SOMETHING!" Slim calmly looked at him and said, "Y-y-you S-so-son of a B-bitch!"

One Monkey Knows Another

The DC-4 was used for many cargo flights, often carrying animals of one sort or another. One such typical cargo was a planeload of monkeys going either to pet stores or to scientific laboratories. A flight with a load of monkeys had landed in Managua, Nicaragua. Preparing to depart, the copilot entered the cockpit and reached way down next to the floor to slide his seat forward. He was surprised to see two little hands grasping the top of his instrument panel. In the small gap between the instrument panel and the glare shield were two beady eyes looking back at him!

One of the monkeys was loose and had found his way up behind the instrument panel. He was a spider monkey and had very long legs and arms as well as his tail to hang on to all the various tubes, electric wires, and maze of gadgets behind that panel. All attempts to prise him loose without doing damage to the panel or the instruments were unsuccessful.

Finally it was decided to delay the flight and to remove the entire panel to extract the spider monkey, a matter requiring several hours. The main flight office in New York would have to be advised of the delay, so a message was sent, "Flight 504 indefinitely delayed due monkey hung up on instrument panel."

The story goes that New York promptly queried, "Which monkey is it, the captain or the copilot?"

One night at Houston several of us were taking our regular six-month check and, with an instructor, were flying ILS (Instrument Landing System) approaches. At the time, when about three miles out, we used a technique of having a speed about 50mph more, than we wanted over the runway threshold. We gradually slowed as we continued the approach so as to arrive at the runway with the correct threshold speed. Each pilot in turn was under a hood, flying only by instruments. We were required to fly down to two hundred feet altitude, at which time the instructor pilot would remove the hood, indicating that we had made visual contact with the runway and could land. If he left the hood up we would fly a missed approach procedure.

The instructor decided to see just how far we could continue while still under the hood. Several of us flew the airplane to touch-down on the runway without ever seeing out.

"Do It Our Way"

Some years later, the F.A.A. decided that allowing the speed to decrease slowly like this was not the best way to do it. They demanded what they called a 'stabilized approach'. This meant that you established the threshold speed several miles out and held it constant throughout the approach. This took less skill and in effect reduced the procedure to the level of the least skilled. It also increased the exposure to wind-shear.

In spite of the recent coverage by the news media wind-shear is nothing new. The condition, if not the familiar use of the term, has been with us as long as the wind has been blowing. It means that the wind is blowing steadily at one speed in one place and then changes abruptly, without warning of any kind, either speed or direction (or both). It is most dangerous to an airplane when it is blowing hard on approach and suddenly drops in speed or even stops. This causes a sudden decrease in airspeed and puts the airplane closer to or even at the stall speed.

If the airplane is being flown faster than the necessary speed over the threshold, then it has some leeway to accept the change. But if it is already at the minimum speed it is susceptible to stalling. While it did require more skill, and sometimes resulted in more speed than necessary at the runway, our original technique, was, in my opinion, a safer way. It is obviously less hazardous to go slowly off the far end of the runway than to crash before even reaching the runway.

Add to this F.A.A. technique the tendency of air traffic control to ask aircraft to slow up further on approach so as to facilitate their traffic flow, and then further exacerbate the potential danger with possible wind-shear in the area, and you have all the conditions present for an accident. In my opinion, many recent accidents, including Delta's tragic crash short of the runway at Dallas in 1985, could have been avoided by making the approach twenty to thirty miles per hour over and above the threshold speed on approach.

I witnessed one airplane land short at Houston. I'm not sure what caused it, but we were in the approach pattern when a Braniff flight was on short final. I was watching as he suddenly swerved to the right off the runway and ended up facing the way he had come. His landing lights were still on but were pointing up in some strange directions. His radio was still working too, for a Texas drawl came on the air to say, "Tow-wer, will you call Bran-iff on the tel-e-phone and tell them to call Dal-las, and have them tell Dal-las that we have had a kind of serious acc-i-dent with this Boe-in." I guess he just assumed that the crash and fire trucks were on the way.

It was a Boeing 707, just nine flight hours out of the factory, and they had hit several feet short of the runway and collapsed the right main landing gear.

Another Braniff pilot whom I knew when we lived in Sangar, Texas, was a farmer tilling some six hundred more acres. The local spot to gather was Johnson's Feed store and on one winter day many of the locals were sitting around the stove there and my friend was one of them.

When he left one of the local farmers said, "Do you all know that fellow? He is teched in the head." Johnson said that he came in regularly and seemed all right to him, and why did he think he was 'teched'? "Well he farms next to me and is just a plain old dirt farmer like the rest of us, but he thinks he is an airline pilot!"

One disadvantage about being an airline pilot is that you can never be sure of being home for any event—Christmas, your kid's school play, July 4th, whatever. I missed the birth of my third child, Nancy, in Houston. By the time I got in from the flight it was all over. 'Chip' West's wife, Mary, had to take Helen to the hospital. When they picked up the bag which had been packed earlier so as to be ready, they found that the cat had been in it, another case, Mary told me, of "when the cat crept in, crapped, and crept out again."

The DC-4 was a good, solid, safe airplane, much larger and far heavier than the DC-3, but it never invoked in me feeling of affection that the 'Three' did. A friend was flying one night as my copilot when we landed at Tampico, Mexico. He was a little slower than I would have liked throughout the approach but I did not say anything. I guess my voice as I called off airspeeds to him gave him a clue, though. We hit pretty hard, and he turned to me and said, "Well you told me all through the approach that I was too slow." Then the purser, a friend of ours, opened the door from the cabin and shouted, "Nobody hurt in the back captain!"

Hurricane

In summer 1950 I was copilot on a flight from Guatemala into New Orleans. A hurricane in the Gulf was expected to hit the jazz capital at any time. We fought our way through and around it and landed just as it reached the coast at Grand Isle, some forty miles south. We were congratulating ourselves on joining our families before the hurricane did. It was forecast to be a big one, and as we came off the airplane, the station manager told us we were not to leave the airport because we had to fly the airplane to Houston to get it out of the path of the storm.

I was not expecting that, and I did not like it. My wife was at home with our two children, and she was pregnant. (Our third child, Scott, was born soon afterward). I told him to find another crew, as I was going home to be with my family, but was told that there were no other crews in New Orleans, because they had already deadheaded every pilot to Houston on Eastern Air Lines. We had flown all day to make it home before the storm hit, and the company had not had the courtesy to send us an advance message that we would have to fly on to Houston.

I thought more of my family than I did of the airplane. I telephoned Helen but before I could say any more than that we had landed, she said,

"Don't you do it!" I asked her what she meant, She said "Don't quit!"She knew me very well, because that was exactly what I had in mind.

I said that I would only fly the airplane out if my family could go too. As things turned out, the storm made a turn at Grand Isle and went more to the east, making things much better for New Orleans, nothing worse than heavy rain. Then we had to fly to Houston, anyway, to pick up all the crews and bring them home. I later found out that only one pilot, Don Mundellow, had refused to leave in the face of the storm. He had stayed home with his family and had stacked all his furniture up in the attic.

Because of the decision of the local station manager, that was one of the few times that I was ready to quit Pan Am.

Cash Money

Many pilots seemed to like farming. Kenny Floro would have liked to be a cattleman. While living at Hemstead, Texas, he ranched with several hundred head of Santa Gertrudis cattle, at a time when, as a DC-6 captain, he was making about $1,500 per month. In the 1950s the country was in the midst of a prolonged dry period. Cattle prices were low, feed prices high. The ranchers habitually met at a coffee spot to discuss the situation. Kenny was right in there with them, cussing the drought, high prices, and the government, but not necessarily in that order. One wizened old cowboy said to him, "Floro, I don't know what you have to complain about. Why, I'll bet you make $200 a month, cash money, flying them there airyplanes."

Kenny said that he simply reached for his hat, got into his pick-up and went home. "I figured that if $200 a month 'cash money' coming in was heaven, it was no place for me to be."

Panic

While flying the DC-4, I experienced one of the very rare critical situations of my career. I was copilot to 'Mike' Carmichael on a flight from Guatemala to New Orleans. Mike was a very capable pilot and a gentlemen of high caliber who had learned true instrument flying fairly late in his career and, though he was certainly competent, I think he may never have been totally at ease with it.

We picked up an F.A.A. flight inspector in Guatemala and while en route, Mike asked me if I would make the approach into New Orleans where we expected to confront bad weather. Of course I agreed, but later Mike said, "No, I expect he wants to see me make the approach, so I'll do it." Mike was a company check captain on both the Douglas DC-4 and the Lockheed Constellation.

As we neared New Orleans, a hurricane was making its way in-shore, but we edged around it and reached the area of the airport without too much trouble. The weather was reported to have a ceiling of seven hundred feet and visibility of two miles, but the wind was strong and not blowing down the runway that we would use for an instrument approach. However, with that ceiling we could approach to the east and then circle to land to the northeast, and that is exactly the clearance we received. "Clipper 504 is cleared for an ILS approach and for landing on runway one-zero or zero-four, your choice." Mike said to tell him we would take zero four, into the wind, and I did so.

The approach continued routinely and we broke into the clear under the clouds at just the altitude that they had reported the ceiling to be. With the runways in sight, Mike started a turn to the right to line up with runway zero-four, to the northeast, and continued his descent. Runway one-zero, now to our left, had bright lead-in lights, while zero-four had none, but we had both runways clearly in sight, and zero-four was into the wind.

We had reached an altitude of about two hundred feet when the bottom fell out. It started to rain as though being poured out of big buckets, and the visibility decreased until we could no longer see the runway, although the lead-in lights to runway one-zero were visible. Mike started a left turn toward the lights and I knew, without being told, what he intended to do. Having lost sight of our intended landing runway, he was going back to the runway with the guiding lights, and where it was still possible to make a safe landing.

Now down to about a hundred feet, and with the lights still in sight, I was feeling comfortable with what Mike was doing. Then, without warning, the F.A.A. inspector, who was seated on the jumpseat between us, reached across me and grabbed my wheel and pulled back on it! At the same time he started shouting, "You are going to hit the ground! You are going to hit the ground!" Pulling back on the yoke without adding power would cause us to stall, and his cries were upsetting—to put it mildly. I then did the one thing that I had said I would never do unless I was willing to defend it with my job. I leaned over to the left so that I broke his grip on my wheel and, with no command from the captain, took four throttles in one hand and four prop controls in the other and applied full take off power.

Mike understood exactly what I was doing and immediately started into a climb for a missed-approach procedure. As he made a turn to the proper heading, the inspector shouted, "You are going to drag a wing!" and again tried to reach my wheel. I was more alert now and leaned to the left so he could not reach it. As we climbed back to altitude, Mike and I quickly agreed

Typical volcano on the Central American route.

Omatepe, the volcano in Lake Nicaragua. The Morse code for the name consists almost entirely of dashes, so the radio operators just sent a continuous signal.

Trio of craters in Central America, a segment of the Pacific's 'rim of fire'.

that neither of us cared to try another approach to New Orleans that day, and he asked me to request a clearance to Houston, where the weather was reported to be clear.

The flight to Houston was routine, except that the inspector was as nervous as a cat on a hot tin roof and kept at us for little picayune things that he did not like. When we landed he said that he was going to file a violation on both of us. The next morning we had a meeting in the chief pilot's office and, when asked what the violation was going to be, the F.A.A. inspector replied, "Going below landing minimums." The chief pilot told him that was all right, but that at the hearing both of us would testify that we had the runways in sight at an altitude above the minimums and, therefore, were entitled to continue. We would further say that as we made the approach, the visibility decreased to the point that we lost sight of the runway, and that when that happened we abandoned the approach and climbed out. Nothing illegal in all that.

He also said that when we testified we would also tell of the actions of all persons in the cockpit. That was all it took, and the inspector decided that maybe there was no violation, after all. But he did insist, probably to show his authority, that Mike should not be allowed to be a check pilot on both DC-4 and the Connie. The company took him off the DC-4, and I always thought it should not have given in on that point, either. The inspector should have been fired, but wasn't. I later had more flights with him on board; on those flights I was never too happy, and was ill at ease the entire time.

Doing a Wheelie

Once when Mike was chief pilot of Aviateca, Pan American's subsidiary in Guatemala, he was flying a Ford Tri-Motor. Somehow the gear—non-retractable—on the right side came loose. By design, it was fastened to the lower edge of the fuselage and also by a long strut to the engine mount; the latter had broken, so the gear was hanging straight down below the airplane. Mike was afraid that if he landed on top of it, hanging down there, further damage would occur. He calmly and coolly approached the end of the runway where there was an abrupt, cliff-like edge and passed over it so low that the broken gear tore off. Then he circled the field and made a perfect landing on the remaining left gear, doing little damage.

Horses Are Cargo, Too

In October 1951, I finally made captain again at our Houston base. On one interesting trip that I made as captain out of Dallas, Texas, to Managua,

Nicaragua, we had every piece of a one-stand cotton gin in the cabin of a DC-4 cargo plane. Only the heavy diesel engine was sent by ship, and barely an inch of space was left on the plane.

Bernie Wilson was my first officer and Les Means was a third pilot, needed in this case because of the length of the flight. When we arrived at the airport we had to enter the cockpit by way of a ladder up to the front door because the cargo took up all the space in the cabin. Only after we were airborne did we remember that the only toilet was all the way back to the rear. Finally, Bernie just had to find a way to it. He found some sort of crawl space through all the machinery and, after being away from the cockpit for about thirty minutes, he returned to the cockpit. I was next and I, too, crawled over, under, and around the various shapes in making my lengthy journey there and back. When Les left the cockpit for his relief, he was back in about two minutes. Bernie and I looked at him accusingly and said, "You didn't go all the way to the back!" Les calmly replied, "Well, you know, they haul horses in these damned things."

I think that was the first cotton gin in Nicaragua, and very probably the only one that ever arrived by air.

Ice

Pilots who flew up north would sometimes say that we did not have to contend with the icing conditions that they did. Perhaps we did not see icing very often, but the Gulf Coast could have the worst ice that I have ever seen. If Houston had a drizzling rain and a temperature just below freezing, ice could build up on an aircraft unbelievably fast.

Once, with T.N. White, we started an approach to Houston and when we entered the cloud tops, ice started to form. The de-icer boots kept the wing pretty clear but, as we slowed down and dropped the gear, we knew it would build up on the wheels and wheel struts. Tom asked for the gear down as we turned away from the airport on a 'radio range' approach. I suggested that we wait, so as to delay the buildup of ice, but he was afraid that the wheel-well doors would freeze over and block the gear in the retracted position. I thought that the hydraulic system would force it down all right, but was afraid that it would then freeze and we would not be able to retract it if need be. Anyway, we dropped the gear and flew for about eight minutes on the approach with it down. The aircraft collected so much ice that we had to keep adding more and more power, just to stay airborne. We were finally on full power as we approached the airport, and wondered whether we could maintain the airspeed until we were over the runway.

When we reached the ramp, great chunks of ice were hanging on the gear, as well as under the belly and in every exposed area. This added substantially to the weight and increased the drag to a critical level. I seriously doubt if we could have pulled out and diverted to an alternate field, had we been unable to land at Houston.

Rice Truck Van Lines

Pan Am pilots usually had to pay their own moving expenses. In 1951 we moved from New Orleans to Houston. In an effort to save money, I made a trip to the Houston area and borrowed a two and a half ton stake bed truck from a rice farmer friend of mine, and drove it back to New Orleans.

We also ordered a moving van and, when it came, I showed the rice truck to the two big black fellows who were working on the van. I asked them to leave me enough to load the rice truck, and to come back the next day and help me with the loading. They were delighted with that arrangement; so much so that they left me about twice as much as my truck would hold.

When they returned the next morning, we loaded up to the top of the stakes and then about four feet higher. We tied all that stuff on with a tarp over it to hold it down. Then we stuffed brooms, mops, rakes, shovels, and whatever else we had, under the ropes. We were loaded too high, too wide, and too heavy.

Then I walked into the back yard and discovered my children's swing set. It was a big one, with two swings, a see-saw, acrobatic rings and more. What in the world could I do with that?

I disassembled it, laid it on the driveway, positioned the truck over it, and tied the swing set up under the axles. Now we were too low, also. We cleared the ground by about four inches.

Our car, a Chevrolet coupe, was loaded to the top with clothes, bed covers, and everything else we could jam into it. At about four o'clock we started out, with Helen driving the car, and the baby on a pallet in the front seat. (We didn't know anything about child restraints.) The other two kids went in the truck with me.

We stopped at a filling station to put gas in both vehicles. The attendant stood looking from me to my wife, and then at the truck with buckets, tubs, and tools hanging from every side. He glanced at the swing set between the wheels and said to me, "Follow construction, do you, huh, Bud?"

Yeah!

We made it to Houston without losing a thing, threw it all into a rented house, and I was soon on my way on a trip to Central America.

Minimal Ground Clearance (Rice Truck Move)

Landing Gear (Discount) Class

I was transferred to Houston, Texas, in January 1951, still flying as copilot on DC-4s. But in October that year I was checked out again, as a reserve captain, meaning that I flew some trips as captain and some as copilot. I did not mind that arrangement except that the pay was prorated, depending upon the number of hours I flew in each capacity. But I felt like a captain, and most of the pilots with whom I flew usually let me do things my way. A few would not relinquish their seats, but I felt they were the ones who had less confidence in themselves, and it really did not make any difference to me. After all, I was the one who was considered competent to fly from either seat. Later I flew both the Constellation and the DC-6 from both seats, often on alternate flights.

During October 1952, at Miami, Florida, I took training for an F.A.A. type rating on the Lockheed Constellation. This air-plane was notable for its beautiful lines and three tails, and is well-loved by historians who remember it as an elegant representative of the piston-engined era.

Pilots usually learn to like every airplane they fly, but in my case this was the one exception. Had it been one of the later models it might have been fine, but these particular ships were well-worn when we took them over and, furthermore, they were the early models (Model 49s). They had no reverse thrust, no nose wheel steering, and the brakes were strange, in that after pressing the pedals there was a delay before any action at the wheels. As we made taxiing turns by using the brakes, this presented a challenge to our finesse in taxiing smoothly.

The Constellation was also, while I was the pilot in command, the first airplane that required a flight engineer. His station was aft of the copilot's seat, with his own panel and his own set of throttles. I might as well say right now that I prefer two-pilot crews. Two pilots working closely together can do a better job than three people.

Originally there was only one pilot, and mechanics were sometimes carried for the purpose of working on the airplane when required. This was the origin of the flight engineer. It made a lot of sense in Pan American's pre-war days when the airline flew to remote locations without adequate maintenance facilities. In those circumstances the flight engineer was a very important member of the crew. But in the post-war era it did not make as much sense when we were flying into stations where there were good mechanics, and where the flight engineer did not stay at the airport to do mechanical work, as he had done, for instance, on the flying boats. However, the Constellation had a station for the flight engineer, and it was something else to get used to.

Un-Hydraulics

Perhaps one of the reasons that I never felt comfortable with this airplane was an incident that happened in training. The 'Connie' had two separate hydraulic systems. The primary system, powered by pumps on Number One and Number Two engines (on the lefthand wing), was used entirely to operate the boosted flight controls. The secondary system, powered by pumps on engines three and four, was used to operate the flaps, gear, and brakes. The secondary system could be 'crossed over' to operate the flight controls in an emergency. But the primary system was supposed to be restricted to control use only as they were considered the most important. We were taught that a loss in the secondary system could not find its way into the primary system.

On our first training flight the instructor was John Hollingsworth who, years before at Big Spring, Texas, had also been my roommate and fellow student. We were doing airwork south of Miami when the flight engineer reported that the Number Four hydraulic pump had failed, for real. Not long after, he said that Number Three had also failed. The other student, Bernie Wilson, and I regurgitated what we had learned in class and said, almost in unison, "That's as far as that can go." But it was not long until we were told that the other two pumps had also failed. I was flying from the left seat with John in the right seat, and we now had an airplane with absolutely no hydraulic pressure. The controls were so hard to move that it took all the force I could exert, even with my knee under the wheel for help, to move the ailerons. The rudders were almost impossible to move.

John called Miami Tower to advise them that we would return for an emergency landing. They said that was nice, but we should know that the airport had a two hundred feet ceiling and low visibility because of heavy rain. While waiting for the weather to improve, we flew the airplane around southern Florida for nearly two hours. We took turns trying to herd that truck around, and learned to make turns by using the engines rather than the flight controls. More power on one side and less on the other did a pretty good job.

Finally we received a good weather report and started an approach to land. John had never taken over from me and he let me make the approach and landing while he acted as copilot.

Our primary concern was to actuate the flaps for landing. The way to do this was to go back into the cabin, take down a long crankhandle from the hat rack, pull up the rug in the aisle, insert the handle into the hole in the floor and make more than three hundred turns. Wouldn't that make a good impression on passengers? Even then, all you achieved for all that effort was only twenty degrees, less than the normal flap angle, for landing. Bernie went back to take care of that chore. The gear could be put down by pumping on a long handle just to the side of the right seat, a task to be continued for about five minutes. John started doing that and told me to start the approach. We had pulled a lever that disconnected the hydraulics from the controls so that they could be moved manually (with great effort) and this also reduced movement of the elevator (the control used to flare for landing) to one-third of its normal movement, but made it easier to move. This would normally have felt strange, but here I was at an advantage. I had flown this airplane so little that I didn't know what normal was.

As I approached the runway, John still did not have the gear down and locked, so we had to abandon the approach, go around, and try again. Everything was in order on the next approach and we landed safely. We had only one shot at stopping, because the accumulator held only enough pressure to actuate the brakes for one stop. We had to be towed to the ramp. During that flight we all prayed that we would not have an engine failure. That would have been tricky.

I flew the Connie until January 1953, sometimes as copilot, sometimes as captain. In spite of my distrust, I must say that it was a pleasure to fly, and especially to land. It had a very good feeling as long as everything worked as it was supposed to, but I just did not trust it. We had many engine failures, but it handled well on three, so that was not really a problem.

Un-Pilot Error

On a flight to New Orleans when I was copilot to Sam Enfield I found another reason to mistrust the Constellation. I was making an approach on instruments with a low ceiling and poor visibility. I was in the left seat, as Sam normally allowed me to fly from there. I felt that the airplane was not responding properly to the controls but I didn't mention it, thinking there might be wind-shear or turbulence. I maintained some extra speed to help. We touched down normally and the main wheels were on the runway, but the nose wheel was still in the air when, without warning, the right rudder pedal advanced itself to the full forward position.

Instinctively I was sure that no force that I could apply was going to help, and I shouted, "The rudder is locked!" The airplane was starting to turn violently to the right. I think most captains would have tried to take control and, before they could have done so, we would have been off the runway. But Sam—never an average pilot in my book—took both throttles on the right side (engines three and four) and went to full power with them. At the same time I was using all the left brake that I dared, trying not to skid the tire. With our combined actions we stayed on the runway, but barely.

Subsequent investigation revealed that a safety wire had broken and allowed a valve to put three thousand pounds of hydraulic pressure to the right rudder. Had it happened a few minutes earlier, when we were still in flight, we would almost certainly have snap-rolled. Theoretically, the hydraulic pressure could have been released, but we would have been on our back before we could have pulled the proper lever. I cannot help wondering whether a crash investigation team would ever have found that broken safety wire. Maybe it would have been just another report of 'Pilot error, stalled and spun in on approach'.

In February 1953 we were again assigned to Douglas DC-4s at the Houston base, and did not see the Constellation for seven months. My logbook shows no more captain trips until April 1956, when I flew a full month as reserve captain on the Connie. Then the next month we received training on the Douglas DC-6B and on May 7 I received my rating. Thereafter I flew a large percentage of my flights as captain on both the Connie and the DC-6. We were operating both airplanes and usually did not know which one we would fly until we showed up at the airport and saw which one was on the ramp. This was not normal for Pan Am, which generally assigned pilots to one airplane type at a time. In contrast, airlines such as Eastern would sometimes have pilots flying as many as four or more types. Pan Am felt that it was too confusing for pilots to do that, and this time at Houston was an exception. In this case I did not feel it was a problem because the aircraft were so dissimilar. Had they been more alike, there might have been some confusion.

Hail In The Cabin

One thing about the Connie: it was strong. To give an example, Mutt Fleming was letting down into Houston and entered the top of a level cloud deck at about nine thousand feet. As he descended he hit what was later deduced to be a tornado, and the airplane went wild. At one time Mutt thought it was on its back. The airspeed was impossible to control and at times exceeded the limits that Lockheed had designed it for. The altimeter read more than twelve thousand feet, but they were still in the clouds. (The low pressure in the tornado caused the altimeter to read much higher than the actual height.) All the papers were thrown out of the crew's briefcases. Everything in the cabin was flying around, including the ice cubes from the galley. A lady passenger later testified that it had been 'hailing in the cabin.'

When they emerged from the clouds they could not immediately locate themselves because so much water had flooded the ground VOR station that it was giving inaccurate signals ninety degrees off the actual direction.

Pan Am pulled that Connie out of service and a ferry crew flew it to the maintenance shops in Miami for a thorough check. They found nothing wrong, and it was returned to service.

The Six B

There is not much to say about the Douglas DC-6B except that it was a very nice airplane to operate, just a bigger and better, pressurized DC-4. It had some good features such as a lever that would change the pitch on all four propellers at the same time. Control feel was very good and pilots liked it. Altogether it was a good airplane and, with more power, would have been a great airplane. In many of our minds, the one fault was that it did not have enough power to take off and accelerate as sprightly as we would have liked; but once up to speed, it performed very well.

Douglas designed the DC-6B to be flown by two pilots but, because of F.A.A. regulations, we carried a flight engineer. Unlike the Constellation, the airplane had been built without a position for the flight engineer, so the manufacturer had to put a rail-mounted seat right between the pilots which could slide back to allow access to their seats. The cabin pressurization was operated by the copilot, as the controls were on the panel above his windshield.

There was not much for the flight engineer to do except to monitor engine power in flight, to feed the engines from the proper fuel tanks, and to shuffle paperwork. On a flight into Houston we had lost the Number One engine and the engineer had put the other three engines on the Number One tank so as to use the fuel from it and keep the airplane in balance. Approaching Houston, he decided to put each engine back on its own tank for landing, as was proper, but in doing so he closed the crossfeed valve before he selected the engines to their own mains. The result was that the other three engines immediately quit—starved of fuel—only long enough, fortunately, for the engines to cough once or twice before some pretty fast hands returned the valves to the correct positions. It was a perfect example of one crew member taking action before he let the others know what he was planning. Trying to land a 'Six' without engine power would have been a memorable experience, but one that I am happy not to have to record.

Language

Having been promoted to full captain again in February 1959, we were on approach to Guatemala one summer afternoon with some rain showers in the area. I had put W.G. (Moose) Stovall into the left seat, a preferred move of mine when I thought the copilot could do a good job. As he started to line up with where the runway should have been, some rain was obscuring our vision and I could not see if we were in line with the runway or not. I said, "Moose, I can't see the fucking runway." Just as I said that, I realized that one of the stewardesses was standing behind the engineer's seat.

We soon saw the runway and landed without incident, but I was embarrassed by my use of that language, especially in the presence of this innocent-looking young lady. We were in the terminal building, in the crowded coffee bar, when I turned to her and said, "Young lady, I am sorry about the language I used in the cockpit, but if you had been in your seat where you should have been for landing, you wouldn't have heard it." She turned to me and, in a voice that was heard all over the coffee shop, said, "Oh, that's okay, captain, I couldn't see the fucking runway, either!"

Free Ride

John Strickland was in a Connie flying into San Salvador. He taxied out for take off and stopped to run up the engines before taking the runway. The purser had checked to see that all the passenger seatbelts were fastened and was just taking his seat in the aft of the cabin. As he reached down for his own belt he saw, through the window on his right, some bare feet topped by some rags that might have been trousers. A man was standing on the landing gear or, to be exact, was standing on the 'scissors', an articulated connection that allowed the wheels to go up and down as the shock strut moved.

The purser made a dash for the cockpit, hoping to get there before the landing gear was retracted. He didn't make it. The gear had just then been tucked up, and all indications showed it to be securely in its place, before he shouted, "Captain, there is a man on the right gear!"

Every man in the cockpit was certain that anybody on or in the gear would now be dead. There was very little extra space in the wheel well with the doors closed (with some three thousand pounds of hydraulic pressure)—

"Captain, there is a man on the right gear."

just a scant few inches behind the shock strut. The man had to be crushed, but there was no way to reach him, nor to see into the wheel well.

John called the tower and explained the situation, and because no one wanted the man to fall into a house or onto someone on the ground, they agreed that John should fly over the runway at five hundred feet and lower the landing gear, so that the body would fall onto the runway.

When the gear was lowered, John asked the tower, "Did you see him fall?" The tower replied, "No, he is still standing on the wheels!" Somehow he had managed to put his head into a 'Y' where the strut divided and he was so slender that he fitted between the strut and the gear doors. When the gear was up, his feet had been above his head, but he had hung on. And was still there!

John quickly circled around for a landing and touched down as smoothly as he could. He also had the presence of mind to cut the switches to all engines and let the propellers stop as he rolled to a stop on the runway—a good spontaneous decision because his hitchhiker jumped off the gear and ran right through the props so that he could salute the captain and say, "Thank you for the ride, Cap-i-tán!"

It turned out that the fellow was out of work and had a family of many children; he had wanted to leave the country only to look for work somewhere else. He was held in jail for a day or two and, as soon as he was released, he tried it again but was intercepted before he became airborne. The government of El Salvador asked Pan American to give him a seat on a flight out of the country and, reluctantly, Pan Am did so. This was a mistake because for several months we had to station someone at the end of the runway to prevent others intent on taking a free ride in the landing gear. Most of us took to doing our engine run-ups while rolling, so as not to give anyone a chance to jump on.

What a Dump!

When we stopped flying the Lockheed Constellation into Houston, one had to be ferried to Miami. On the way, the crew had quite an experience when they lost two engines. I am not sure whether they were the two outboards or the two inboards, but they were symmetrical. The airplane did not fly very well with two engines out, so they decided to dump the fuel out of the corresponding fuel tanks to lighten it.

The controls for fuel dumping were on a bulkhead behind the pilots' heads, and alongside those were four more controls for shutting off all fluids to an engine in case of fire. The captain called for the fuel to be dumped, and the flight engineer pulled the valves. An extra crew member who happened to be on board kept going back to the cabin to look out of the windows, but no stream of fuel was visible. This went on for several minutes; they badly needed to jettison the fuel and reduce the weight because the plane was beginning to lose altitude. At long last, someone finally realized that instead of activating the fuel dump valves, the fluid shut-off valves had been pulled by mistake. Only because the valves pulled were for the same two engines that were already stopped did they avoid losing the other engines. I thought it was a suitable curtain call for that airplane.

Easy Street

During this time the Pan Am crews at Houston had one of the best schedules in the airline business. We would fly to Panama, making stops at Mexico City, Guatemala City, San Salvador, Managua, and San José. Then we would have a day off in Panama and return to Houston the third day. None of us carried a suitcase, but left one in the hotel in Panama. We stayed at the El Panama Hotel and all the bellhops knew us. As soon as they saw who was arriving they would be off to retrieve the suitcase from storage and, before we could check-in, it would be in the room. We did carry a briefcase, our 'brain bag,' but seldom opened it as we knew by heart every elevation, course, and radio frequency.

Several of us pooled our resources and bought a car (wreck) for $200. We used it to go to the beach for snorkeling, or anywhere else we wanted to go on our days off. Sometimes we drove across the isthmus to Cristóbal or up into the mountains for sightseeing. The Grace Steamship Lines allowed us to board its ships at one end of the Canal and ride through to the other because Pan American and Grace were partners in PANAGRA, an airline which flew down the west coast of South America to Peru.

At first we agreed to leave the car, full of fuel, in the hotel parking lot. Of course that was, to be polite, impractical; so we changed the rules and tried to see how little fuel we could leave in it. Some of the guys became near-perfect at that. They could leave it without enough gas to reach the nearest gas station.

All in all, it was a very satisfactory way of making a living, and it sure beat working.

Chama

He was called 'Chama' although nobody knew if that was really his name or even if he had a name. He was totally deaf and had only one eye, the other having apparently been punctured by something like a sharp stick. Where he had come from was also a mystery. There was a report that his family had brought him out of the remote hill country to the city of San Salvador and, either by accident or by design, had abandoned him there. He could make a few sounds but, because of his deafness, had never learned to speak.

He showed up at the airport and Gus Longoria, station manager for Pan American, had let him do a few chores around the office such as sweeping up, running errands, and carrying baggage to and from the airplanes. He was paid small stipends from the petty cash.

Chama was also an artist of sorts. He could draw pictures of the various airplanes he saw arriving and departing. And he could draw recognizable likenesses of crew members. He would often present such drawings to us during our ground time at San Salvador and be rewarded with a few coins.

Crew members would occasionally give him a gift of cast-off clothing that our children had worn, or soap and towels, or even a small bill or two. Most of us did not go beyond that.

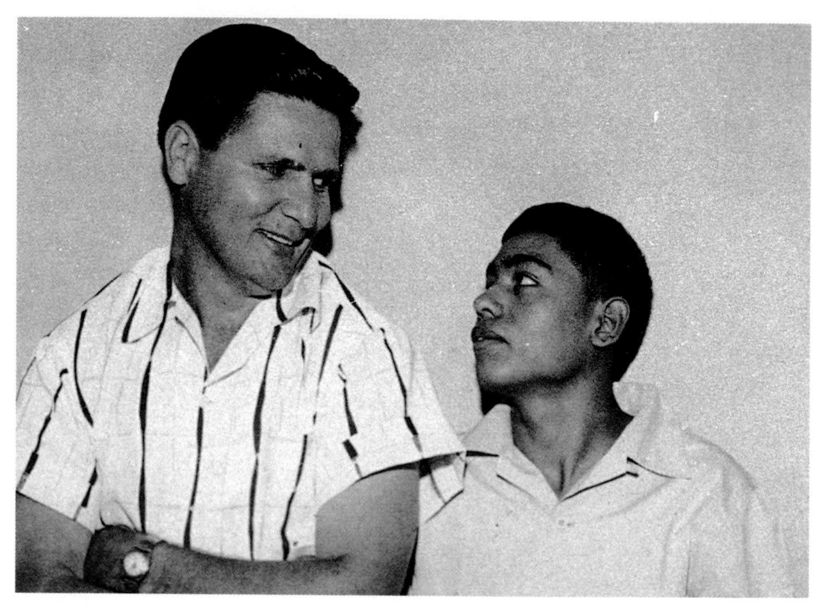

'Moose' Stovall and 'Chama'.

But William G. (Moose) Stovall had a wider vision. Bill was called Moose, I guess, because of his size and appearance. He had that tough exterior look that is often described as 'a diamond in the rough.' In any case, Bill had a marshmallow heart.

He took Chama under his wing and wangled some sort of papers from the government of El Salvador to permit his leaving the country. Bill arranged for a seat for Chama to Houston, Texas, asking the rest of the pilots and other crew members to contribute to a fund to pay the bills. Bill's idea was to take Chama to the Children's Hospital in Houston to see if anything could be done for him.

Upon arrival in Houston, Bill took Chama into his own home; he had also arranged for another pilot to share his home for part of the time but, when the other pilot found out how much trouble that could be, he kept Chama only a few hours and then returned him to Stovall's home.

As Bill later told it, having Chama in his home with his family was a real adventure. Chama had never known regular baths, how to brush his teeth, or had a regular change of clothing. Bill's family bought Chama a toothbrush and taught him how to use it. He thought that was so much fun that he wanted to do it six or seven or even ten times a day. But there was a problem—he did not care whose toothbrush he used--and the family members had to hide their own utensils. He would also use up all the hot water taking baths several times a day if they let him.

To keep Chama busy and take up some of his time, they taught him to run the lawn mower and cut the grass in the yard. Grass grows quickly in the Houston summers, but not fast enough to keep up with Chama. When no one was around to stop him he would start up the mower and cut the grass again. Bill said that he scalped his yard so badly that they had a hard time persuading the grass ever to grow again. He also cut the neighbor's grass without permission, and did a good scalping job on that, too.

From his size, we had guessed Chama to be about twelve years old. When Bill had him admitted to the hospital and the doctors examined him they concluded he was probably about seventeen. Part of the reason was his bone structure, but another was that he also took a great deal more interest in the female nurses than would a twelve-year-old.

Unfortunately, the doctors concluded that there was nothing that could be done to help Chama. He had apparently been born deaf and there was no known way to give him any hearing. His bad eye had been punctured beyond repair. A speech therapist might have been able to teach him to speak, but there was not enough time, and also no one to teach him Spanish. English would do him no good in El Salvador.

The time for Chama to remain in the United States was limited and so, reluctantly, he was returned to El Salvador where he picked up where he had left off. The Pan American employees continued to help as they could. The flight crew members who knew him were gradually transferred to other locations and, inevitably, lost track of Chama.

A sad postscript to this already sad tale: when Bill Stovall returned Chama to San Salvador, a small amount of money was left over from the contributions which we had made. Rather than trust the money to Chama, Bill left it in the safekeeping of Gus Longoria's secretary. She was to dole it out to Chama as he, as best he could, indicated his needs.

By sign language, he let her know that he needed money to have some laundry done. He must have used the money not for the laundry, but for the laundress. When Bill next came through on a trip Chama indicated that he was sick and motioned to the lower part of his body. The remainder of the money had to be used to provide treatment for venereal disease. I wish that I could provide a happy ending to Chama's story, but we lost contact with him. Pan Am no longer flies into El Salvador and, with the recent war situation, Chama's current status is a matter for conjecture.

No-Parking Know-How

We were approaching Houston at the end of a trip, and the copilot offered me a ride home from the airport. I thanked him, but said I had brought my own car to the airport. I then began to test my memory in the hope of locating just where in the parking lot I had left it.

I remembered: four days earlier I had parked right in front of the terminal building while I took my bags into the baggage room so they could be taken to the airplane. Somebody had called my attention to some sort of a problem on this particular flight, and I never thought of my car again until I was now offered a ride home—I had left it in a No Parking zone with the keys in it.

"Well," I thought, "surely some Pan Am person would have seen it and moved it into the parking lot." As soon as I left the customs room I made a beeline for the curb in front. It was still right there where I had left it. The windshield wiper was perched high in the air over a stack of parking tickets. It had been ticketed every eight hours since I had been away—a total of $48.00 in tickets. The judge thought it was funny when I explained the circumstances. I told him that I would be glad to pay one ticket, but that I hoped I would not have to pay more, because I was out of the country and could not have done anything at all to have that car moved. He asked me if Pan Am provided a parking lot. I told him that it did, but that I had simply been distracted and forgot the car. He laughed and cautioned me not to do it again, and dismissed the charges.

My story is topped by a captain in New York who drove a jeep to the airport and left it in front of the terminal. It was winter, and he inadvertently left the engine running as he threw his overcoat over the steering wheel and departed for Europe.

In his case another employee did move his jeep to the parking lot. His friends knew when he was due back, some three weeks later. They took his jeep out of the lot, put it back where he had left it, started the engine, and put his overcoat back over the steering wheel. They watched with gleeful anticipation to see his reaction, only to see him walk calmly to the jeep, slip on his overcoat and drive away, just as though this were an everyday occurrence.

(left) The Fuego Volcano in eruption, photographed from 20,000 feet near Guatemala City on a southbound run. The smoke and steam rose twice as high. (below) Volcán Fuego photographed two days later on the northbound flight.

Sex, Salary, and Seniority

Sex, salary, and seniority: these were the three 's' words that were supposed to comprise the entire repertoire of a pilot's conversational bag. Sometimes this was only too true, but at least one other 's'—scheduling—was often a fourth element just as important as the others. Well, maybe not to some.

Was there sex among the crews? Some, but no more, I'm convinced, than among any other group that you would care to name. No more than in any small town. People's morals and character do not necessarily change because they are confronted with a special situation. Some pilots married stewardesses and I found them, in general, to be the most successful of marriages. One or two of our pilots might have overdone the marrying habit. At the last count, one had had, I think, seven, and is perhaps still counting.

Many times, at the end of long flights and with adequate layover time, a get-together often ensued, sometimes known as a 'debriefing'—alternatively, a crew party. It was one way to relax and unwind, and discuss events that might have happened during the flight, or the latest gossip on what might be going on in the company. The subjects usually covered technical aspects of the flight; the whims and habits of our passengers; unusual working problems and, as we were an international airline, the unpredictability or the keen insight of the customs inspectors. Some of us had drinks and some of us didn't.

Many people were often surprised to find that the flight crew had to go through customs everywhere we went; and at times there were problems. We were not permitted the normal duty-free exemptions that our passengers enjoyed. The privileges varied from place to place but in most cases we were not supposed to bring in more than ten dollars' worth, free of duty. I once had a copilot who brought into Houston a radio on which the duty would have been $9.00, had he declared it. He gave it to a stewardess who was to overnight in Houston and go out on a Mexico flight the next day. She would maintain that it was something she carried with her for use on the layover. When she reported for the next day's flight she gave the radio to a baggage boy to take into the office and leave for the copilot to pick up from there. Customs watched the whole deal and filed a violation on him, on the stewardess, and on me, because I was the captain on the flight and was, in their eyes, responsible.

Pan American fired him. I was in an awkward position because at the time I was also the local union chairman, and I had to defend him. We were able to have his penalty reduced to six months' furlough without pay; he paid a fine; and the radio was confiscated by customs. The stewardess got off with a reprimand, and I was cleared, as I actually knew nothing of the arrangement they had made. All to save a $9.00 duty tariff! The pilot later wrote to thank me for saving his job.

Foreign customs procedures were usually less severe on us than their American counterparts. One exception was at Delhi, India. They would usually clear the cockpit crew, all males, quickly, but would hassle and hold the flight service for some time, usually until the girls offered a 'present', a bottle of wine from the airplane, or playing cards, or whatever they could come up with. Pilots had transport separate from the flight service personnel, and we would be urged by customs to go on to the hotel. We soon found that if we refused to go until our entire crew had cleared customs, staying to watch what happened, the girls were promptly cleared.

Wooden Boxes

People played little games all the time. I once arrived in San Francisco on a cargo flight where I had been checked by a check pilot. He had bought some speaker cabinets in Tokyo for use at home. He declared them as 'wooden boxes.' The customs agent said, "Captain, these wooden boxes are actually speaker cabinets, are they not?" "No, they are just wooden boxes." The agent tried again, "But you do intend to use them as speaker cabinets, do you not?"

The check pilot told him that they did not have speakers in them and that they therefore were just plain, wooden boxes. The customs agent said, "Well, I'm sorry they aren't speaker cabinets because the duty on wooden boxes happens to be 75%, but the duty on speaker cabinets is only 10%." The captain immediately began to backpedal, "Well, but of course I do intend to put speakers in them when I get home." The customs officer said, "Captain, I tried twice to tempt you to say they were speaker cabinets, but now they are just plain, wooden boxes."

Hands Off

I was copilot to Roger Sherron on a DC-6 flight out of Panama when the flight engineer showed up in a condition unfit for duty. As we drove to the airport it was obvious that he had over-indulged in the not too-distant past, and I won-

The Douglas DC-6B, pressurized development of the DC-4, was acknowledged by pilots, engineers, and economists alike to be the 'thoroughbred' airliner of the four-engined piston generation, before the arrival of the jets.

dered what action Roger was going to take. I did not have to wait long to find out. As soon as we had checked our baggage, he told both of us to accompany him into a small room near the dispatch office.

He said to the engineer, "This is how we're going to work today. You are going out of this room and straight to the airplane without speaking to anyone. When you get there, go into the cockpit, lock the door and do not open it until you hear my voice. Ned will do your walk-around (inspection of the airplane) and he will also check and verify the fuel load. When we come into the cockpit you will slide your chair back as far as the rails will permit, where you cannot reach any control, and you will sit there and do nothing while Ned and I fly the airplane. Now, are you willing to do this, or do you want me to have dispatch call for another flight engineer?"

Calling for another flight engineer would very likely have resulted in his being fired, and he had enough sense to know that he was being given a break, so he agreed. Roger and I flew the first several legs without his services and it was no problem. Roger asked him, after some hours and several cups of coffee, if he felt better and he said, "Yes, I am ready to go to work," so Roger told him to pull up his chair and take over his duties. I thought this was both a compassionate and very effective way of handling the situation. Many years later that engineer was still working, and I never heard of his having drinking problems again. We had stuck our necks out for him, and it had worked.

Roger Sherron was one pilot whom I greatly admired. He was a perfectionist and very much an instructor. I flew with him as his copilot on many flights, and with him checking me when I was a captain, and once or twice with me checking him. Not everyone felt as I did; some thought he was 'too nit-picking' and dreaded flying with him. But I learned something from him every time we flew together. I did not hesitate to tell him if I disagreed with him on any issue, and he seemed to appreciate that. For his part, he simply wanted you to know how he thought things ought to be done, but if you had a safe way of your own, that was fine with him.

On one flight to London he was checking me and my crew, and he probably told me at least a hundred things that could have been done differently. As we were walking into the hotel lobby a friend of my copilot, who apparently did not know Roger by sight but did know him by reputation, rushed up to us and said, "How did your flight go? I heard that you were being checked by Captain Sherron." My copilot said, "I guess it went all right. Every time he told Captain Wilson to do something, Ned just told him to go to hell."

Buy It As A Hobby

In the early days, when I was working for $220/month as a copilot, or $604/month as a captain, I did not think we were overpaid. In later years I was told many times by newly-hired pilots that in those early years the dollar was worth much more and they were worse off than I had been, though they were, on paper, making many more dollars. All I knew was that they were living in much better houses and driving much better cars than I had been able to afford at the same stage in my career. The first place that my wife and I lived in was a walk-up apartment with a shared bathroom down the hall, and it was the best we could afford.

As contracts improved, and pay was based upon the gross weight and speed of the aircraft flown, the salary for flying larger equipment reached higher levels. I would have to admit that, as a Boeing 747 captain, I was probably overpaid. But my pay never reached the astronomical heights referred to in the press. In my last full year, flying as a very senior captain on the heaviest airplane, and as fast as any, I made $91,793.52, never topping $100,000/year. Some airlines paid better than Pan American did and there

The Lockheed Constellation, fastest of the post-war long-distance piston-engined airliners, and remembered for its fine aerodynamic lines. This one, Clipper Winged Arrow, *was transferred to Cubana, and subsequently sold to El Al.*

must be many pilots who made more. But I was never envious of any of them, as I liked the type of flying that I was doing, and I liked the company that paid me.

One of my copilots expressed my opinion pretty well when he said, "If I didn't have this job, I'd have to buy it as a hobby."

There were bad times, too, and occasionally I thought of quitting, usually because of the excessive time spent away from home. I often heard the argument that "You only work fifteen days per month," but many a time during the early years I spent twenty-five days away on trips during a single month. Later contracts provided that we spent fifteen days at home, and sometimes it worked out. I would sometimes respond by pointing out that an office worker always enjoyed two days off each week—104 days per year, plus special holidays. And of course that same office worker was on the job only eight hours per day, while the other sixteen hours could be spent at home. If I had 180 workdays a year, they were twenty-four-hour days, and I had no guarantee that I would be home for Christmas, my wife's birthday, my children's graduation, or any other special day.

If any crew members were overpaid they were, in my opinion, the flight service people. A senior purser on Pan American could make about $35,000 per year, which was a lot of money for a young person to serve coffee and hang up coats. Our flight service did more than that, of course. In my flying days, Pan Am used to serve real meals, not the quick beverage and bag of peanuts which is all I see on most flights today, at least on the shorter routes. On long flights our people sometimes had to serve two full meals and perhaps a snack in between. We had some really outstanding people, and Pan Am's first-class service was as good as any in the world. It seemed to me that, once on the airplane, our passengers received excellent service; only on the ground did many of us think that they were sometimes poorly served.

One of our flight service people once maintained that she should be paid the same as I was because she "was on the plane just as many hours" as I was. A few of them could not see beyond that; to them, the experience, the training, and the responsibility, all acquired only through rigorous tuition, training, constant discipline, and continuous surveillance by our peers, seemed to count for nothing.

Flight engineers also were paid, in my opinion, more than the job deserved. We had many very talented and fine men in that position, but the job itself was intended only to relieve the pilot of the routine jobs. They had little or nothing to do in the decision-making or manual control of the airplane, on which so much safety depended. I will say, however, that they were always eager to accept any chore that was offered them, or should I say, sometimes imposed upon them. Pilots hated to make out logs or keep records or read the checklists (they wanted to be the ones doing the checking), but engineers would gladly do all those tasks. Perhaps they knew their jobs were not too essential and they sought to add to their responsibilities, and so make themselves less dispensable.

The flight engineers were usually paid about seventy five percent of the captain's pay, and the copilot or 'first officer' received about the same. The first officer was second in command to the captain; he assisted in flight decisions, normally flew half the flight legs, and made the take offs and landings. He had more responsibility. I think he deserved a good deal more pay than the engineer.

Once, on a polar flight, a member of the earlier astronauts, 'Pete' Conrad, was on board and he spent a lot of time in the cockpit with us. He made the flight engineer mad when he maintained that the Boeing 747 did not need a flight engineer at all, and could be flown by two pilots alone. Boeing is just now coming out with a model, the Boeing 747-400 (bigger and heavier than the one we were flying), which is designed to be flown by two pilots—no engineer.

Seniority

The word can invariably start an argument among almost any group of pilots. Application of the rules can be claimed either to restrict the talented, or, on the other hand, to be the only fair way to promote people. A big company, as Pan American was, with pilot bases worldwide, could hardly manage to maintain a just system in any other way. Without it, an opening for promotion in one base would, more often than not, be filled by someone the bosses knew. This was quite natural—they could hardly be expected to reach across the world and take someone they did not know.

In our case, though, seniority, pure and simple, was modified by the fact that no one could be promoted without passing rigorous tests; and if anyone failed those tests, he could be passed over in seniority by someone more junior. This was done many times.

When I went to work for Pan American, I hardly knew what the word seniority meant. Subsequently, however, it became paramount in all aspects of my life—where I lived, what I flew, when I flew, and how much I was paid. I would like to think that I could have done as well or better in my career if promotions had not been based on seniority. But overall, I suppose it was necessary.

The years did pile up. On one flight in a Boeing 707, with three cockpit crew members and eight flight service people in the cabin, I found that I had more years of service than all of them put together. We figured it up after a stewardess came to me and asked, "Captain, when did you start with Pan Am?" I told her, "1942." That was two years before she was born.

Your Husband Will Arrive Tonight

Scheduling was also very important to us. When I started in Brownsville, Texas, one girl did the scheduling for a base of more than forty crews. She very simply made up a list each week of who would fly which flights and so advised us. We had no say at all in the matter.

From this elementary approach, scheduling evolved over the years into a complicated system, requiring a huge staff to operate. Finally we were able to bid, according to seniority, on bases, airplanes, trips, days off, and so on. This gave the pilot more control over his life, provided that he was senior enough. If he was junior, forget it. He got all the garbage left over.

Over the years there were horror stories about pilots whom the company 'lost'; that they had stayed for a long vacation in some place or another; or that a pilot who had been killed in a crash was due in on such-and-such a flight. Scheduling was alleged to have called one woman to tell her that her husband would arrive that night. She said, "I don't think so, he isn't out on a trip." On the clerk's insistence that he had the right information and that her pilot husband would indeed be in on a specific flight that night, the wife said, "All right, then, I guess I'd better tell this fellow in bed with me to leave."

Sometimes they called out two pilots for a flight, or sometimes none at all. But, considering the fearful complexity of handling countless flights all around the world, they did a good job, especially with delays, weather, crew illness, and a thousand other factors affecting crew scheduling that they had to deal with all the time.

French Accent

Through Central America when we had only a couple of flights each day, it was a welcome diversion to know who was on board a flight that we might be passing. We would swap information on the radio about weather or other conditions over the route, and sometimes also discuss less important matters. One pilot had been on vacation in Europe and had been a passenger on some flights of Air France. Jokingly, he made the familiar reference to 'Air Chance', a disparaging nickname for the French airline, a mild insult shared by dozens of other reputable companies, whose acronyms can be humorously explained. I picked up the microphone and, with what must have been a passable French accent, said, "Will zee aircraft makeeng zose remarks pleeze identify?" Silence reigned the airwaves. We tried contacting the other aircraft by call sign, predictably without success.

We were flying into Mexico City and the other airplane would be there in a couple of days. I took the station manager aside and told him that when that flight arrived he should tell the captain that the Air France office had been calling to ask the name of the pilot on that particular flight. He did so, but denied that he knew any reason for the request. I think we had the pilot worried for some time until, again passing him in flight, I made a comment with my best French accent. He promised dire retribution.

The Power of Hot Air

I had had 'Jet Fever' for some time and at last, in December 1960, we at Houston were assigned to fly the Douglas DC-8. I went back to co-pilot again because only three Houston crews were assigned to the new four-jet. But the copilots had to have the same F.A.A. rating on the airplane, so we were to receive the same training as the captains.

Pan American Airways had been the first U.S. airline to order jets. The initial order was for twenty-five DC-8s and twenty Boeing 707s. I was pleased that we drew the Douglas, as I had flown Douglas aircraft for years and had confidence in them.

Transponders

We went to Miami for the training. As usual we had about three weeks or a month of classroom study about the airplane, and had to pass an oral examination with an F.A.A. inspector before we would be allowed to take flight training. I spent a lot of time learning all about the airplane's systems and how to operate them. I had paid little attention to a new item: the transponder. I suppose all my readers now know what that is, but at the time I just regarded it as something to help the air traffic controllers and felt that it had nothing to do with safe flying. So I did not spend any time reading about it, thinking that there would be plenty of opportunity for that when I was actually flying the airplane.

The night before I was to take my oral examination I asked my friend Fred Knotts, whom I relied on heavily and who had just finished his oral, if he had been asked about the transponder. He told me that he had not been asked about it at all and, in fact, the inspector who examined him did not seem to know anything about it himself. A telephone call asking something about the transponder had been received while Fred was in the office, and the inspector had to refer to a manual to answer the question. So, naturally, I did not worry any more about that.

Early next morning I reported for my examination and sat down opposite the inspector at his table.

"Mr Wilson, what do you know about the transponder?"

The Douglas DC-8. Pan American originally ordered 25 of this first generation jet, but reduced this number to 21, two of which went to its associated airline, Panair do Brasil. Although the Boeing 707 became Pan Am's standard jet in the 1960s, the DC-8-30s were used throughout Latin America.

I could have been more discreet, but I thought I might as well let him know, so I said, "I can tell you all I know about the transponder in one sentence. You turn it on before take off and you turn it off after landing."

"What is the emergency code?"

"I don't know."

"What is the code for being unable to communicate?"

"I don't know."

"If you are coming into the U.S.A. from overseas, how far offshore do you turn on the transponder?"

"One hundred miles?" That was wrong; it was two hundred miles.

It went on and on. I could not believe that there was so much to know about transponders. Finally I was told that, if I missed one more question, I would have to go back to ground school. I had not been asked a single question about the DC-8.

The next question was, "What is a high density area?" At last! This was something I thought I knew. I told him it is an area designated by the F.A.A.

where traffic was considered heavy. He did not like that answer, though it was correct, and asked me if I could identify the high density area symbol on a chart, showing me a chart of Arizona. At that time there was very little heavy traffic in Arizona, but I found the symbol around Phoenix and showed it to him. He did not think I was correct and told me that unless I could show him the symbol on the legend I had flunked the examination. I showed him the symbol, and I'm sure he thought I was wrong, but when he uncovered the legend, there it was, just as I had said. So I was right on that one, but I had no hope of passing with this inspector.

I was quite literally saved by the bell: the telephone bell. A call came in for him. He turned to another inspector in the room and asked him to continue with my examination until he returned. This second inspector had heard all of our previous conversation and told me to bring my books over to his desk.

"Have you heard enough about the transponder?"

"Yes, sir, all I ever want to hear."

"Okay, let's see what you know about the airplane."

And we started to talk about all the systems on the DC-8 and how to operate it. This man was reasonable. When I did not know an answer I would say so, and he would refer to the manual and we would read it together. When the first inspector came back into the room he sat at his desk and kept looking in our direction, but neither of us ever met his eye and we just kept on with what we were doing. This went on for three or four hours (which was about normal) and finally the second inspector signed off my sheet to say that I had satisfactorily completed the oral test.

The following day I started into flight training. I was lucky to have Lew Oates assigned as my flight instructor. In my opinion, Lew was the finest flight instructor that Pan American had. Most of them could demonstrate how to perform a maneuver, but Lew could explain it to you, and if you followed his instructions exactly, you could do it. He once told me that he could tell if a person could fly the airplane by the time he had sat down and fastened his seatbelt.

On the first day, when we sat in the cockpit, Lew told me to disregard all the rumors--and there were plenty--that I might have heard about the jets. He said that this was just another fine Douglas airplane and that we were going to have fun learning to fly it. And we did.

Straight Eight

One day we were practicing take offs and landings when a friend in the tower asked one of the trainees how he liked the jet. He answered, "I never knew the power of hot air before!"

The performance was far in excess of what we had been used to with the piston-engined types. Basically, a jet engine just takes air into the front, compresses it, adds fuel, and when it burns ejects hot air with tremendous force out the back end. And it certainly generates power.

We flew the DC-8 higher than we had ever been before, and we did stalls up there, but they were really only approaches to stalls. Whenever we recognized that a stall was imminent, we were supposed to add power and recover flying speed immediately.

One day I told Lew, "You are scaring me about this airplane. What does it do if it actually stalls? Flip on its back? Dive uncontrollably? What?"

"Do you want to see a full stall?" I said I did. He told me to pull all the power off and to stall it and, when I recognized the stall, to pull back on the yoke as far as it would go, wrapping my arms around the wheel if I had to hold it there. I did so, and that Eight would drop its nose and then recover on its own, with the nose going up and down, but never losing control. It felt, though, as if we were flying into one brick wall after another, and the flight engineer was jumping up and down and shouting at us to stop because we were going to 'shake the engines off'. Lew ignored him and told me to add just a little power. When I did so, all the roughness stopped and the DC-8 flew as smoothly as silk even though descending at several thousand of feet per minute. The ailerons were still active and, even though stalled, we could roll left and right under full control. I never again had the least doubt about the safety of the DC-8.

No Simulator

After eight hours of training, Lew said that I was ready for a flight test by the F.A.A. We showed up at about six am to meet the F.A.A. Inspector, Harry Taber. He took one look at my application and said that he could not give me a flight test because I had only eight hours training. At the time, Pan American had agreed with the F.A.A. that it would give every student at least sixteen hours of training. This qualification level was later abandoned and many pilots were given less time than I took.

Lew told him that I was ready for the test. Mr Taber suggested that Lew write him a letter saying that he considered me qualified, but Lew refused, observing that he had signed my application and that plainly indicated that he considered me ready or he would not have signed it. He did not want to start something that could be considered setting a precedent.

In an effort to find a way around this, Mr Taber asked me how many hours I had in a flight simulator. He didn't like it very much when I told him that I had never even seen a flight simulator. Simulators are a great invention and are much cheaper to 'fly' than the airplane, but the airplane is the real thing. One advantage of the simulator, however, is that a pilot can be given one problem after another, cumulatively, until he cannot help but crash. But nobody is hurt and no property is lost.

This argument went on for about an hour, and I was becoming very nervous, as I could see myself being failed just to prove a point. Finally, though, Mr Taber turned to me and said, "Ned, I know this has to have you upset, but I am going to ride with you, and if you can do the job I will give you a rating. Since Quesada (a reference to an earlier F.A.A. administrator who had been considered very tough), I don't even think I'm God any more. We will work this out with Pan Am later."

The flight went very well. As soon as we had gained some altitude, Mr Taber asked me to show him a steeply-banked turn to the left. The idea is not to vary altitude while doing this. But when I had the turn established he asked me to maintain the bank, but to climb at a rate of 500 feet per minute. Then he asked me to reverse the turn to the right and then descend at the same rate. When I had leveled out, he turned to Lew and said, "That's a pretty good indication of ability to fly, isn't it?" I thought then that I was going to make it, and was fairly confident as we did the routine maneuvers such as approaches to stalls, engine-out landings, no-flap approaches, and all the rest.

After about two hours we taxied in and, as I shut down the engines, Lew reached out to shake my hand and said, "Congratulations, you are a DC-8 pilot." He had not waited for a decision from the inspector who, of course, had the final word.

In training we only made approaches while simulating the condition of not being able to extend the flaps. We never actually touched the wheels onto the runway. This was because the approach speed was so high that we could possibly have blown out the tires.

Jet Glider

Soon after I was flying the line, Ed Swenson and I were approaching Mexico City. We had put down partial flaps and lowered the landing gear when we noticed that the flaps were coming back up. In fact, we had a broken hydraulic line in the flap system and had lost all our hydraulic fluid. The gear was down and locked, and we had no way to retract it. With the gear down we would burn too much fuel if we tried to fly to any other airport, so we were committed to a no-flap landing at Mexico City, altitude 7,500 feet. Altitude and temperature (it was a hot afternoon) cause the actual speed to be higher than that

Pilot Ed Swenson, seen here with 'Conche . Porres', ace mechanic at Guatemala City. He could identify and repair a defective part in less time than most maintenance crews would take to realise that something was wrong.

shown on the airspeed indicator. This made our actual approach speed, as I recall writing to Lew Oates, no less than 194mph, fairly close to the speed at which the Space Shuttle lands at Edwards Air Force Base, with a three-mile-long runway.

It was my leg to fly and Ed did not take the airplane away from me, but allowed me to make the landing. We touched down as near to the end of the runway as I thought prudent and, using slightly more than normal braking, stopped in about two-thirds of the runway. We did not blow a single tire.

One difference from the piston-engined airplanes that we noticed immediately in the jets was that we could pull the power off entirely as we approached the runway, without abruptly losing much speed. If you do this with propellers they go to flat pitch and cause very high drag, which drastically slows the airplane. But jet engines, having no propellers, do not increase the drag as the power is reduced.

By the time I had become a line pilot on the DC-8, some of my colleagues were already having a lot of fun by closing the throttles at cruising altitude and 'gliding' all the way into a landing. It took some skill and judgment, but actually the Eight was a pretty good glider. With power off (in idle) we could go more than one hundred miles from an altitude of, say, 35,000 feet, and land without ever touching the throttles.

I do not wish to give the idea that we were being reckless. It was not recommended procedure, but I never considered it dangerous. If you ended up a little low, very little extra power was needed to correct it, and if high or fast, earlier application of flaps would correct that. If you really 'blew it' and were not even close, then you simply went around for another approach.

One unusual feature of the DC-8 was that reverse thrust could be used while in flight. All engines could be put into idle reverse and the outboards could be used almost all the way to take off power. This would permit unbelievable rates of descent, which meant if weather or anything else made us stay very high, we could then come down in a hurry. One night, after arriving in Houston we were talking in the customs room about having been in reverse thrust all the way from Palacios, a check point about eighty miles from the airport. A customs officer spoke up, "I'll never believe you guys again. Are you trying to tell us that you flew backwards all the way from Palacios?"

We had nine pilots at the Houston base because we were carrying a second officer. An argument was going on between the Air Line Pilot's Association (ALPA) and the Company. The union wanted the professional flight engineers (those who did not have pilot's licenses) to be replaced with pilots. As one might guess, a power struggle was involved here. The flight engineers were not in the pilot's union and ALPA wanted the entire crew under its jurisdiction. Some of us truly felt that crew coordination would be better if all crew members were pilots. The matter was before arbitration and Pan American had agreed in the meantime to carry both the flight engineer and an extra pilot as well. Frankly, it was a waste of money. The extra pilot sat in the jumpseat and handled the radio and that was about all. But all nine of us had been captains before, so we just took turns, and whomever was flying at the time used the lefthand seat.

Take Me To Cuba

One of the early hijackings took place out of Mexico City. The hijacker entered the cockpit armed with a gun and asked to be taken to Cuba. Carl Ballard was the captain but, as he was the third pilot on

This was the notorious tower that was too close for comfort to the approach path to Guatemala City. Intended to be a tribute to the French engineer's Eiffel Tower, the pilots had another name for it.

that leg, it fell to Sam Enfield to try to talk to the hijacker. Sam said that the man was so nervous that he was afraid he might shoot at any time. He appeared to be on drugs.

The F.A.A. then required us to wear oxygen masks around our necks so that they could be donned in a second or so. Carl casually pulled his up over his face. When the hijacker did not object, the copilot and then the engineer did the same. Through internal microphones they could now talk to one another without him knowing it, and they held a discussion about the possibilities of fooling him. They talked about going to Miami instead of Cuba, but were afraid he would recognize the terrain. They talked about depressurizing the airplane. A switch in the cockpit could release all oxygen masks to drop down in the cabin, and the flight attendants were trained to ensure that all passengers used them. The hijacker (and possibly Sam) would be the only one not on oxygen and should pass out. But they were afraid that some passengers would be hurt or that the fellow might become irrational and shoot, as he began to pass out. They did not want Sam taking the risk of trying to overpower him so, in the end, they thought it best to go to Cuba.

On arrival in Cuba they were met by Fidel Castro himself, who gave everyone in the crew a big black cigar and a bottle of Cuban rum. The hijacker unloaded his gun, spilling bullets on the floor, and Sam asked him if he could have one. The fellow said, "Sure, I intended for you to have it, one way or another." Sam took the powder out and fashioned it into a tie clasp which he wore for many years.

My view on hijacking was that no concessions of any kind should be made. The hijacker should be informed that once the airplane landed, and when he came into sight, he would be shot, then and there, by the security force or the military or the police. There might be one tragedy, but I do not think it would be tried again. I told my family that if I was ever hijacked, they were to inform Pan American and any law enforcement units that I preferred no concessions be made, but then I never had to find out if I could maintain that attitude under fire.

The Douglas DC-8 was enjoyable to operate. For several reasons, it was not as efficient for the airlines as the Boeing 707. It would not carry the same load to altitude as quickly as the Boeing 707, and the cross-section fuselage was not quite as large, thus cutting down on the volume of baggage and cargo that could be put into the belly holds. Because of these considerations, and even counting the larger 'stretched' DC-8s, it did not sell quite as well to the airlines as the Boeing, but it was a real 'pilot's airplane.' Many of us who had flown both preferred the DC-8 to the Boeing 707.

Some of the routes over which we operated the DC-8 were not really long enough to be efficient. For instance, we flew from Panama to San José, Costa Rica. If we departed with only enough fuel to be down to landing weight at San José and the weather there turned out to be bad, we would have to come back to Panama. We found a way around that by carrying enough fuel and filing a flight plan to Managua, Nicaragua. On arrival over San José, and if the weather permitted a landing, we would then dump enough fuel to bring down the landing weight; not very efficient perhaps, but the practice kept us on schedule and the passengers arrived at their desired destination.

Frosted Glass Landing

Near San José was the volcano, Irazú, which was more or less active all the time. On a dark night one of our pilots, based in Miami, went into what he thought was just a cloud, but he never seemed to come out of it. After a while he realized that he had flown into smoke and ash from Irazú. It had etched the windshields so that they were opaque and he could no longer see out. It would have been preferable to go to Miami, which was the closest place with an ILS (instrument landing system), and there he could have come very close to the runway before he actually had to see it. But with insufficient fuel to reach Miami, he had to settle for Panama, where he had only a VOR approach, not as precise in runway alignment as the ILS. He flew carefully and at about two hundred feet above the runway he began to see the lights and safely landed the DC-8, seeing through a glass, darkly.

The Douglas DC-8 rates as a very fine airplane in my book.

Tears In My Hair

The emphasis in the term Air Traffic Control should be on the word Traffic, which is all that the professionals in that field were meant to control. Had they been called 'traffic directors', or something similar, I would have no objection, and I do not like to hear the news media call them controllers. I really cringe when I hear a reporter say that "the controller brought the airplane in." A.T.C. does not, or should not, do anything except give the airplane a clearance to land in such a manner that it does not interfere with any other airplane.

Even that much is unnecessary when the conditions are such that the pilots can see each other, under conditions termed Visual Flight Rules (V.F.R.). Even when one airplane has filed a flight plan for Instrument Flight Rules (I.F.R.), if he is flying where it would be possible to fly V.F.R., then A.T.C., according to its own rules, is not required to keep him separated from other V.F.R. traffic. The only exception is above 18,000 feet, where all airplanes must be on I.F.R.

In the early days, we had little or no traffic control throughout Central America. Our dispatchers were supposed to relay to us any knowledge they had of other airplanes in our area but, communications being what they were at the time, we had often passed the other aircraft before we received the message.

Even when we were in the United States, where A.T.C., a comprehensive system existed, clearances had to be received first by our dispatchers who then sent them on to us by radio: a slow process, to say the least.

Finally, of course, voice radio procedures were developed so that we could talk with A.T.C. directly. I remember the first time we were given a clearance to "take up a heading of X degrees for vectors to Houston." The pilot I was with thought it was wonderful not to have to follow the radio signals we had been using; but my thought was then, and my memory is today, that we had come to the end of an era. The pilot had lost some of his freedom and, furthermore, pilots would become complacent because some of their navigational chores were being taken over, at least partially, by someone else. The pilots were always assured that none of this took away any of their responsibility, that they could always refuse any directions that were unsafe; but the real world was a little different. Any pilot who refused any clearance had to defend his position and to write a report to explain his decision. Usually it was not worth the trouble.

Many times these clearances to proceed 'direct' had nothing to do with traffic. I proved this many times by replying, "If that heading is necessary for traffic separation I'll accept it but, if not, I'd like to follow my flight plan." Almost always the answer was, "Proceed as filed."

Close Call

The only close call I ever had—what is called a 'near miss'—was under A.T.C. control, going into San Francisco one dark night. I was not flying, but was sitting behind the captain and handling the radio. Approach Control called to say that we had "traffic at two o'clock." We all looked to the right of the nose, saw nothing, but then, looking left I did see the flashing lights of an airplane. I replied, "no contact at two o'clock, but we do see traffic at ten o'clock."

"Oh. Okay."

We all assumed that he had made an error in direction, and his reply seemed to confirm it. So we all watched the lights passing to our left, which were not nearing us. Then, suddenly I looked to the right and the windshield was full of airplane. The copilot saw it at the same time and pulled back on the wheel just enough so that we cleared the Cessna 310, on a collision course with us, by maybe one hundred feet. I could see into his cockpit and saw the lights of his panel.

The confusion of the call had caused each of us to make the mistake of looking in the same direction and watching lights that were not pertinent to us. We should have maintained a vigilant watch in all directions, and the controller should have asked again if we had seen the aircraft to our right, or suggested a turn. There were errors both in the airplane and on the ground.

I told him that we had nearly hit a Cessna and his laconic reply was, "Well, I told you that you had traffic at two o'clock."

Getting It Down

But that is the only time in more than thirty-nine years of airline flying that I had a near miss. Much of the talk today is about the obsolescence of the 'see and avoid' concept. I do not think it is obsolete. You have only to go to Oshkosh, Wisconsin, where thousands of airplanes converge for their annual convention and land, sometimes three at a time on one runway, to realize that if pilots can see each other they can handle their own traffic. Oshkosh far exceeds the number of airplanes per hour of any airport in the country, and they are not all of the same type or speed. There will be everything from slow Piper Cubs to military fighters and usually some airline traffic, too.

Sometimes you could hear a 'funny' on the air. Once in Honolulu I heard a tower operator ask a Delta flight, "Can you get it down?" Apparently he was high and the tower's concern was that he might have to abandon the approach and would have to circle for another. The Delta flight came back in an exaggerated Texas drawl, "We-ell, I haven't left one up here ye-et."

Foreign Tongue

Language could be a problem in foreign countries, but some-times it was a problem at home, too. Once on a flight out of Detroit, I was having trouble, as a Texan, with a Yankee voice. He was giving me a routing by V.O.R. (very high frequency, omni-directional range) names and I understood most of them, but I just could not decipher one. After asking him several times, he was becoming irritated. I looked at my map and located the missing station between two that I had understood, and there it was, as big as life—'Gardener.' So I said, "Okay, I've got it now, Gar-den-er." Back he came, still plenty irritated, "That's right__Gahdneh__Gahdneh__Gahdneh!"

Getting the Message

If I had to give a gold star to any A.T.C. group it surely would go to the guys at London, England. They always seemed un-flappable, no matter what happened. On my very first flight there, I was given a clearance to a certain location, but when I looked at the map I saw that there was no direct route to it. It seemed that I needed to make a dog-leg by another location, called Woodley. Not wishing to make a mistake on my first arrival to Heathrow, I asked, "Do you want me to go direct, or via Woodley?" A calm voice slowly said, "Oh, I say, old man, why don't you go either way you'd like?" That is my kind of traffic control. If I had to make an approach to the lowest possible landing minimums, I would like it to be at Heathrow.

To be given a clearance so fast that nobody could follow it was annoying. One pilot recorded a clearance and then transmitted it back to the source. "Hey, wait a minute, I can't take it that fast," said the controller who had just given it to him.

At Los Angeles I was once read a clearance that sounded something like this: "ClipperonetwozeroclearedtoLondonHeathrowviaDaggetOneDeparture DaggetLasVegasMilfordDeltaBakerGreatFallsflightplanrouteclimbtoandmai ntainthreeonezerocontactdeparturecontroltwofourpointsix." And there was more.

Nobody could have deciphered that clearance as fast as it was given, but my copilot grabbed the flight plan and by following it, saw that it was our planned route. He opened the mike and started v-e-r-y slowly, "I understand-Clipper-One-Two-Zero-to-be-cleared-as-follows. To-London-Heathrow-via-Dagget-One-Departure---------------." He read the whole thing as slowly as possible and took about two full minutes to do it. With our microphone open not another radio in the area could transmit on the same frequency. By now I was concerned that, when he let the ground controller in, we would be asked to return to the ramp and come up to the tower for a conference. When he finally finished, he said, "Now, did Clipper One Two Zero get the clearance correctly?" I would not have been surprised at anything the controller said except what he did say. He almost giggled as he said, "Yes, Clipper, you got the clearance, and I got the message!"

Many times direct communication between two airplanes would be more efficient and safer than relying on an in-between controller. The awful accident at Tenerife, where one Boeing 747 was taxiing on the runway in heavy fog and another was thought to be cleared for take off, is a case in point. Part of the problem was that three persons from three parts of the world (two of whom were speaking what was to them a foreign language), were also trying to coordinate through the tower. Would the accident have been avoided if one pilot, on entering the runway, had called directly to the other, with a statement such as: "I am on the runway, don't move until I tell you I'm clear?" An accident might have been avoided, even though by improper procedure. Had I been there, I would have done exactly that.

This Approach Is For Shit

On a flight from London to Los Angeles I heard a United Air Lines flight trying to add a little publicity to his calls. On every transmission he would identify himself as 'United Long Range Jet Sixty One.' Everyone listening got a little tired of it until, finally, Los Angeles Center said to him, "United Long Range Jet Sixty One, what was your point of departure?"

"United Long Range Jet Sixty One is non-stop New York to Los Angeles."

"Roger. Clipper One Twenty One, what was your point of departure?"

I replied, "Clipper One Twenty One is non-stop London to Los Angeles."

"Roger." Perfectly deadpan.

On his next transmission United identified himself only as "United Sixty One."

An American Airlines retiree took off in his private air-plane from Fort Worth and asked the weather service to give him the weather at El Paso, Del

"Da! I haff the runway in sight, but this approach is for shit!"

Rio, Corpus Christi, Houston, and New Orleans. This confused the weather station, which asked, "Bonanza, what is your destination?" The reply was "Well, I'm not going to know that until I find out what the weather is."

There is the story about Aeroflot coming into New York. The pilot was making an approach called the 'Carnarsie Approach' which requires a rather tight turn to the runway following some lights on the ground. The tower felt that he was not turning sharply enough and might miss the runway, and asked, "Aeroflot, do you have the runway in sight?"

"Da! I haff the runway in sight, but this approach is for shit!"

Some airport controllers in foreign countries really took their jobs seriously. On a beautiful, clear night we were coming into Rangoon, Burma. As we came close, the lights of the city were beautiful, like diamonds in the night. The runway was in sight, yet we were told the airport was closed because the runway lights were out. We could see the runway and maybe five or six of the lights alongside the runway were not burning. This did not concern us as we could see the runway just fine and, in any case, our landing lights would illuminate the runway once we were down low.

But to no avail: we were not about to take their authority away, and they insisted that the airport was closed. We had some thirty or forty passengers bound for Rangoon and just as many were awaiting us. But the airport was closed, and that was that. I tried to tell them as I circled, burning up fuel, that I could see the runway just fine. No deal. I finally asked if they had any flare pots available and suggested that they fill in the blank spots with them. No deal. But I guess that gave them an idea. They would light another runway, one that had no electric lights on it, with flare pots.

Never mind that this runway was much shorter than the regular one, nor that it was also much rougher, having been made during the war out of poured concrete squares. Had this been in the United States, I would, by this time, have been mad enough to land on the main runway without a clearance and take my chances that I could talk my way out of it. In Burma that might land me in jail, so I circled some more while they put flare pots along the sides of the shorter runway. When they had finished it was not half as well-lighted as the main runway, even without its few missing lights. But they had exercised their authority and proved that they were in charge; and I landed on the shorter and rougher runway.

In Paris we would call for start clearance and invariably the tower would reply, "We will call you bek." Then we would wait for two to five minutes until they called us back to tell us we had their permission to start engines. My copilot caused total confusion by transmitting, "Clipper One Two Zero is ready to start, will you call me bek?" They did not know what to say, but finally said, "We'll call you bek."

Another U.S. airline asked Frankfurt Tower for directions on where to taxi. The tower said, "Have you never been to Frankfurt before?" The reply was, "Well, I was here in 1945, but they wouldn't let me land."

I recently heard a light airplane preparing to take off from a nearby airport. He was asked if he was, "Ready to copy the clearance?" I liked his reply, "I'm ready to copy, do you want to give it to me five times fast, or once slowly?"

A Pretty Poor Show

I have already remarked that I liked London's traffic control, but I did draw their ire once. It was a trip where I was checking a new 707 captain. We had been around a large part of the world and were approaching London from

"...my tears are running into my hair."

Frankfurt. The pilot asked me if it would be all right if he let the autopilot make an approach. Because that requires a skill all its own, I agreed and he set up the autopilot to intercept the inbound course of the I.L.S. and turned it on.

As we approached the beam the controller said, "Clipper, you can start your turn to intercept the I.L.S. now." As we were all set up and expected the autopilot to start turning momentarily, I did not think it necessary to explain this to the controller, but just said, "Roger." But our autopilot malfunctioned and did not intercept at all. When it became evident that it was not going to do so, the pilot disengaged it and made the turn manually. and the turn was now too wide.

The controller spoke up, "Clipper, I told you when to turn and you went steaming right through the I.L.S. localizer." I explained that we had been attempting an autopilot approach and that the autopilot had failed to capture the I.L.S. His reply was classic British, "Well, I say, that was a pretty poor show!" I still prefer the control at London's Heathrow Airport.

Much has been said of controllers who have aided pilots who were lost or who had wandered into instrument flying conditions without being qualified to handle them. And there have been many instances when they have done a fine job in this regard.

A joke made the rounds that one pilot called in to say, "I am not instrument rated, but I'm in the clouds and I think I'm upside-down." The controller said, "If you are not qualified on instruments, what makes you think you are inverted?" "Because my tears are running into my hair!"

A Little Help From My Friends

On 7 November 1969, I reported for a flight from Los Angeles to London. The forecast over the route showed a strong tailwind in excess of 100mph, and apparently we could easily break the existing L.A.-London speed record, perhaps by as much as fifteen or twenty minutes.

I called the chief controller in LAX (Los Angeles International Airport) and advised him of this possibility and requested take off to the east because records are based on 'wheels up' to touchdown. Winds on the runway were light from the east, but traffic was taking off to the west, over the ocean, which is normal at LAX. He told me to advise ground control when I was ready to taxi. I did that and was told that if I wanted to take off to the east, there would be a 45-minute delay. We had already boarded passengers and I did not wish to subject them to the discomfort of sitting so long on the airplane, so I agreed to take off to the west. I asked for an immediate turn on course to the east.

After take off I again asked for an early turn, without results. It was eleven minutes before I was abeam of the field and headed east. That cost us at least ten minutes of flight time. Such an attitude was in striking contrast to our reception in London. I had no more than made contact with the London area controller when he said, "I understand that you are about to set a record. You may make any approach you like to any runway; just tell me your intentions."

We made the flight in eight hours, forty-four minutes, covering 5,580 miles at a speed of 640mph. With a little help from Los Angeles it could have been ten minutes faster.

Clipper One and Clipper Two

Early in 1964, while still at Houston, I bid for a captain's job on Boeing 707s, to be based in San Francisco. At first I was told that I could not go right away because I was needed in Houston but, as often happens in the airline business, I received a call one Friday telling me that I was expected in San Francisco on the next Monday morning to begin training. I caught a flight to SFO and left my family behind to be moved later.

I spent most of March in ground school. One feature was known as a 'walk-around', or learning how to check the airplane before a flight. This consisted of, among other things, knowing all the holes in the airplane: inlets for air, compressor ducts, pitot tubes, small orifices for measuring static pressure, or the outlet for pressurized air. These exercises usually took place in the wee small hours of the morning at the airport which was built on reclaimed land and thus protruded out into San Francisco Bay. I had not brought enough warm clothes from Texas and I thought that the Bay area was the coldest place I had ever been to. I also had to take some time in the Boeing 707 simulator. Until then, I still had never seen a simulator. They told me to fly it gently because it was more sensitive on the controls than the actual airplane. It seemed to have no 'feel' at all, had minimal pressure to move the controls, and was seemingly almost impossible to fly. I kept complaining and would be told repeatedly that "Yes, we told you, it's very sensitive." Finally, though, the instructor said, "Here, let me show you," and he took the wheel. "Oh," he said, after a couple of seconds, "I forgot to turn on the hydraulics." All the control response in a simulator is artificially supplied and there had been none at all. In its normal condition the simulator flew very much like the airplane.

Fred Knotts and I were sharing an apartment in San Francisco and neither of our families was there; so we were both eager to extract as much out of our training as we could. One day we went up to the lady who scheduled the training flights to say, "Berkie, if you have any extra seats on a training flight, put us on as observers."

The Boeing 707, which dominated the world's air routes during the first jet era throughout the 1960s.

"Captain Knotts and Captain Wilson, my name is Miss Berk-land, and I do the scheduling around here!"

"Yes, Ma'am, Miss Berkland, we understand." In April, after ground school was completed and I had gone through the process of an oral exam, I was considered ready for a 'rating ride' with the F.A.A. The inspector was John Bowers, known to be tough but fair.

I decided to use a little psychology. As he sat down in the jumpseat behind me I told him, "Sir, that seat is usually occupied by a second officer and I expect him to watch me and if I'm doing something wrong or missing something, I want him to speak up. Now I know you will not do that, but his other duty is to watch for traffic and to warn me of what he sees. I do expect you to do that, and it's all the more important as I will be under the hood and can't see out." I am sure that John Bowers knew what I was doing, but I also think he liked me showing that I could take command.

The flight went all right and after we landed we started to do a 'walk-around' check. The first thing he asked me was about a small square plate on the side of the engine. He asked me what it was for, and I was not sure. I said, "Well, I think it's hinged and opens inward." And with that, I reached up and bumped it with my fist. It came out and fell into the engine cowl. It was designed to do just that if it was hit, because it was where a ground crewman was supposed to push the end of a fire extinguisher if the engine caught fire when it was being started. And it now had to be retrieved from inside the cowling and installed back where it belonged.

Bowers told me to hurry up to the cockpit, where they were preparing for another flight, and to tell them that they would have to wait for maintenance to replace the panel. Then he said, "Let's get the hell away from this airplane before you tear it up!" That ended my check ride, but he gave me a rating for Boeing 707s, which also included 720Bs.

I always admired John Bowers because at the end of a flight during which he might have checked four or five different pilots, and perhaps ending up in Sacramento where we did much of our training, he would, if given the chance by Pan Am's flight instructor, fly the airplane back to our base. He would take the captain's seat and, just before he started the take off, would glance back at all those pilots to whom he had just given a hard time and say, "After V_1, it's open season." You may rest assured that he had an engine cut on take off, instruments failed, hydraulic systems wouldn't work, the gear wouldn't go down normally, and anything else the guys could think of. But he would handle it all and fly the airplane back to base in short order.

Can You Spare a Match?

One day a crew was at Sacramento practicing landings, and around and around the airport they went. A group of interested onlookers was hanging on the fence in front of the terminal building, watching this jet come and go.

In the cockpit were several smokers and nobody had any matches. As smokers will, this group was becoming jumpy without a cigarette, so they decided to taxi over to the crowd and beg some matches. They stopped near the fence, and as there were no stairs, the flight engineer opened a hatch in the cockpit floor and dropped out onto the nose wheel, then to the ground, and collected a book of matches from someone at the fence. As he turned to go, he said, "We had an engine flame out," then struck a match, threw it into the engine intake, then climbed back up into the airplane, and away they went.

English-speaking World

My first trip out of San Francisco was a polar flight direct to London, with Dan Pierson as check pilot. I was a very unusual Pan Am pilot at that stage of my career. I had almost twenty-two years with the company but had never crossed either the Atlantic or Pacific Oceans; nor had I flown into New York, which was the company's headquarters. I could not believe all that ice and snow that we flew over for many hours without seeing so much as a light.

Then, several hours over water. The only time I had been out of sight of land before was over the blue Caribbean.

I fell in love with London which, to me, seemed like a group ofsmall villages rather than one of the largest citiesinthe world. I always enjoyed coming into Heathrow Airport in the very early morning and gazing at that beautiful English countryside, not to exclude London itself, which had so many green areas scattered through the city.

I had been asked by a neighbor whose brother was in a London hospital if I would go by and visit him. So after sleeping for a while in the Kensington Palace Hotel, I called the hospital and found that I had to wait a couple of hours before visiting time. I left the hotel, just walking in any direction that looked inviting, neither knowing nor caring where I was. After two hours of this, I stepped into the street, hailed a cab and asked the cabbie, "Can you take me to the Princess Beatrice Hospital?" He looked at me strangely and replied, "Well, I could, Yank, but I think you might walk it." I was standing right in front of the hospital. And this was before the introduction of Inertial Navigation.

Before I was allowed to fly around the world on PanAm's routes I had to take yet another check trip to Bangkok and back. Bill Saulsberry was the check pilot and we left San Francisco for Hawaii. I did not know there was that much water in the world.

At the time (the mid-1960s) we were still using navigators who took star shots to determine our position. About thirty minutes after we left the coast and were losing signals from the coastal V.O.R. stations, a hand came over my shoulder holding a piece of paper with a number on it—a heading to fly. I did not know what I was supposed to do with the paper, so I flew with one hand and held the paper in the other. Bill took pity on me, reached over and stuck it up on the glare shield above the compass. Successive pieces of paper collected there, one on top of the other, as headings changed until we reached Honolulu.

From Honolulu we left the next day for Tokyo, over yet more expanses of water and when we arrived we were issued a clearance by a controller who did not speak Texan. I did not understand a word he said, and told Bill to ask him to "Say it again." When he repeated the message I still did not comprehend, so I asked Bill if he understood the clearance, and he said "No." I was unsure whether he just wanted to see what I would do, so I said, "Well, tell him that I am going into a holding pattern over Tokyo V.O.R., and that I'll stay there until I can understand the clearance." When Bill told them that, a different controller came on, probably a supervisor, and in better English (and passable Texan) repeated the clearance so that I could understand it.

I always felt very lucky that English was and is the universal aviation language for, even as a Texan, I do have a reasonable working knowledge of it. Every major air control center in the world has to employ staff who can speak English. If I had had to learn Japanese to fly into Japan, or Arabic to fly in the Middle East, I am sure I could never have made it. I did learn enough Spanish for the control towers in Latin America, but I could always fall back on English if I had to. Though they did not have to, I have heard pilots of Japan Airlines speaking to the Tokyo tower in English; it did help everybody to know where everyone else was.

Bare Skin

In Tokyo we checked into the Hotel New Japan and, when told I could have either a 'western' room or a 'Japanese' room I chose the latter as it was my first time in Japan. They escorted me to a small room with a table about knee-high and no bed. The room boy showed me how to roll out the sleeping mat on the floor and asked if I wanted a massage. Having heard from other crew members how wonderful the Japanese massage was, I sure wanted one. I told him I would have one in an hour, took a hot shower, put on my pajamas, and waited.

Right on the dot the bell rang and I opened the door to find a young lady about twenty years of age. She spoke no English and I knew no Japanese, but she motioned for me to lie down on the mat. She seemed perplexed to find me in pajamas, but managed to work around them and proceeded to give me a wonderful massage. I do believe I went to sleep in the middle of it.

Those massages had nothing to do with what goes on in 'massage parlors' in some stateside locations. The masseuses generally knew enough English to ask if you wanted a 'Japanese' massage or a 'soft' massage. The former could be so rough as to be uncomfortable. Sometimes they beat the living daylights out of you. The person giving the massage could be male or female, but most were women. They never had to be told if you had a sore muscle or a catch in your neck--they would go directly to it and work away on it. The normal procedure was to take a hot shower before the masseuse arrived and to wrap a towel around yourself and lie on the bed. They did prefer to work on bare skin.

I have been told that they were better and cheaper in the years before I visited there, but they were plenty good enough to satisfy me. They would work for about an hour, and at that time cost about five dollars, as I recall. I seldom spent a night in Japan without having a massage. I often paid at the beginning because I knew I would be so relaxed (or even asleep) by the time they finished that I would not want to get up. In Taipei, massages were given by very young blind girls who would be led to the room, but who would find their way back alone. They, too, gave good massages, but I couldn't help feeling a little uncomfortable with them.

Hong Kong Approach

I have been asked so many times what was my most dangerous flight. Did I ever have a near-accident? Well, folks, this is it.

When we left Tokyo for Hong Kong in a Boeing 707C there had been a bad storm in the area. Called in the Pacific a typhoon, it is the same phenomenon that in other places is called a hurricane. No flights had landed at Hong Kong for several days and it looked as if we would be the first since the storm. Hong Kong was one of only two places where the F.A.A. required a pilot to make a 'physical entry' before he could fly into it in command. The other was Guatemala, where I had flown for years.

As we approached the Hong Kong area we received a weather report giving us a ceiling of seven hundred feet and a visibility of about two miles. The wind was reported as being from the south at about twenty-five knots, which meant that we had to land to the southeast and the wind would be across the runway at a forty-five-degree angle from our right.

The usual landing at Hong Kong was to the northwest, and that approach could be made with the help of the I.L.S and came into the runway over the bay. Because of the wind, we had to make what was known as the 'back door' approach, more properly called a 'Chung-Chou' approach. It started over the island of Chung Chou and a let-down could be made toward another radio beacon to an altitude of seven hundred feet. That was exactly what we had been told the ceiling was. From there we proceeded by visual contact with the surface directly toward a mountain until we saw a 'checkerboard' on the side of the mountain. This was an actual figure on the mountain consisting of white and red squares, lit at night by floodlights. It was used as an aiming point so that the pilot would not be too close in or too far out from the runway when he turned to the runway heading.

When we approached the checkerboard we made a forty-five-degree right turn and that was the first time that the runway would come into sight. We were down to about three hundred feet at that point, and then went over some apartment houses situated right on the approach to the runway. We would be so close to them that it seemed we would take down the clothes that were hung in huge numbers from lines supported by bamboo poles on the tops of the buildings. I should mention that this 'over the rooftops' approach from the west is one of only two curved approaches into any major airport of world standing. The other is the Canarsie approach at JFK Airport which is not surrounded by mountains or rooftops, nor is it as notorious as Hong Kong.

Before we started the approach, Bill and I had considered our fuel situation and had agreed that we had only this one chance for a Hong Kong landing and, if we missed it, we would have to go to Manila, our alternate. Manila was far off our route and would seriously delay the flight, so we very much wanted to get into Hong Kong.

I was not overly concerned about the approach, thinking that I had made many difficult approaches to airports in Central America, and I did not think this could be any worse. Everything went well until we made the turn in front of the checkerboard, and then the wind coming over the hills caused some very bad turbulence and it became difficult to control the airplane. I remember saying to Bill that I did not want the airspeed to fall below one hundred and sixty knots. I did not mean that I could not fly more slowly, but that we might hit some wind-shear and lose control if we were any slower. Bill knew what I meant and said, "I don't want to see it below one-sixty."

As the runway came into sight I forgot about the wind being a bad crosswind, and straightened out the airplane, lined up with the runway, at which point the wind promptly blew me off to the left. When I crossed the threshold I was actually over the grass area between the runway and a parallel taxiway. I was afraid to touch down in the grass; first, because there is practically no braking on grass, and second, because we might mire down in mud. It was raining very hard. So, being too low to bank and turn, I side-slipped the airplane to the right until I thought the wheels were over concrete. Bill was calling out to me, urgently, to "Put it on, put it on!"

I did put it on, fairly smoothly, but too far down the runway. Bill tried to help at this point. While I was putting my hand on the lever to raise the wing spoilers and thus put more weight on the wheels and make the braking more effective, he reached over to bring the throttles into reverse thrust. When I too reached for the throttles I found that he had only three of them in reverse. I fumbled in front of the throttles to find the one he had missed and then brought all four back to full reverse power. I was applying all the brakes I could, practically standing on the pedals.

We had done all we could to stop the airplane and I looked at the runway ahead. I had never seen so little runway ahead of any airplane going that fast, and I remember saying to Bill, "We aren't going to stop." His cool reply was, "Well, there is some overrun, but I don't remember how much." Overrun is not runway, but an extension of it, with a surface that is supposed to support the airplane if you are forced to use it. We later looked it up in the manual and this runway had two hundred feet of packed shell at the end of it. After that, there was nothing but the cold water in the bay.

The correct procedure was to bring the throttles forward, out of reverse, when we were down to fifty knots, but I just kept pulling hard back on them until we came to a full stop. We were still on the pavement but with so little left that I had to open the side window and put my head out to see if we had room to turn the airplane around without going off the end.

At slow airspeeds the engines will backfire if held in reverse, and all four engines were banging away loudly. I finally rectified that, turned the aircraft around, and started to the terminal. My knees were banging together so hard that I could hardly use the brakes. Bill, the check pilot, had not said a word. When we were about half-way to the terminal I said, "Bill, I guess you must have some comments, but may I make one first?" He said, "What have you got to say?"

"That is as close as I have ever come to hurting one of Pan American's airplanes."

Bill said, "I think that is as close as I have ever come, too." And no other comment was made. I'm sure that he was aware that I knew as well as he did where our mistakes were.

We went on to Bangkok, arriving after midnight, and left at noon on the following day on our way back to Hong Kong and Tokyo. Up to this time Bill, as the check pilot, was still in command even though I had been flying. When I checked the flight plan and the weight-and-balance documents in the office at Bangkok, I found my name where the captain was to sign. I asked Bill if they had made a mistake. His reply was revealing. "You don't think I'm going to ride with you back through Hong Kong with me being responsible, do you?" So, there in Bangkok I again became a captain for Pan American Airways and, for the first time, on jet equipment.

There was a sequel to this story several years later on a trip into Hong Kong. Somehow the subject of near-accidents came up, and my first officer had a funny look on his face. I asked him if he might have been on a certain approach into Hong Kong with me. He said, "Right behind your back, Captain, right behind your back."

When I hear of airplanes going off the runway into the bay at Hong Kong, as a foreign airplane did some years later, I think, "There, but for the Grace of God, go I."

Physical Entry

Now that I was fully checked out, I could bid for trips instead of being arbitrarily assigned to them. But my seniority was not very high and the first trip

I was able to bid for was back down through Central America to Guatemala. I had flown in this area for over twenty years, but it was also the other place on Pan Am's routes that required a 'physical entry.' Never mind that I had been there a thousand times, that was the Latin American Division and this was the Pacific Division. It was decided that I had to have a check pilot aboard again.

I was told he would be either Don Kinkel, the chief pilot, or Ira Anderson, assistant chief pilot in charge of training. The day before I was to leave I asked again, only to be told that it had not been decided. When I showed up for the flight, I did not have a check pilot. They had called Miami, the headquarters of the Latin American Division, and had been given assurance that I knew the area and had made many 'physical entries.' So they finally agreed to send me out alone. The airplane was not a Boeing 707, which I had flown for my rating, but a 720B, a smaller version of the 707, more of a hot-rod.

My two copilots, first and second officers respectively, were Bart Barrier and Bill Walling. When I returned to San Francisco I found a note in my mailbox from the lady who kept the records. "Who was the check pilot on your flight to Panama?" Having had no check pilot on the flight, I wrote on her memo, "Black Bart Barrier and Bill Walling" and put it in her mailbox.

Making Good Time

One of the best of the navigators was Russ Parks, who had been a captain in the Western Division and I had flown as his co-pilot many times. He had decided, years back, that he did not want to fly as a pilot, but preferred to be a navigator. One day he gave a heading slip to the pilots and the captain was doubtful about it and asked, "Russ, are you sure about this heading?" Russ replied, "If you don't like it, captain, I have three hundred and fifty-nine more. Which one would you like?"

A navigator's standard reply, when asked where we are, was "We are lost, but we are making good time." One dark night a certain navigator, bent over his table, felt the presence of someone looking over his shoulder, and who asked, "Where are we?" He gave the standard reply and heard a chuckle as the person said, "I pioneered many of these routes." He turned to come face-to-face with Charles Lindbergh, who had indeed pioneered many of Pan American's routes worldwide and who was still an advisor for Pan Am. One of the disappointments of my career was that I never met Charles Lindbergh.

Fly Around It, By Gum

The best story about navigators happened in the days of the flying boats, when the navigation was more difficult because these aircraft were slow and therefore more vulnerable to being blown off course by the winds. Also they flew at lower altitudes, below the clouds, often for long hours without being able to see the stars well enough to take a bearing. But they had a very large navigation table at their stations and once, while the navigator was bent over his charts, the captain came by, and did not like what he saw. Taking a wad of gum out of his mouth, he threw it down on the chart, saying, "I could find our position like that better than you are doing." About two hours later the navigator handed a heading slip forward which called for a forty-five-degree turn to the left, an excessive correction. The captain grumbled, but made the turn. A few minutes later the navigator sent up another slip asking for a ninety-degree turn to the right. The captain exploded. "What the hell is going on back there?"

"I'm sorry, Captain, but there is an obstruction on my chart and we have to fly around it."

Around the World

In July 1965, as soon as my seniority permitted, I bid for a round-the-world trip. The San Francisco base flew them in both directions. You could go eastbound, first to London on a polar flight and then to Frankfurt, Istanbul, Beirut, Teheran, Delhi, Rangoon, Calcutta, Bangkok, Hong Kong, Tokyo, Honolulu, and back to San Francisco. Or you could go the other way around. The flights did vary, the stops depending on the day of the week, or when schedules changed seasonally, sometimes landing either in Karachi or Bombay, for instance. The flights were numbered PA1 westbound and PA2 eastbound—commonly called Clipper One and Clipper Two. They became a criterion of reliability and scheduling dependability for seasoned travelers the world over. Any businessman marooned at some point in Asia, or wishing to change his itinerary to an earlier or later flight, could always rely on PA1 or PA2 to take him home.

I preferred these flights for the variety they offered. Some pilots liked to do the easy flights over and over, going back and forth; from Honolulu, for instance. I always liked the changes and would bid for different flights as often as I could. I had to spend more time staying qualified on the different routes, but I thought the time well spent. The F.A.A. required a trip into representative airports on each route at least once a year or you had to re-qualify by watching movies of every approach at every airport on the route.

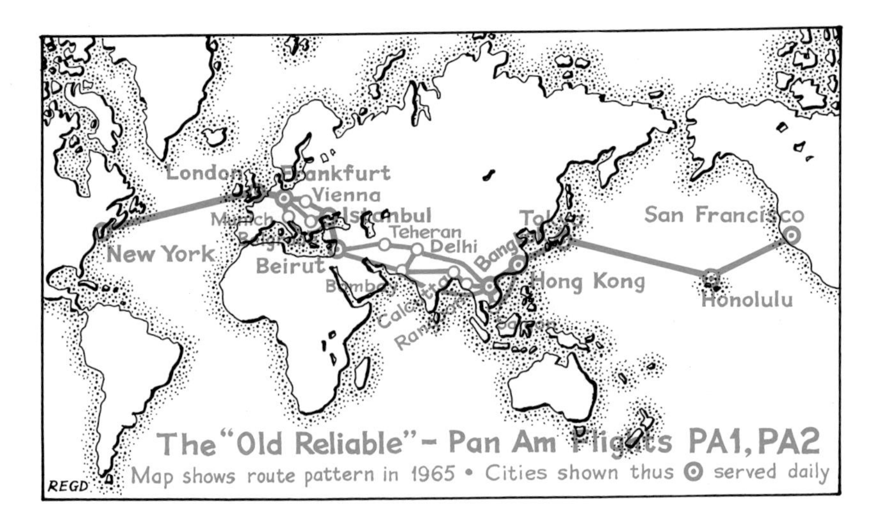

It all sounds very romantic, but unless you spent a layover at a place, you saw little of it. I have been asked, for example, if I have been to Rangoon or Calcutta. I would reply that I had; but when asked to describe what they were like, I would say, "Well, they both look just alike: two rows of white lights in the middle of a dark night." I never made it to town in either place and the only daylight landing I made at either place was one at Rangoon when we were behind schedule.

Pilots who flew these routes usually preferred one direction over the other. I think the favored direction was westbound, but I liked to go east. You could have a daily time change of five hours or more. Going west always made the days so much longer because you traveled with the sun. When you arrived at a station you had a tendency to stay up until you dropped. Going east, it was always later by the clock than where you had come from, so you would cut your day short and go to bed. I found that sleep was the only answer to jet-lag. I slept much more on trips than I did at home. It cut down on the sight seeing, but it helped to make the trip less arduous. My first round-the-world trip brought me to many new places. I had been east to London and west to Bangkok, but everywhere in between was new to me. I liked it all, but I particularly liked Beirut. My copilot knew the route well and laughed at me and my Texas accent as I would ask him over and over, what was that "Over yonder."

I learned to love many of the places where we stayed. London was a favorite, but Beirut was high on the list. Our schedule there was such that I often found myself awake in the middle of the night. I have walked the city and waterfront many times at two or three in the morning with no uncomfortable feeling at all. I am sickened, now, when I see pictures of the destruction of that once lovely city and of the Phoenician Hotel where we stayed. The crowded hustle and bustle of Hong Kong was fun. Bangkok, while hot and humid, had a lively feeling and was unlike anywhere else. Tokyo was a great place to spend hours just walking through the streets, and stopping at any little sidewalk cafe for some excellent and clean food. I liked the food almost everywhere I went, but, then, it has been said of me that I'll eat anything that does not eat me first.

I would have to write two books if I tried to describe all the cities in detail and tell of all the different kinds of food. But this book is supposed to be about flying.

Backing Turn

On each round-the-world trip I usually tried to make at least one of those power-off gliding approaches that I spoke of earlier. Istanbul was a good place to do it because the traffic was not heavy and the traffic control people left you alone. I did one in a Boeing 707 at Baghdad one day, with my copilot, Bus Mills, who would later become the chief of training at San Francisco. I told him of my intention to close the throttles at cruise altitude and see if I could land without touching them. It worked out beautifully and I circled the field and made a nice landing, using only about two-thirds of the runway. Then I started to turn around to taxi in, but when I was part way around, too far to turn back, I realized that if I continued I would go off the runway and into the sand. That runway was only one hundred and twenty-five feet wide, and it takes one hundred forty five feet for a 707 to make a complete turn. That would not do at all, so I stopped and asked Bus, "What do I do now?"

He said that all he knew to do was to shut down the engines and call for a tug to tow us to the ramp. I said that I was not going to embarrass myself like that. "Well, what else can you do?" "I am going to back it up." And I did, using the reverse thrust. Carefully, because if you put on the brakes while backing, the airplane could set down on its tail. We had been told never to try backing one, but nowadays I see it done routinely to back away from the gates at terminals.

On the Wing

On a cargo flight to Vietnam I also did a power-off approach at Da Nang. The pilot in the right seat was a newly-hired ex-Air Force pilot who had flown jets in the service. I could see that he was nervous and when I asked for some flap down, he said, "Put some power on!" I did not need power and told him so, finally persuading him to put partial flaps down. But when I asked for more flaps, he again insisted, "Spin the engines up, put on some power!" I was now actually too fast because we had been slow in putting the flaps down. I shouted, "PUT THE DAMN FLAPS DOWN!" We landed without a problem and, as we taxied in, he turned to me and said, "Do you know what I thought would happen when you put full flaps down without the power on? I thought we would stall and fall right out of the sky." I suggested that he buy a good book on aerodynamics and read it. "This airplane, like all others, does not fly on the engine, it flies on the wing." Some modern fighters, though, do fly more like a rocket, straight up.

I intend, of course, to tell only of the good approaches and landings, the ones that made me feel good. I am sure there are plenty of tales from other sources about the other kind.

On one trip I had two ex-Navy pilots with me as first officer and engineer. They were good pilots and they had a good rapport going between them, as would be natural. We were coming into Tokyo and received an unfavorable weather report. There was a low ceiling and we would have had to make a circling approach and land with a bad crosswind, and in heavy rain.

We had been taking turns landing. The copilot asked if I wanted him to land it, and I said "It's your turn." So he flew down the I.L.S. beam and did it better than I could have done. Such approaches are difficult with a strong wind from the tail, and it was turbulent, too.

When we broke into the clear he reached over and started to push the throttles up. I grabbed his hand and asked him what he intended. He said he was going to our alternate. "You don't think you can land here?" He said, "No, not in these conditions." I said, "Maybe I can't either, but let me give it a try."

I continued down to five hundred feet and went right over the runway, turned forty-five degrees to the right and flew for a minute, then turned back to the runway heading. The runway had disappeared in the rain, but I knew that it would come back in sight with this maneuver, and it did. Our calculated speed at the threshold should have been about one hundred thirty-five knots, but I did not want to come in that slow. As it was, in the turbulence, our indicator was fluctuating from one forty to one hundred eighty knots. The runway looked as if it had whitecaps on it from the rain and wind. We landed, fairly smoothly, and started to taxi in. The copilot turned around to the engineer and made a remark I shall never forget: "Well, I guess that is what twenty-five years of experience can do."

Right Hand, Left Hand

I campaigned to allow copilots, with the captain's permission, to fly from the lefthand seat. I had done so much switching back and forth in my career that I thought it would be to the company's advantage to do this. My suggestion was that, during the six months training periods, a senior copilot should be given training in the left seat, while at the same time, captains should be qualified in the right seat, but only if they volunteered for the program. Then when a crew consisted of two pilots who were cross-qualified, and even then only at the captain's option, the copilot might be allowed to fly from the left seat.

I had many discussions about this with the chief pilot for training. We ended up the same way every time: he would say that, because the airplane flew the same way from either seat, copilots did not need to fly from the left before they checked out as captains. And I would reply that if the airplane flew the same way from either seat, why did the company object if the pilots traded seats? We never did resolve the argument, but before I retired I did see such a program put into effect.

There was some sort of psychological effect in doing this. You could tell a copilot that he was in command, but leave him in the right seat and he would always be looking around to see if you approved of what he was doing. Put the same man in the left seat and he would really take control. Some people's personalities changed completely when they were put in command. A nice, easygoing fellow when flying as copilot, could become a tyrant when he became captain. Allowing him to fly on the left might give him an inkling of this tendency and perhaps prevent it, or maybe he would not check out.

Personally, I continued to allow selected first officers to fly from the left seat. Once in Beirut when I was in the right seat, the landing gear gave us an unsafe indication when we put it down. We recycled it, up and down, and still had the same indication. I remember thinking that we would have to change seats and fly around for thirty minutes before trying an approach, because the cockpit voice recorder (which recorded conversations for the last thirty minutes) would reveal which of us was where. If I had to land with an unsafe gear indication, I wanted to be where I belonged. It would not make a bit of difference on the landing, but it would be 'legal'. We recycled one more time and the gear locked down fine.

Federal Air Regulations Trespasses

We still had some occasional conflict with flight service personnel wanting to be in command of the airplane. Some of them considered the cockpit crew merely 'drivers' and thought that they themselves should direct the entire operation. Once they actually tried to form an organization. They were going to call it 'CART' for 'Civil Air Regulation Trespasses'. They asked the chief pilot to attend their meeting, and explained how they intended to monitor the pilots' activities and report to the authorities whenever they thought there had been a violation of any kind. When they asked the chief pilot to comment he said, "If you are going to go ahead with this project, you should know that the name 'CART' is inappropriate. The Civil Air Regulations have been renamed and are now called '*Federal* Air Regulations'. It broke up the meeting, and nothing further took place.

Try A Tractor

Arriving over London early one morning before daylight on a polar flight we found beautiful weather, but snow during the night had left about six inches on the ground, completely covering the runways, including their lights which were flush to the ground. We would have to wait while the runways were plowed so that we could see them. We had flown from Los Angeles so we did not have enough fuel to hold for very long. When it became evident that they were not going to finish the snow-plowing any time soon, we diverted to Prestwick, Scotland. There we refueled and I told the station manager to put on fifteen thousand pounds of stored fuel; that is, fuel over and above that required for the flight. He did not want to do so because he had a message from London saying that the runway would be cleared by the time we could return there. I insisted, which was my prerogative, and we put on the fuel and headed back to London. When we arrived, the runways were still not plowed and a real comedy of errors ensued. Pan Am would tell me the runway would be cleared in fifteen minutes, so I would ask Approach Control for an approach. They would not give it to me because they said it would be another hour before the runways would be cleared. Back and forth, back and forth.

Meanwhile, more and more flights were arriving from the U.S. and from Europe. Jets burn more fuel when down low, so everyone was asking to go up high where they could hold and use less fuel. Because we had plenty of fuel, I would say, "Clipper One Two Zero can accept lower." The result was that when they finally opened the runway I was the lowest and in line for the first approach, saving my passengers much hassle on the ground, as they would be first through customs and immigration.

But when they said the runway was operational they also told me that there would be another hour's delay because they had to plow the taxiways, too. I told them that I could taxi in six inches of snow if I could know where the taxi strips were. I suggested that they just mark the taxiways by driving a tractor down the middle of them, and that I would follow the tractor. That was one of the few times that I had anyone take my suggestion. I landed and taxied in without a problem.

But you should have seen those taxiways the next day. Because they were continually in use, they were never plowed. The snow piled up on the wheels of every airplane in huge chunks and then fell off and froze that way. As I taxied out the next day when departing, it was like rolling over a rock quarry, the roughest ride I ever had in an aircraft on the ground.

On a cargo flight into Cold Bay, Alaska, I was warned as we started our approach, on a dark and moonless night, that there might be polar bears on the runway. I had seen dogs, rabbits, and even burros on runways, but how in the world would one see polar bears against all that snow? We did not see any but I'm not sure that they weren't there.

U.F.O.s

I had wanted to see a U.F.O. for years and kept looking for one. Leaving Bangkok for New Delhi one night I had my best chance. We had just leveled off at 29,000 feet and put the airplane on autopilot. The night was clear and we had commented on how beautiful were the lights of Rangoon, which we were approaching. I had relaxed and was just watching the world go by when, suddenly, the sky ahead of us seemed full of lights! They appeared to be traveling toward us in a kind of loose formation. I had never seen their like, and all I could think of was a bunch of space ships. I shouted for the crew to look. The engineer's seat is somewhat lower than the pilot's, so that when he looked up he saw the windshield full of lights. He thought it was the lights of Rangoon and therefore that we were in a steep dive. He started to holler for me to "Pull it out!"

We watched as the lights came toward us, went a little to our left and gradually faded out as they came abeam of us. None of us could account for these lights from any of our experiences. We were discussing the possibilities when suddenly there came another group just like the first.

This time we were a little better prepared. I checked the time and asked the crew to count them. I called the purser and told her to look out of the window and to ask the passengers to look out, also. I wanted as many witnesses as possible. There were seventeen of the lights and they followed the same path as the first ones, slowly disappearing as they passed on our left.

Now I realized that there was a voice in my headset. It was a T.W.A. flight and he was saying, "I'm seeing strange lights in the sky, does anyone else see them?" I replied to him and we compared notes. The lights which had been to my left were to his right and his course was paralleling ours. This meant that the lights were between us and it was the first indication we had of their true location. At night it is very difficult to determine the distance of a light.

As we were talking, each afraid to say the words, 'space ships', a British Airways airplane joined in the conversation. He said that he had once before seen a similar thing and thought he could tell us what it was. He said it might be the second stage of a rocket re-entering the atmosphere.

Back at home I consulted with some scientists and found that that was, in fact, the best explanation. The fuel tanks and second stages in re-entry would burn up into individual parts and enter the atmosphere as fireballs. I was told that, though they seemed to be at about our altitude, they would probably burn up before they fell below about 75,000 feet.

So I am disappointed to have to report that I never saw any-thing that could be considered a 'flying saucer' though I have talked with several pilots who would swear that they had seen them. A copilot with me on a flight to Venezuela related in detail how he had seen a cigar-shaped ship, complete with windows, that he believed was so close to them that he feared a collision.

Jake

Jake Nagel was a colorful flight engineer. He was with me on a Boeing 707 trip around the world. Stories abounded about Jake. It was said that he had stolen a streetcar in Rio de Janeiro. I asked about that and he said, "No, I didn't steal it, I only borrowed it to get back to the hotel." The conductor had walked off at the end of the line, probably for a cup of coffee, and Jake simply drove it back to his hotel.

On a flight into Iceland where they had landed a DC-6 to refuel, Jake went up on the wing to check the fuel quantities. The wind was blowing hard and the snow was several feet thick. Jake had left a line boy holding the ladder against the wing, which was so slick that Jake slipped and fell off into a snowbank. He wasn't hurt, and walked around to climb the ladder again. The line boy said, "I wouldn't go up there if I were you." When asked why not, he replied, "Because there is the meanest son-of-a-bitch in the world up there."

Jake was disappointed that, when the company was forced to train engineers to fly, they would not go further and check him out as a captain. On my flight we left Frankfurt for London with a very light load on a 707. We had picked up an F.A.A. inspector for a routine check. The copilot was flying and as we took off, with the airplane climbing rapidly, he asked me to retract the flaps, which I did. Jake reached up to slap his shoulder and shouted, "You just did something wrong! You aren't supposed to retract the flaps in a turn!"

I tried to keep him quiet, telling him that we were so light that the copilot had no choice; that we had to turn and were gaining speed so quickly that the flaps had to be brought up so we did not exceed the speed permitted with flaps down. But Jake would not be placated, and pulled out the manual, insisting that I take time right then and there to look at it. I had to tell him to put away the manual and that we would discuss it later. All this time the F.A.A. man was looking from one of us to the other but he never made a comment, either at that time or after we arrived in London.

Cheek-en

We grew tired of the American-style meals served at many of our crew hotels. In Teheran the copilot and I decided that we would leave the hotel and find some typical Iranian food. We walked around town until we spotted an interesting-looking garden restaurant with beautiful lights hung in the trees. We seated ourselves and scanned the menu which, of course, we did not understand at all. The waiter apparently knew only one word of English, "Cheeken." We did not want chicken, we wanted local food. Seeing some platters being carried to a group of men in the back of the room, we motioned that we wanted the same. The waiter kept saying, "No, cheek-en." But we insisted, and he did finally bring us a platter of whatever it was. Awful, that's what it was! Some kind of steamed vegetable like eggplant, but tasteless. We sent it back and said, "Cheek-en." We got broiled chicken.

We later learned that the men in the back of the room were waiters employed by that restaurant, and that they were being fed the cheapest thing the restaurant served.

Pioneers

On 16 February 1976, when I reported for a trip to Honolulu, I was informed that I would have on board a group of seventy-five people grouped under the name 'Aviation Pioneers Bicentennial.' They were celebrating America's 200th birthday, and this group comprised prestigious persons, such as ninety-year-old Charles F. Willard, holder of pilot's license No. 4; 'Tiny' Broadwick who, in 1908 at the age of fifteen, was the first woman to make a parachute jump; Ed Granville, builder of the famous 'Gee Bee' racing planes flown by Jimmy Doolittle in the Thompson Air Races; Steve Wittman, renowned pilot and builder of racing aircraft; and others—every one of them an outstanding aviation pioneer.

In spite of the F.A.A.'s admonition to keep the cockpit door locked in flight, I simply could not refuse cockpit access to such notabilities. In cruise I made the announcement about who these people were and that the cockpit door would be open and that they would be welcome to visit in twos and threes. Both during and after the flight I heard some wonderful stories, including eye-witness accounts of the Dole Race to Honolulu, when only a few lived to tell the tale. I offered Tiny Broadwick a glider ride, but found that one had already been arranged for her and she later sent me a newspaper write-up about it.

The rest of our passengers were very understanding and did not try to crowd the cockpit. After all the pioneers had been up, I walked to the back and through the cabin. As I passed one gentleman he handed his card to me. It read, 'Robert A. Byrd, F.A.A.' I just looked at him and said, "Well, I knew that there had to be one of you on board today." He gently said, "But I'm retired, Captain." And his wife added, "And he would love to see the cockpit." And, of course, he saw it. He was actually a member of the pioneer group and he was the one who later helped me to locate my first flight instructor.

Flight To Trece Aguas

I had tried to teach my children that they needed to do their part in this world by helping others whenever and wherever they could. Christ told us that whatever we did for others we also did for Him (Matthew 25:35-40). So we were pleased when we heard of a program where they could really 'make a difference'.

Based as I was during the Sixties in San Francisco with Pan American World Airways, I lived in Danville, to the east of the Bay Area. We heard of an organization called, 'Amigos de las Americas' with headquarters in Houston, Texas, and which had been started by Guy Bevil, Jr., the son of a Pan Am station manager.

In this organization teenage high school students were trained to administer vaccines such as D.P.T. and polio, to give vision tests, and to distribute eyeglasses. They also taught children basic hygiene measures such as cleanliness and brushing teeth. They dispensed medicine for expulsion of pinworms and taught preventative measures to families. These young people did all of this in small villages in foreign countries from Guatemala to Paraguay.

We wanted our children to have the benefit of this wonderful experience, but there was no local chapter of the organization in our area. Determined to have them take part, I traveled to Houston to obtain information about the group. We organized a chapter in Danville, with meetings in the Alamo Methodist Church.

We easily obtained the support of local doctors who, under the direction of Dr Byron Zaharias, trained these youngsters in such procedures as how to give hypodermic injections. Using sterile water, they practiced with oranges and upon each other. They spent months in training that included a basic knowledge of the Spanish language, as they would be working in Spanish-speaking countries. Actually, we found that many of the areas in which they worked were so remote that the natives spoke Quecha or some other Mayan dialect, and knew little Spanish.

Two volunteers were assigned to each village, often so remote that they had to walk in. They stayed there for a period of three weeks, after which time they would be replaced by another pair. They were expected to set up a clinic and to attend it every day, giving shots, binding wounds, teaching hygiene, distributing toothbrushes, and whatever else was necessary. None of these villages had access to a doctor or to any kind of medical services.

Two of our children were of the proper age to participate: our son, Scott, and our daughter Nancy, who was actually a few months shy of the sixteen years which was supposed to be the minimum age. The first year we trained twenty-eight volunteers, with the understanding that Nancy would go only if we were able to obtain funds for all of them.

We sought to raise funds in every possible manner. We had garage sales, collected paper, promoted walks, sold work time of the volunteers for yard work, and any other things that we could think of; and we learned to be bold in asking people to sponsor these young people in this humane project. It would require more than $20,000 for us to send them all, and we came up with almost exactly that amount by the end of training. Doctors and trained medical people were very generous in donating their time.

We had collected old eyeglasses and they were then sorted into four grades of far-sightedness and four grades of near-sightedness. I remember one day that Dr Rod Abernethy lectured them on how to fit eyeglasses. Rod told them his history of having spent four years in medical school and then more schooling on top of that to obtain his degree as an opthalmologist. He said, "Now I'm going to teach you in thirty minutes how to do what I do."

He taught them how to evaluate the patient's vision and to give out the correct eyeglasses. I remember that he assured them that they could not harm a person's eyes, that the worst that might happen and that the person would discord the glasses if they did not fit comfortably.

Guy Bevil used to tell about being in one of the villages where eyeglasses were being dispensed. He stopped an old man who had just been fitted, and asked him how he liked the glasses. The man replied, "I cannot read my book." Then he pulled out what must have been the smallest Bible ever printed. Guy took him back to the young people and asked them to give him eyeglasses two numbers higher than the first pair they had given him. The old man then agreed that he "could read his book."

As the old man went up and down the street of the village, he accosted every person he met to say, "Americans are wonderful people. The first ones I met gave me my book, and now these young people had given me my eyes so that I can read it."

So for four summers Scott and Nancy both went on assignments and I was very proud of them. One of Nancy's assignments had been to a small village called Senahú, high in the mountains about one hundred miles north of Guatemala City. I had never had any doubt as to the positive impression these

The waterfalls at Trece Aguas—alleged to be thirteen, but who's counting? The approach to the landing strip is to the left, and round the back of the fog-capped mountain.

The landing strip at Trece Aguas, looking out towards the valley.

Pilot Molina indicates a successful completion of the Cessna 185 Skywagon flight to Trece Aguas.

Daughters Nancy and Joanne negotiate the creek (and creaking) bridge between the Trece Aguas airstrip and the coffee plantation.

Truly 'away from it all'. The plantation, high in the mountains of Guatemala, owned and operated by Erica Fickert-Forst.

The coffee processing shed at Trece Aguas.

young people had made in their villages, but I wanted to see for myself just what sort of ambassadors for the United States they had made.

We took a vacation to Guatemala and I made up my mind to see if we could go to Senahú. Some investigation discovered, about seven miles from the village, a small mountain landing strip called Trece Aguas, serving a coffee plantation that was owned and operated by a German lady, Erica Fickert-Forst. I tried to rent a small airplane but found that while I could fly a U.S. registered airplane in Guatemala, I must have a Guatemalan pilot's license to fly one with Guatemalan registry. So I rented a Cessna with pilot.

Like most of my profession, I felt uneasy entrusting my family with an unknown pilot. I told my wife that it would be all right because I was going to sit up front and would have a set of controls that I could use if I had to. But the controls for the righthand front seat had been removed, so we were at the mercy of the local pilot. I need not have been concerned. He was excellent and naturally he knew the country much better than I did. By the time we reached the area of Trece Aguas I was glad he was doing the driving.

We were flying down a wide valley with a very steep, almost vertical wall on one side. Trece Aguas, which means Thirteen Waters (or Falls) was located in a narrow side canyon in this wall. When we arrived, a low cloud covered the entrance to this canyon and we had to fly back and forth below the clouds, waiting for the cloud layer to rise enough for a chance to fly into the canyon. On the face of the canyon wall we could see the waterfalls for which the site was named. It seemed many more than thirteen, and it was a beautiful sight.

We were finally able to enter the canyon mouth and approach the landing strip, strictly a one-way pattern, into the mountains, and no room to make a turn. You had to land and then turn the airplane around on the ground so that you could depart the other way—no place for an amateur pilot or someone like me, who did not know the site very well.

We landed at one of the most beautiful spots that it has ever been my good fortune to see: a beautiful runway of emerald green grass, alongside a swiftly-flowing mountain stream. The clouds were barely above our heads. The whole scene seemed to have been stolen from a fairytale.

We crossed the creek on a single log footbridge and walked up to the house that served this coffee plantation. Mrs Fickert-Forst welcomed us warmly and invited us in for tea, complete with beautiful English silver. We sipped tea as we watched workers, just outside the windows, raking the coffee beans on a cement slab so that the sun could dry them properly for shipment. She told us that her grandfather had left Germany after the government of the time had confiscated his land. He had emigrated to Guatemala and moved to the mountains because he reasoned that no government would ever want the land and he could be secure in his ownership. It had been developed into this wonderful spot, producing coffee.

We were given use of a Land Rover and started the drive into the village of Senahú. With me were my wife Helen, daughter Joanne, and our 'local' daughter Nancy. A mile or so from the village, youngsters along the roadside recognized Nancy and began to shout, "Nancee! Nancee!" We continued to the village square and parked alongside a long, low building which proved to be the local school. Children of every age started to pour out of the schoolhouse, through doors and windows, and perhaps more than a hundred surrounded us. I was embarrassed at having disrupted school and, seeing a man who turned out to be the school principal, apologized, saying, "I am very sorry that we have caused a commotion, we had no desire to disrupt your school." "That is perfectly all right, Mr Wilson, Nancy is here and I am going to turn the school out for the day."

The kids crowded around Nancy, holding her hand, pulling on her cloths, demanding her attention, with great affection. I wished that we could have stayed longer to savor the love that they were pouring out, but we had to return to Trece Aguas and fly back to Guatemala City.

I never again doubted the fine impression these young people left for our people and our country in places like Senahú. And I knew that they had made a very real difference in the lives of the people there. During these times when the younger generation is too often criticized for almost every sin known to mankind, we should remember that for every street bum picked up for petty crimes, there is a dedicated youngster in some remote corner of the Third World, serving as an anonymous ambassador for the United States.

Under the Bay Bridge

I had previously been a check pilot on DC-3 aircraft while in Pan American's Western Division, but I considered it a compliment that the Pacific Division regarded me as competent to do the job there too.

I almost lost the opportunity because I liked to fly the line in command, but I was told that if I turned down the request I would not be asked again, so I first went to the chief pilot, Don Kinkel, and asked him how he wanted the job done. His answer was clear and simple. "When you take out an applicant for captain, you are going to be with him for at least eight days. On one of those days—it may be the first or it could be the last—you will say to yourself, 'I can put my wife and children on this man's flight on a dark and rainy night and then go home and have a good night's sleep.' When you decide that, check him out. But if you can't come to that conclusion, turn him down. Don't feel that you have ruined his career because we will send him out with another check pilot for another opinion before we take any action."

Sometimes, if there was a doubt, the chief pilot or an assistant chief would go with him to make the final decision. I have always thought that to judge whether a pilot is a safe one or not is very difficult. It is not just a case of ensuring that he follows the published procedures. Some pilots can do that very well and yet leave doubts about their ability to handle an unusual situation, especially one that is not covered by the regulations. Some can do all the right things and still leave the impression that their 'feel' of the airplane is not all that it should be. Some can make small deviations from the published procedures but they know exactly what they are doing and give no cause for concern. I repeat something I have said before, "Following all the rules is not necessarily the same as being a good pilot."

Some pilots can handle the airplane very well, and be a near-perfect copilot, yet cannot take command. I had a case of this on a Boeing 707 when I had been asked to give someone an informal check ride, not to put him in command but to judge how he would react to an official check ride. I found that as long as I flew the airplane he could be an excellent copilot, alert and helpful, always ready with anything I needed. If I asked him to fly the aircraft from the righthand seat while I maintained command, he would do a good job, adept at discerning what I thought he should do. But if I told him that he was to make all the decisions and I would act only as his copilot and would do only what he told me to do, he went to pieces. He would forget to ask for weather reports, fail to start a let-down when he should, or to call for the proper checklist and, in general, simply lose control of the situation.

I had to report to the chief pilot that I doubted if he could pass a check ride for captain, and in fact he did not, and took early retirement as copilot. The strange aspect of this case was that he had an excellent personality. Everyone liked him and was pulling for him, from the chief pilot down to the most junior stewardess who flew with him. He was a fine man and it hurt everyone concerned to see him fail to advance, but it just could not be done.

There were routine route checks, on a leg or two with another captain. All of us had to have a route check at least once per year, usually more often. The F.A.A. inspectors also accompanied us periodically and documented each time they checked us and noted the date of the last time they observed our performance. Airline pilots must have more people watching over their shoulders than those in any other profession.

I found this kind of checking pretty dull. These men were experienced professionals, well trained, and seldom needed any correction. We just sat in the jumpseat and watched. Occasionally we might be able to call attention to an overlooked regulation or to suggest how a thing might be done better. But in general there was little to do. We were entitled to stay on for more than one leg if we had any doubts, but this was seldom necessary.

I once found myself bawling out a pilot for making a power-off approach and landing, something that I did not think was dangerous, and which I did myself, at times. I told him that I liked to do that, too, but not to do it with me on board as check pilot because it put me on the spot. I either had to write him up for making an unapproved procedure; or to ignore it, and I did not want to do either one.

Another type of checking was to upgrade copilots to captains. I liked that much better. To be able to say to someone, "You are okay. I can make you a captain" was very satisfying. We worked from the copilot's seat and acted as the copilot, giving advice as necessary, or just sitting there as a silent partner if we wanted to.

I usually had a short conference before we left the base and said something like "We will start out today with you flying, but I'll feel free to give advice or to call to your attention something I think you are missing. Each day I will give less and less instruction and it will become more and more a case of checking you. I will expect several days, at least, of your doing it all without help from me." Usually this was accepted very well, but not always.

Most of these trips were a pleasure. By the time a pilot flew with me, he had passed all the previous hurdles, and was rated on the airplane by the F.A.A., having passed his ground examinations and a flight check. He would have been given a pre-command check by one of the chiefs, and all he now had to do was to satisfy me that he could put it all together on the line. I often said that as far as I was concerned they were already captains and that they would have to prove to me that they could not do the job for me to turn them down.

Hello, Folks, Goodbye

Sometimes we would encounter an amusing situation. One candidate, for example, did not like to use the public address system (P.A.) to tell the passengers anything. The check pilot told him that, unless he used the P.A. to communicate with the passengers, he was not going to check him out. To make it easy, the check pilot offered to fly the airplane while the captain wrote down what he intended to say and then make his speech without distraction. When they were in cruise flight he took a stenographer's notebook and began writing; one page, then another, and another, then four, five pages. The check pilot was becoming nervous. What all was this guy going to say?

Finally he was ready. He picked up the microphone, cleared his throat several times, and said, "Good morning, ladies and gentlemen, welcome on board." Then he hung up the mike.

My first candidate on the Boeing 707 was Leo Sant. Leo was a quiet, very conscientious fellow and, I thought, fully competent to be a captain. I reasoned that he would be very upset if he was found doing something wrong, just at the start, so when he did make a mistake even before we left the ramp, I overlooked it.

Each engine had four basic instruments on the pilot's panel. To depart with one of those instruments inoperable was permissible, but to depart with two was not. The first engine had one such inoperable instrument and it had already been noted in the logbook. But when Leo started that engine, another was also found to be inoperable. I thought the flight engineer would surely catch it, but he did not say anything, either. So we started the other engines and took off for Anchorage, Alaska.

An hour or so later the flight engineer was making out the logbook and suddenly said, "Hey, we took off illegally! Too many instruments out on number three engine." I thought Leo was going to faint, thinking he had already busted his check. I told the engineer that I knew it, and would take the responsibility, and told Leo that we would discuss it during our layover in Anchorage.

At the hotel, I took Leo aside and we discussed it. I told him that I had expected him to be nervous and had not wanted to make a big issue of it at the start of the trip. I didn't consider it really dangerous as we had plenty of other indications if the engine gave us real trouble. I assured him that though he could not continue to make mistakes like this, this one was not going to cause me to turn him down. We had a fine trip thereafter and Leo became one of Pan Am's better captains.

It was quite normal for a pilot to have what is known as 'check-itis'. It affected me as badly, if not worse than, anyone else. Nobody I know likes to have his competence judged by someone else, especially when his livelihood is at stake. Most pilots have more than a fair share of ego, and this trait may well be necessary in the job. Those who maintained that they did not mind being checked were lying, or were so unconcerned as to be dangerous.

Sometimes I could quickly make up my mind if a pilot was all right or not. I told Joe Sceili after only one day that he had done so well that the only way he could bust the check ride was to make a serious mistake and have some kind of incident that would damage the airplane. He had an answer for that; he said that as he was the captain, he was going to assign to me all the rest of the take offs and landings. We had a good laugh, but he still had to fly the rest of the trip.

To this date, happily, no pilot whom I approved has ever had a serious problem or accident.

To continue telling about all the successful flights I had as check pilot would be of little interest. Most of them were a real pleasure, but if I tell a couple of horror stories it is only because they stand out vividly from the rest. They were certainly not typical.

One pilot to whom I gave my pre-flight speech replied that I could "Just start checking right from the first take off." This would have been fine if he could have made good, but he did a number of things that I did not like, even though his handling of the airplane was technically acceptable. He did not handle his crew well, and could easily make them angry and uncooperative. On the way into Tokyo at night he had not made any P.A. announcements and the purser called to say that the passengers wanted to know where we were, what time we would arrive in Tokyo, and what the weather was like there. I had taken this call and told him that we would give them the information. I waited several minutes and the pilot made no move, so I asked him if he was going to make the P.A. announcement. He said, "No." I asked why not and he said that he did not have anything to say. I told him that the purser had explained what the passengers wanted to know, but he still refused to communicate. So I made the announcement. This was on a Boeing 747 and there was a policy on these aircraft that the last leg had to be observed by the chief pilot and an F.A.A. inspector. So in Tokyo I turned him over to the chief pilot.

For the return flight to San Francisco we all met in the hotel lobby and, as we boarded the crew bus, Bill Monan, the chief pilot, tried to put this guy at ease. He said, "I've put aside a Honolulu trip for you for your first command trip and I'm sending one of our best to be your copilot." I thought it was courteously done, showing his confidence that the pilot would be checked out. But Bill received an odd response.

"I don't want your best copilot. Just give me a dumb S.O.B. who will sit on the right and keep his mouth shut." It was a stupid thing to say to the chief pilot, and more so in front of the F.A.A. inspector. I could not help but laugh, even though I knew his barb had been aimed at me.

This guy did not like to be told what to do, and I had done plenty of telling on our trip. As we climbed out of Tokyo, I was sitting in the back eating dinner, my services having been dispensed with, and we had been in level flight for half an hour. The air was smooth as silk, but the seatbelt sign was still on. A stewardess asked me if I thought the captain still wanted it on. I told her that he had probably forgotten, as the cockpit was full of people and a lot was going on. I suggested that she go quietly into the cockpit and ask if it could be turned off.

In a couple of minutes she returned, proclaiming that she would never again enter that man's cockpit. He had publicly bawled her out in front of everyone, telling her never to try telling him how to run his airplane. I wondered if he thought that would make points with the chief and the F.A.A. They would have thought more highly of him had he thanked her for reminding him and turned off the sign.

He made two serious mistakes on that flight. While on descent he failed to make an altitude assigned by A.T.C., and he landed too far down the runway in San Francisco. He was not checked out as captain then, and I thought it was the right decision.

What's the Heading?

The worst trip I ever had was a round-the-world flight. The pilot could fly the airplane, but he had other problems. Round-the-world flights are always arriving at unfamiliar areas and a review of the charts and let-down diagrams, along with advice about the airport, is always advisable. A pilot should be able to fly into airports he has never seen, provided he has the proper charts, and studies them ahead of time.

This was obviously not being done. There was often some confusion because he had not read the charts thoroughly. En route from Hong Kong to

Tokyo we were nearly at the point where we should have started our let-down to land at Tokyo. He searched through his route manual for several minutes, then several minutes later repeated the performance. He just could not find the right chart because it was not in the airport pages.

I finally asked him if he had a problem. He said that his Tokyo area chart seemed to be missing and did I have one? I checked through my manual in the same place and said "No". And on we flew, approaching the time when we would receive clearance for descent and would need that chart to comply with the correct procedure. He made no comment as to how we were going to handle the problem, so I finally asked him what we were going to do, as neither of us had an area chart. He said, "I guess we will have to ask Tokyo radar to give us vector headings to where they want us to fly."

I refused to broadcast to the world that Pan American pilots were flying in the area without the proper charts, so I told him where to find it. Later on, in Tokyo, I had a session with him in the hotel and told him that the trouble could be cured if only he would spend an hour on each layover looking over the charts for the next day's flight. I told him I was not satisfied with his performance at this point, but that I would make him a deal. If he gave me the last two legs, Tokyo–Honolulu and Honolulu–San Francisco with virtually no errors and with a clear indication that he knew the routes, I would approve him for captain.

The next day was fine, but when we were preparing to leave Honolulu we were given a Standard Instrument Departure (S.I.D.) by Honolulu tower. I copied it and read it back. "Cleared to San Francisco as filed, S.I.D. Molokai Two departure, climb to and maintain flight level three-three-zero." This was standard procedure, but this guy did not set up any radio frequencies to fly the correct departure, which required a right turn after take off until we crossed a certain bearing on the Molokai VOR station, then a turn to intercept a given course. I did not help him, as most copilots would have done, by setting up the radio frequencies for him or reading to him the departure procedure. It was his responsibility.

When we took off, he turned almost to the correct heading, as that was normal on a take off to the east. But he flew right through the Molokai bearing. I gritted my teeth and just let him go until A.T.C. called. "Clipper Two, you have flown through the Molokai radial; turn left, NOW!" I said, "Captain, they want us to turn left, now." He started a left turn and I asked, "What heading are you going to turn to?" He replied, "I don't know, ask them what heading they want."

At that, I did something I had never before had to do. I reached up and took the wheel. I told him that our jobs had just been reversed; that I was the captain and would fly the rest of the trip, and that I would not approve him as captain.

Check pilots were entitled to review the files of a pilot they checked, but I seldom did so. I did not like to be influenced by what someone else had said. This pilot was required to ride as copilot for six more months, then he was checked by a different check pilot and made a captain. So on his first six-month review I took a peek at the report and could hardly believe my eyes when I saw the comment, "Could not locate the Tokyo area chart."

Several months later he was separated from Pan Am for reasons that I never knew, but I admit to a big sigh of relief.

Scrubbed Stew

There are not many funny stories about checking because it is a serious business for all parties. To the pilot being checked, not only is his livelihood on the line, but his ego is also being challenged. The check pilot is certainly conscious of his responsibility to the company, to the pilot being checked, and most of all to the passengers who put their very lives in that man's hands. No check pilot that I ever knew ever took his duties lightly.

Check pilots were hated by some pilots more than others, but nobody looked forward to having one on board. In one case, two captains had the same surname and for various reasons were referred to as the Good ____ and the Bad ____ . On one trip a stewardess who had only recently joined Pan Am went into the cockpit and said, "I understand there are two of you and one is known as the good captain and one is the bad captain. I have been watching you and I have decided that you are the good one." He replied, "On the contrary, my dear, I am the bad one."

In London one morning I sat down next to this captain at breakfast. I was in uniform and when I told him that I was going to ride to San Francisco with him, he was very direct. "I don't like check pilots." I said, "Well, I don't think much of them, either."

When the crew showed up for the bus to the airport, one stewardess had more paint on her than many a circus clown. The captain walked up to her in the lobby and quietly said, "Young lady, I'd like for you to go upstairs and wash your face. If you don't want to do that, then put on civilian clothes and you can dead-head to San Francisco."

"Well," she said, "I just won't go on this flight."

"I'm sorry, but I didn't give you that choice. You may work this flight with a clean face, or you can deadhead in civilian clothes, but I'll not let you represent Pan Am on my flight looking like that."

She went upstairs and came back with a scrubbed, if teary look. I thought the incident was neatly handled.

This captain was a little unorthodox, but I saw nothing that I considered unsafe in the least. Several times he said, "I guess you'll write me up for doing thus-and-so." I answered, "It looks safe to me and I think you know exactly what you are doing." He was simply an individualist, and the deviations were really very minor.

When we reached the ramp at San Francisco, I passed my report over to him to read before we left the airplane. He read it and noted where I had identified those minor variations that we had discussed, but that I did not consider them unsafe and thought he was a good pilot, with control throughout of both the airplane and the crew.

I will always treasure his remark as he handed the form back to me. He said, "I still don't like check pilots. But if we have to have them, I guess you are as good as any." Coming from him, this was high praise indeed.

Cockpit Resource Management

During the last few years while I worked for Pan Am there was an emphasis on what was called 'crew coordination', because of a tendency, in the early days, for too many 'one-man shows'. The captain ran the whole operation with little regard for what the rest of the crew thought. There is nothing wrong with a captain using the opinions of his crew, and he should do so in making his own decision, but I do not think flying an airplane can be done by popular vote. The Federal Aviation Administration (F.A.A.) delegates to the captain the total responsibility for the airplane, its crew, and its passengers. During the flight, he is responsible for any action taken by himself or by any crew member. In my years of checking crews I much preferred a strong, competent captain in full control over a weak captain who depended on his copilot. A good captain will gather from his crew all the information that time allows, but the final decision should be his, and his alone.

If television reports are correct, there was a recent case when one engine of a twin-engined aircraft caught fire. The captain shut down the correct engine, but the copilot mistakenly thought he had information that the other engine was on fire and he shut down that one also, without being so instructed to do so by the captain. This lack of discipline effectively turned the aircraft into an overweight glider, and many lives were lost in the resultant crash.

My Kind of Pilot

Al Fritz, a check pilot, was a few months from retirement when he was assigned a trip to London. After an engine failure on take off he took some non-standard actions. The company chiefs did not approve and, as a result, Al accepted early retirement instead of re-training on the Boeing 747, as would have been required.

A few months later I attended a retirement party where Al was one of the retirees. I was wondering just what he would say when it was his turn to come to the podium to receive his plaque. He was dressed in a black suit and tie, very much like our uniforms. He removed his coat to reveal a uniform shirt, but the epaulets were like little knots, looking as if they had been through the washing machine a hundred times. The shirt was torn and had what looked like bloodstains in several places. Normally a dapper man, Al was obviously making a statement—that he had been in a battle. In his own words, as I recall them at the time:

"While I'm up here, let me tell you about my first trip with Pan American Airways. It was on a flying boat out of San Francisco Bay. The boat was fully loaded and the water was smooth. The captain made several runs down the bay before he could get that seaplane up on the step, so that it would break

The Martin 130 China Clipper. *Only three 130s were built, but they gained fame out of all proportion to their numbers.*

"Check altitude, Al."

loose from the water. When we became airborne we were headed right at one of the stanchions on the Bay Bridge. The captain made a small turn to the right, then back to the left, and we went between two stanchions under the Bay Bridge. We went down the Bay at about two hundred feet and flew by, not over, Alcatraz Island. We also went under the Golden Gate Bridge, and we were several miles out to sea before we got as high as one thousand feet, and went on to Hawaii."

I thought that was an interesting story, but there was more: "Now let me tell you about my last trip with Pan American Airways. It was with a Boeing 747, fully loaded for a trip to London. We left about midnight, taking off on Runway 28 (to the west). At the most critical point on the take off run, number one engine exploded—not just quit—exploded. It scared the hell out of everybody on board. Me, I was the most scared of all. But I'm a well-trained pilot. I yelled, "Feather number one engine! Retract the tail wheel! Put the hydraulic pump on number two! Full low pitch!"

He recited about a dozen commands, none of which pertained to a 747. He was poking fun at himself and had, of course, used the correct commands at the time. But then he became serious.

"I doubted if we could clear the hills ahead, and I am a command pilot, I am not a committee pilot. I decided that the thing to do was to get that big bird back onto the ground. I made a steep turn (about forty-five degrees of bank) at about two hundred feet and went back down the Bay. I told the flight engineer to start dumping fuel and not to stop until we were on short final. I flew at two hundred feet as far down the Bay as I dared, then turned back to the runway and landed. So you might say that my first trip with Pan Am and my last were alike, both were spent flying over San Francisco Bay at two hundred feet altitude. I have no other comment about that flight, except to say that I am surely going to enjoy my grandchildren in my retirement." People stood in line to shake his hand.

The following day I had a scheduled four-hour training session in the Boeing 747 simulator. We had a few minutes left after doing all the required maneuvers and the instructor asked if I would like to try anything else. I told him to line me up with Runway 28, loaded to full gross weight, and to cut number one engine at the critical time. I said that I intended to over-rotate (as if I was startled by an explosion) and let the airplane decelerate to a speed that was ten knots too slow. I wanted to see if I could ever recover the airspeed and climb out over the hills ahead.

In this simulation of Al Fritz's experience I would not have made it—I would have hit the hills. On Al's flight, on the other hand, nobody was hurt, nor was there any damage to the airplane. It is hard to argue with success. Al Fritz was my kind of pilot.

Check pilots were paid a little extra and were generally expected to check one month and fly the line themselves for two months. It often worked out the other way around. I enjoyed flying my own trips so much that I resigned as check pilot about a year before retirement.

The Boeing 314, designed specifically for Pan American—which operated a fleet of twelve.

Side Trips and Celebrities

Some flight service individuals think that they should be in command aft of the cockpit door. Of course, the F.A.A. regulations are hard to overcome when they say that everyone on board, and that includes the passengers, is under the command of the 'pilot in command' of the aircraft whenever it is in flight.

A steward once told Captain Russ Parks that while Russ was captain in the cockpit, he, the steward, was 'captain of the cabin'. Russ said that was okay, but that there was a difference: "When you come to the cockpit, that does not make you captain of the cockpit; but when I come to the cabin, that makes me captain of the cabin."

I normally got along with the flight service people very well. Theirs was a very important job because passengers formed their opinion of Pan American Airways from impressions made by the service personnel. I tried to support them when I could and I received their support in return.

There were other times, though. On one occasion out of Panama I was told in the flight office that we would have ten new-hires who had just finished their training in Miami and were on their way to San Francisco for their first assignment. I thought our flight service would like to welcome them to the company and mentioned this to our purser, a red-headed girl. Her response shocked me. "Well, they are not going to ride first-class."

No thought had been given to putting them in first-class, for as new-hires they were at the bottom of the pecking order and nobody would ever have thought about putting them anywhere except in the tourist section. However, her remark made me angry and I asked, "Why not?"

"Because I do not intend to serve them, that's why not."

"You won't have to serve them. You go back and work the tourist section and send the other purser to first-class."

"I'm the senior purser and I'm not going to work tourist."

"I'm the captain, and you will work tourist."

Then I went into the cockpit and called operations on the radio to ask if they had empty seats in first-class. They did, so I requested that they put those ten new-hires up there. I was careful to go back for my own coffee during that flight.

The first-class seats on one of our airplanes had a strange control for reclining. Instead of pushing a button as on most seats, a small lever had to be pulled out from the lower end. A very irritated passenger was trying to recline his seat and was too upset to listen to the attendant who was trying to help him. Finally, in desperation, she shouted, "PULL UP ON THE BOTTOM."

That got his attention and he asked, "What happens if I pull up on your bottom?"

"I'm sorry, sir, but I don't recline that easily."

It took a certain kind of person to do that job day in and day out, maintain poise and keep the passengers happy.

On one occasion when leaving Guatemala, I received a report from the cabin that one passenger refused to sit down because she could not have the seat she wanted. Instead of going back to try to resolve that one, I used the P.A. system, announcing that we were going to return to the ramp because one person was not seated and that I could not take off until everyone was buckled into his seat. I had gone only about a hundred yards when she took her seat. She was a Mexican movie star, and after we were in flight she insisted on taking over the microphone and apologizing to the entire cabin.

Lockerbie

As I write this, Pan Am Flight 103 has just been destroyed by a bomb over Lockerbie, Scotland. I never thought I would live to see the day when the passengers would be the most dangerous thing on the airplane. I flew that 747, N739PA *Clipper Maid of the Seas*, many times, over that very route.

Much as I would like to see flights made one hundred percent secure, I doubt very much if it is possible. Terrorists can keep pace with any technological advance in security. Rather than spend huge sums in trying to make the aircraft secure, delaying flights, and inconveniencing passengers, I would rather see that money spent in finding every terrorist and ensuring swift and severe punishment. In my own mind, nothing less than death, immediate and certain, would suffice. Hardly anywhere are trains, buses, or boats subjected to the security measures that are accepted as normal for airliners; yet the surface carriers are subjected to fewer terrorist threats.

Regulations such as a locked cockpit door, which the F.A.A. requires, do little good. Any terrorist will gain access to the cockpit, one way or another, if he or she wishes to. And as long as the rule is not required on all airlines worldwide it hurts U.S. carriers. I have been told many times by people that they chose to ride an overseas airline because "They let us see the cockpit in flight, and you won't do it."

Lost

It is said that there are two kinds of pilots: those who have been lost and those who will be lost. My time came on a flight from Miami to Brownsville with an AVENSA DC-3 that we were delivering for maintenance. I elected to go straight across the Gulf of Mexico to New Orleans where we intended to refuel. We had no navigational aids for that route, but I thought holding a heading would get me there okay.

Over the water the weather worsened until I had to go low to stay below the clouds and that reduced my visibility. I began to worry about missing New Orleans too far to the south which could put me over water until I ran out of fuel. So I started 'leaning' to the right, just enough to be sure that I hit the coastline. When we did hit it I made my next mistake. I thought I recognized a ground feature that would have been only a few minutes' flying time from New Orleans. I called New Orleans tower and reported an estimated arrival time.

Then we flew on and on without finding New Orleans. I started to deviate from side to side in the hope of finding some feature that I knew. I was finally reduced to some very basic techniques of the times to determine if I had passed New Orleans or if it was still ahead. This consisted of tuning in to the New Orleans station and turning the volume down as low as I could hear it. If, as I flew westward, the volume increased, the station was still ahead. If it decreased until I could not hear it, then I has passed the station. This took time, and the tower personnel were wondering where I was. So was I. I determined that I was east of the field, and just as they called me to ask if I knew where I was (I'm sure they knew that I didn't) I spotted an airport. So I replied, "I know exactly where I am. I am over Biloxi, Mississippi!" It was a good lesson and one from which I profited many times.

Split Liver

We had arrived at Papeete at about six in the morning, directly from Los Angeles, a Boeing 707 crew of eleven, and most of us had never been to Tahiti before. We were scheduled to leave at ten o'clock that night, but some of us wanted to see what we could of the island, so we rented five motor scooters. Ten of us started out to circle the island on the only paved road, about thirty miles long. We planned to be back at the hotel by noon and to sleep away the afternoon so as to be rested for our flight back to Los Angeles.

We only made about five miles. Just after passing the air-port, the flight engineer, John Garibaldi, and one of the stewardesses had a wreck with their scooter. He was playing about, zigzagging back and forth, slipped on the gravel at the side of the road, and the machine ended up in the ditch. John landed on some big lava boulders and a barbed-wire fence. When I reached him he appeared to have some very serious wounds from the wire and from branches of a trimmed hedge that had penetrated his body. But worse, he couldn't seem to breathe. I sent the copilot to the airport for assistance, including some oxygen. The stewardess was knocked out for a few minutes, but was not seriously hurt.

People kept stopping along the road, wanting to help by putting John into a car to take him to the hospital. I thought he was too seriously hurt to move that way and asked them to call an ambulance. They kept telling me that this was Tahiti and that the ambulance might not arrive for hours. Fortunately it took only about half an hour. I rode with John and the stewardess, as there was no attendant, and the driver drove like a madman. Had I not been there to keep a tight grip on the patients, I am sure the ride would have killed them before we reached the hospital.

A French doctor examined our patients and the stewardess was released. He said that John had some bad cuts and three broken ribs, but that if he stayed in the hospital overnight he could probably go back to Los Angeles the next day, as a passenger.

I spent hours with a policeman trying to make out a report of exactly what had happened. They wanted every little detail, measuring all the skid marks and distances to the fence from the shoulder of the road, and a dozen other items. I hated to think how complicated they would have made it had there been more than one vehicle involved.

We were having a language problem, too, as the officer spoke French, no English. One of our stewardesses spoke a little French and she was attempting to translate until something the policeman said made me think he might speak some Spanish. Sure enough, his mother was from Spain and we managed very well with my limited use of the language.

We could not leave on schedule because we had to wait for an engineer to arrive, and we were to leave at nine o'clock the next morning. Back at the hotel I was awakened at about two a.m. by a telephone call from the doctor, who informed me that John's blood pressure was falling, he had internal bleeding, and they were going to operate immediately on John's damaged liver. The fall on the rocks had caused a split about ten inches in length.

I went to the hospital at six and John was still unconscious and looked awful. So did the hospital. In his room there were holes in the floor, through which I could see rats running around on the ground beneath. I begged the doctor to put John on a stretcher and onto my flight, telling him that I would have him in Los Angeles within eight hours. The doctor, who had served with the French in Vietnam, said that John would not survive the trip if we insisted on moving him. He told me that he had seen as many split livers as any doctor and that John's best chance was to leave him there, though he did not give him more than a fifty-fifty chance of recovery.

John did recover. The wife of the Pan American station manager was a nurse and she practically moved into the hospital and acted as his private nurse. When John was finally transferred Stateside, he underwent further operations and was eventually put back on flight duty.

The Tahitians were wonderful. At the rental place, they were not at all concerned that we had left their motor scooters all over the island; laying by the road, at the airport, everywhere. They just laughed and said that the island was small, that they would gather them up, as they were not going anywhere.

Cut Foot

On another trip to Tahiti some years later, we rented a sailboat from a local yacht club for a rental fee of three dollars for half a day. One of our cabin crew said that she had been a sailing instructor in France, so she would sail the boat. It turned out later that she had never sailed anything bigger than a 'Sunfish', a surfboard with a small sail on it. We managed to capsize the boat on a coral reef and scratched it up a little. We had to be towed into the dock, with the boat full of water. I had cut my foot on the reef. Coral cuts can easily become infected and be sore for a long time.

At the dock they laughingly pulled the boat out of the water to examine it. When I asked what I owed for the damage, they said that their policy was to double the rent in the case of damage to the boat. Even if we had sunk the boat and lost it, the rent would have been six dollars.

They put fresh lime juice on my cut foot and told me that it would promptly heal without infection, and it did, giving me no trouble. I can understand why people want to live in Tahiti. It's a great place for losing scooters and cutting feet.

Tidbits in Transit

Flight crews could always find interesting places to eat, some quite out of the way. Next door to our hotel in Auckland, New Zealand, in the basement of a house, there was a little sandwich shop which served delicious omelets, a welcome treat when we had just arrived from an overnight flight. A palm-thatched hut on the beach at Maiquetía, Venezuela, had the best broiled prawns and hearts of palm salad. The Phoenician Hotel in Beirut had the finest assortment of fruit for breakfast, although we seldom ate in hotels unless we could not find anything else or were in a hurry.

In an out-of-the-way, rundown part of Sydney, Australia, near the docks, there was a restaurant called The Wooloomooloo Wool House, and the woman who owned it specialized in mutton. Because of the location it was about to go broke when a Pan Am crew wandered in. They loved it, passed on the word, and soon it was crowded with crews every night. Pan Am crews invariably got the royal treatment there.

One of my favorite places was in Tokyo, where they served pork loins, called 'toncatsu'. I never knew the address, but if you caught a green train, rode seven stops and got off, turned left two blocks, you were there. It was a big, square, plain room and in the corner was a square counter; no individual tables. A very old Japanese lady nodded to you when you came in and noted how many were in your party. No list, no reservations, but she knew when it was your turn and she would direct you to your place at the counter. She never spoke a word. The pork was cooked in huge cauldrons in the center of the counter and sliced up in great style in front of you by a man who, miraculously, still had all of his fingers. Served with hot mustard and accompanied by miso soup and shredded cabbage, it made a very satisfying meal.

Seat Fit for a Dog

As seniority increased, so did our privileges of reduced-fare travel. Pan American never did use the term 'passes', preferring instead the term 'service charge' and we paid an amount that was sufficient to cover the cost of issuing tickets and the food aboard. My wife and I took our children to London for a vacation. We could not all board on the first day. Some stations were good about putting 'sublos' (subject to load) on and some were not. The latter would not check you in until they knew there were open seats and, by the time they knew, there would be a delay to accommodate you, so you were left at the check-in counter.

Our six-year-old daughter, Joanne, stayed behind with me to try the next day, but we were once again left standing in the terminal, facing the airplane as it prepared to leave the gate. When the purser came into the cockpit to make her cabin report, she saw us through the plate glass window in front of the aircraft's nose and told the captain, "Ned Wilson and his daughter are wanting to go to London and we have two seats left." The captain held the flight and put us on. But there was a problem. One of the seats was actually one that a lady passenger had bought for her dog. But she was very accommodating and pleasant, she allowed Joanne to take the seat if she would hold the dog in her lap. So Joanne ended up being a caretaker for the dog all the way to London.

This Flight Stinks

I always found, on our airplanes at least, that the more important persons are the easiest to get along with. Celebrities were not usually the demanding type.

Celebrities of one sort or another were often on board. One of the most interesting was Danny Kaye. On a flight from Honolulu to Los Angeles I was about to leave the cockpit to take an informal look through the cabin, as was my custom. I always considered it part of my duty to do this, and did so on almost every flight. I normally stayed about fifteen minutes, checking the cabin and observing how the passengers were being served.

In this case, just as I left the cockpit, the first officer made a normal course change, making a turn that was emphatic enough for everyone on board to be aware of it. I opened the door to the cabin to find Danny Kaye in the lounge, holding court. He was as funny there as ever I saw him when putting on a stage performance. As I came through the door, he turned to the other passengers and said, "Do you folks know what they are saying in the cockpit just now? 'Now the old man is out of here, so let's get this damn thing back on course'." Then he pulled out his wallet and showed me his Air Transport Pilot's license, just the same as mine. He said that when he tired of being a comic, he wanted to be the world's oldest airline pilot.

On one of my forays into the cabin during the middle of the night, and over the Atlantic, I met Don Rickles in the galley area, taking a cup of coffee. I asked him if everything was all right and he replied, "Do you think I'm going to tell you at 39,000 feet over the ocean that this flight stinks?"

Seeing Stars

On another occasion, on the same route, Red Skelton was flying first-class. Other passengers found out that he was aboard and kept trying to enter the first-class cabin section to ask for his autograph or talk to him, and flight service was having a hard time keeping them out. Red Skelton went to the back and made an announcement, "They say that you can't come up to visit me, so

I'll come back and see you." He stayed there talking and signing autographs for almost an hour. A real gentleman.

Leaving London one morning on a Boeing 707, I saw Elizabeth Taylor boarding the plane. My first reaction was, "Oh, no, nothing but trouble!" I had heard of some problems between her and Richard Burton on other flights. She had two first-class seats and when I went back to talk to her, I found that she was returning to Los Angeles because her father was in the hospital with a stroke. Her only special request was for us to try to determine his condition and let her know. We found her quite delightful and she captivated the entire crew.

Flight service was having difficulty in trying to remove the armrest between her two seats and I sent a cockpit crew member back to see if he could help. Miss Taylor was sitting in the aisle seat and he reached over her, while struggling with the armrest. As she pulled back out of his way as much as possible, she said, "Am I sitting on something?" He replied, "Well, I certainly hope so." She smiled and said, "That isn't what I meant, but I do know that it is ten pounds too heavy."

On a trip to Panama, John Wayne was handing out autograph cards. He carried a handful already signed and passed them out to anyone who wanted them. I did not normally ask my passengers for autographs, but I had a young friend who was a big fan of his. I told him that I really did not want one of those signed cards, but would appreciate a personal note to my friend, and he promptly wrote her a note.

Peter Graves (Mission Impossible) was on board as we were preparing for departure for Sydney, Australia. Dolle, a crew scheduler and my future wife, asked him for an autograph before we left the ramp. During the flight I spent some time explaining to him and his family the concept of the International Date Line. After Dolle and I were married, he was aboard again, and he remembered, saying to her, "I understand that you are a 'Mrs Captain', now."

On an early DC-4 flight through Central America, Billy Graham was on board and he preached at every stop, even standing on top of the airplane boarding stairs to deliver his message, with an interpreter who would repeat each sentence in Spanish. Twenty years or more later I was riding on Delta Air Lines and met him again. He remembered our flight and even my invitation for him to visit the cockpit.

Out of Saigon one morning I spotted an individual climbing the boarding stairs. He could be, I suppose, considered a celebrity. Certainly his face was familiar because it had been on the cover of a major magazine and in many newspapers all around the world. He was the policeman who had shot a Viet-Cong in the head right on the streets of Saigon. We had all kinds.

One night out of Guatemala, heading for Panama, the vice president of Guatemala and his entourage were aboard, sitting in the upstairs lounge on our Boeing 747. They wanted to take their meal there, but meals were not normally served in the upstairs lounge on that flight. I persuaded the flight service that they needed to make an exception in this case, in the interests of Pan American, which had many flights into and out of Guatemala, and whose status in that country could be jeopardized. Guatemala was an important Pan Am hub in Central America—long before, incidentally, the hub concept became standard practice in the United States.

On another flight, a group of Middle East sheiks were playing poker in the lounge and when we made a stop they left the cards and money on the table while they went into the terminal. There seemed to be thousands of dollars there, and they just walked off and left it. A stewardess asked me what to do about it and I told her not to touch it, but to ensure that nobody else picked it up. When the sheiks returned from the terminal they insisted on giving her a $100 bill—against the rules, but I turned a blind eye on this occasion.

Astronauts

The most interesting celebrities were the astronauts. The original seven often traveled with us on their way to Panama, where they trained for survival in the jungle, in case, on their return to Earth, they landed in some remote part of the world.

As a group they were the most inquisitive people I had ever met. They were far from reticent about their own work, and were always asking us about our operation, spending a lot of time in the cockpit with us. I remember that John Young had a million questions about the DC-8 we were flying.

One of my favorites was Gus Grissom, who seemed somewhat more serious than the others and was very concerned with the safety of all aspects of their flights. We discussed the coincidence that both of us had sons named Scott. I told him how, when once gazing at the moon with my son, I had told him that before he was grown someone would have been there and back, and that my son had replied, "Yes, and it might be me."

Gus asked for a piece of paper and wrote my son a note. I later bought his book and pasted that note on the fly-leaf for Scott. When Gus died in a fire on the pad, along with the rest of his crew, I felt as if I had lost a close friend.

I followed every flight they made with great interest and was glued to the television when they first circumnavigated the moon. I could not help wondering—quite illogically—what we would think if that module went behind the moon and never re-appeared. I almost held my breath during the time they were out of communication.

When Neil Armstrong landed on the moon with only a few seconds of usable fuel left it set me trembling. Just think: at about five hundred feet above the surface, he first sighted the landing place and, instead of the smooth surface that had been predicted, it was a boulder field. He took over manual control of the Lunar Lander and flew this strange vehicle over an unknown surface, thousands of miles from Earth, looking for a suitable touch-down spot. He had only seconds to do so. It was a good example to demonstrate the advantage of having a human pilot to make decisions that no computer could manage to do. Neil was also a glider pilot, which pleased me. I had visited with him at some glider meets.

There were times when I wished I could have been an astronaut, but I did not have the education or training required. Anyway, their careers were too short, and too much of what they did was directed from the ground, or accomplished by computer. I would have preferred to be a Shuttle pilot. I think I could have done that. General Joe Engle did his first glider tow at Marfa, Texas, flying my Cessna 180. I was the one being towed in my glider, a Laister Nugget. I have Joe Engle's signature in my logbook to that effect. I may never have had the privilege of traveling in space; but I did have the privilege of meeting many of the superbly trained and accomplished men who did.

The Old Man's Cadillac

My last 707 flight was made in January 1972, and I started training for the Boeing 747. I asked Freddy Knotts, always a little ahead of me, what he thought of the 747. He said, "Ned, if you could redesign the 707 and make it as you would like to have it, you would end up with a 747."

Whenever Fred and I met we had long discussions, mostly about flying techniques, and seldom did we disagree. Incidentally, as a high school student, he wanted to be an airline pilot for United Air Lines. He informed the company of his ambition, and repeated his desire when he started college. Fred started flight training in a Civilian Pilot Training (C.P.T.) course, continued to advise United of his progress, and when he finally received his commercial pilot's license, promptly went to see the airline. When he walked in and gave his name, the receptionist said, "Oh, we know about you," and he was immediately entered into a training class. However, after only three weeks United elected to discontinue that entire class. And so Fred Knotts became a Pan American pilot instead, a move that he never regretted. Sadly, he died of cancer soon after his retirement.

I flew the Boeing 747 for the rest of my career and called it, 'The Old Man's Cadillac'.

There are airplanes that will always hold a soft spot in a pilot's heart, and the Douglas DC-3 holds such a spot in mine. But the Boeing 747 would run it a neck-and-neck race. In my opinion, it is the safest airplane ever built. And surprisingly, it is downright fun to fly, so big that it has been said that it does not fly, the earth just drops out from under it. And yet you can circle the airport as slowly, if not more slowly, than any large airplane and feel that it is under full control, solid as a rock.

The Simulator Takes Over

When I took my rating, most of the training was done in the simulator. Only a few maneuvers were actually done in the airplane. We used the airplane for emergency descents and for take offs and landings. My log shows that I had three hours and fifty minutes airplane time when I went for my F.A.A. rating. Later the F.A.A. approved the simulator for all maneuvers and gave the rating

The Boeing 747. This aircraft, introduced to the world's airlines by Pan American, and ahead of its time, has dominated long distance air routes for a quarter of a century—and still counting.

rides in the simulator, too. The first time when the pilots actually flew the airplane was on their route check, and with passengers aboard.

The simulators had become very realistic, so much so that some pilots would become excited and shout when it seemed as though someone was going to stall or crash. The beauty of the simulator is that the instructor can load you up with problems until no pilot can handle them, yet the inevitable crash does not hurt a thing. You just start up and go at it again: wonderful for learning procedures, but still not quite an airplane. A friend of mine once said that there are two things that they will never build into a simulator. One is the G (gravity) forces that are felt in an airplane when it makes a tight turn or a sharp pull-up. The other is the feeling of stark terror when it seems the ground is rushing up to hit you.

My actual flight test for a rating in the 747 took only an hour and twenty minutes with F.A.A. inspector Dick Fulton.

My check trip, in March, was to Tokyo, on a route that was by then familiar to me. As we flew away from the coast I remarked to the check pilot that the airplane had a wonderful 'feel'. He reminded me that there were no mechanical connections between the wheel that I was holding and the control surfaces on the wings and tail. Boeing had done it all with hydraulic pressure. All the 'feel' was artificial, designed and built in by engineers just to satisfy us pilot types. It had four separate hydraulic systems, each with its own fluid supply, pumps, lines, and everything; and arranged in such a way that any two of the systems would operate all the essential components such as landing gear, flaps, leading edge flaps, brakes, and so on.

Landing At Thirty Feet

The only trouble that I found in learning to fly the 747 was that enormous height above the ground of the cockpit. On a landing the eye level was some twenty-nine feet above the runway. On all other airplanes I had had no trouble knowing where the wheels were in relation to the runway on approach. But the 747 took some getting used to in this respect. It was just difficult to tell how high the wheels were above the runway. Nearly all the pilots used the radar altimeter to help. The copilot would call off 'fifty feet' and 'thirty feet' from the radar altimeter. At 'fifty' you would pull the throttles closed, and at 'thirty' start to flare for landing. It was fairly mechanical, but it resulted in passably good landings until you learned where the wheels were, which usually took about three months.

On our way back to San Francisco the next to last landing on my check trip was at Honolulu. W.D. (Bill) Saulsberry, checking me, told me that on this landing he was going to cover up my radar altimeter, and make no call-outs. Also he was not even going to let me use the glide slope portion of the instrument landing system. He wanted me to do this landing purely by 'eyeball'.

I told him that was okay, but not to cover up his own radar altimeter. When he asked why not, I told him that he was going to have to read it to know when we were on the ground—pure bluff. I aimed the airplane at a point about one thousand feet from the approach end of the runway and, when I thought we had covered half that distance, I pulled the throttles back and then gently started to flare. The only indication that we had landed was a microswitch near the gear handle which clattered several times, not being able to make up its mind whether the gear was on the runway or not.

A stewardess came running up to the cockpit and said, "I've been on the 747 for eighteen months and that is the smoothest landing I have ever seen."

I told Bill that I had instructed her to come up and say that even if I had hit so hard that the landing gear struts came through the wings.

My joy at flying the 747 on the line myself did not last long. Bill Monan, the chief pilot flew with me on the last leg of my check trip and asked if I would be a check pilot on the type. I suggested that I would like to have three months of flying by myself before I started checking. This was in March, but I found myself checking other pilots in May; and April had been my vacation month, during which time the only thing I flew was a Cessna.

Low Ceiling, and Icy Runway

My first trip in command was on March 14. We were supposed to fly from San Francisco to Tokyo nonstop, but we had a heavy load and the westerly winds were strong, so we had to land for fuel in Anchorage, Alaska. The reported weather was as good as I had ever seen and I was glad of that. Anchorage reported, "No clouds and a visibility of sixty miles." I liked that, because I was restricted by what was known as a 'one-hundred-hour override'. Until a captain had one hundred hours on a given airplane type, his minimum weather was somewhat higher than normal. Whereas the normal minima at Anchorage were a two hundred foot ceiling and half a mile visibility, I had to use three hundred and three-quarters.

As we proceeded up the coast I apologized to the passengers for having to land in Anchorage for fuel, but thought they would enjoy it because the weather was so good and the sunset over Cook's Inlet would be very beautiful. I gave them the published report of "Sixty miles and no clouds." As we passed abeam of Seattle, I again checked the weather: "Sixty mile visibility and no clouds."

As we reached Middleton Island, about one hundred and thirty miles from Anchorage, which was our point to start descent, I once again asked for the weather, anticipating the same, only to be totally shocked by the reply.

"Anchorage weather is seven hundred and fifty feet overcast, visibility one mile, blowing snow, runway braking reported marginal."

We started the descent, and at about fifty miles out I requested another report: "Five hundred feet overcast, three-quarters of a mile visibility, braking poor." I did not wish to hear any more, as the visibility was already down to my minimum and seemed to be worsening. But soon another report was forwarded: "Now three hundred feet overcast and three-quarters of a mile visibility, heavy blowing snow, braking poor." I was at the absolute limit.

The rule was that if we were past the outer marker we were permitted to continue the approach down to minima even if the weather was reported to be below those limits. If, when we reached the minimum altitude, we could actually see the runway, we could land. Any weather reported to be below minima before we reached the outer marker precluded our continuing the approach.

You have probably guessed what happened next. Just as we were approaching the outer marker, here it came: "Two hundred feet overcast, half-mile visibility, braking nil." This is the time you earn your salary.

Discontinue the approach, pull up and go to your alternate? That would be the proper, legal decision. But our alternate was Fairbanks, only a couple of hundred miles north. What if this sudden weather change coming from the west hit Fairbanks before we get there—and maybe worse? Then we have nowhere else to go and will have to try a landing regardless of the weather. It will cost Pan Am many thousands of dollars for us to divert to Fairbanks, and the diversion may not be any safer for our passengers. Perhaps even dangerous?

I said to my crew, "I think there is something wrong with the radios, I didn't hear that transmission." I continued the approach and landed. I reasoned that I was fresh out of training and probably as sharp as I would ever be, and another one hundred hours on the 747 would not make me a safer pilot. I still think it was the right decision, though I knew when I did it that if we so much as blew a tire or did anything that triggered an investigation, then I was in trouble. If we had slid off the runway or anything like that, it could have been the end of my career.

As it was, we landed normally and those sixteen wheel brakes on the 747 helped us to stop in about three quarters of the run-way. I reported the braking to be 'fair'. Another airplane, a 707, landed just behind me and the pilot bawled me out for that report. He said he slid all over the runway and nearly did not stop at all. I told him that all I knew was that I pushed on the brake pedals and the airplane stopped. I considered that at least 'fair'.

The first time I ever saw all those wheels on the 747 I thought it strange, but they made for wonderful landings, reduced pressure on runways, and all those brakes made stopping much easier.

Five-Engined 747

There was also the Boeing 747SP. This was a 747 from which forty-seven feet, in two sections, fore and aft of the wing, had been removed from the length of the fuselage. It had the same wing, and as much fuel, but was shorter and weighed less, and therefore had more range. We considered it a great performer. I flew the first one seen at the Dallas-Fort Worth airport. It had what we called a 'fifth pod' on it. This was a way of carrying a spare engine from one place to another. Too big to go into a freight hold, the engine was hung under the wing between the fuselage and number three engine. It didn't function, it just hung there.

As I taxied out, one of the tower operators asked, "Clipper, what kind of airplane is that?"

"This is a Boeing 747SP."

"Oh." (pause) "What does the SP mean?"

"SP stands for Special Performance."

"Oh." (pause) "Why does it have five engines?"

"That's what makes the performance so special."

(above) The Boeing 747SP. Known as the 'Fat Albert' by its rival manufacturers, it was not a success, as its extreme long-range capability applied to only a handful of the world's routes. (left) The 'Fifth Engine'—the Boeing 747 could ferry an engine in this manner, thus saving freight charges for specialized loads.

Inertial Navigation

After I had flown the Boeing 747 for a year or so, we received inertial navigation systems (I.N.S.), a tremendous technical advance. When I started flying across the oceans we were still using the same celestial navigation that had been on the flying boats. Since then we had used, among other devices, LORAN, (Long-range radio navigation) which depended on earth-based stations, or Doppler, which used radar beams to and from the surface of the earth. An inertial system is totally self-contained. It calculates every movement that the airplane makes, in every direction, and decides, "If I started there, I must now be here."

They have to be aligned (told where they are) before every take off, a procedure that takes nearly twenty minutes, with the airplane standing still.

One pilot had a short layover in Pago Pago and allowed the flight engineer to align the system so that he himself could take a few minutes longer before going to the airport. The engineer put in the correct numbers, but failed to note that the latitude should have been south, not north, because Pago Pago is south of the equator. The pilots did not catch the error.

After they were en route to Honolulu the navigation information they received was nonsensical. The only thing to do was to dump about 100,000lb of fuel and return for a landing to re-align the navigation system.

The pilot on this flight was a good one but an egotist who thought he could not make such an error. On his written report he said as much and warned other pilots they too should be alert; and he offered to pay for the fuel if Pan Am would take it out of his pay a little at a time. I quote his last sentence: "If you intend to publish this letter in 'Cross Check' (a company publication) please edit it, because I can't spell for shit."

My log shows that I flew the first flight which used inertial navigation on the Honolulu to Tokyo route. We had previously flown some 'proving flights' with the inertial system. On one such flight to Hilo, Hawaii, I was instructing pilots on the use of the I.N.S. with the F.A.A. observing. The F.A.A. inspector had warned me that only the Doppler system that we were then using was approved, so if the two deviated by as much as twenty miles, we had to abandon the I.N.S. and use the Doppler. I had used the inertial system enough to know that it was much more accurate and reliable, so as we went along, if the Doppler showed us some miles off track, I would 'dial' out some of the difference while he was not looking. He would say, "That's odd, the difference was twelve miles, now it's only seven." "Yes," I would reply, "The Doppler position wanders back and forth like that." When we arrived at Hilo the inertial was within one mile of our actual position.

There is not much to say that was especially remarkable about the 747. It was such a dependable airplane that everything was routine and so consistently reliable.

Admittedly it took more finesse to make a power-off approach with the 747 than it did in the DC-8 or 707. Slowing for landing started earlier and required lowering of the flaps sooner. It was easy to be too early with the flaps and if that happened a small amount of power had to be added to compensate.

Auto-Brakes

After I had flown the Boeing 747 for some years, the manufacturer convinced Pan Am to put on an 'auto-brake' system, with the excuse that this saved tire wear by doing the braking instead of letting the pilot do it. Many of us hated the auto-brakes. As one said: "When I put the brakes on nobody knew it, now everybody knows."

The auto-brake system had three possible settings, Minimum, Medium, and Maximum. Those of us who disliked the system never used anything but Minimum. Even then we had some landings, like one of mine in Hong Kong, when the brakes locked and shook up everyone in the airplane with a panic stop. Usually I did not turn on the system at all, and all the check pilots knew that I did not use it.

I have in my file a report by a check pilot (my ex-copilot, W.G. Stovall) who wrote that he refused to grade me '100' unless I used the auto-brake system on at least one landing. I turned it on, but landed with my feet on the brake pedals. Any such usage would turn the auto-brakes off at once, so they stayed on for only a split-second.

They did give me one source of satisfaction. When landing before the introduction of auto-brakes, I normally started to brake as soon as the main wheels touched the runway, even though I was told many times not to use the brakes until the nose wheel was on the runway. But after we had the auto-brakes I was never told that again because they also did it my way. As soon as the main wheels spun up to 50rpm, the brakes came on.

Neither Boeing nor Pan Am ever gave us any figures to show that the auto-brakes saved tire wear.

Un-Check Pilot

I kept advocating a program to allow first officers to fly from the left seat, and such a program was finally approved, but for selected captains only and even then, only with certain first officers. I liked to do this, but on one flight I found out that I was not everybody's favorite.

I had been swapping left seat days alternately with this one crew member. True: I was not very fond either of him or his flying, but I did not know it showed so plainly. After several days when it was his turn, he told me he did not want to fly from the left, so I asked him if he did not like flying from the captain's seat. He answered, "Not with you, I don't. You act as though you're giving me a check flight." I told him that I would sit on the right and never say a word unless I felt that I had to take over the airplane for safety reasons, but that was not good enough for him. We just went back to my being the captain and letting him be the first officer. I was trying to help, but maybe I overdid it.

He spent his time trying to sell me a tax-avoidance scheme that I thought had at least the possibility of being on the far side of legality. He told me that he was paid $500 for each person that he signed up. I told him that I thought he was a parasite, living off of his fellow pilots. I hope he is never the pilot on a flight I intend to ride. I may just get off.

Too Old At Sixty

The age sixty rule was put into effect by the F.A.A. in about 1955. Many of us thought it then to be a mistake. There was little evidence to suggest that a pilot's ability deteriorates with time. Today, there is reliable evidence that the older pilots are the safest. The determination to terminate a pilot's career should be based on his physical examinations and his ratings on his flight checks each six-month period.

A United Air Lines pilot has safely brought back a Boeing 747 into Honolulu after the side had ripped off. He lost two engines, and apparently had some other problems as well. He was on his next to last trip before he reached age sixty, and performed superbly. How much sense does it make that, two weeks later, he was considered incompetent, by law, to fly that same airplane, or even to be permitted on the flight deck?

Single Crew 747

I had a fantasy about the Boeing 747. I wanted to fly one solo and would dream up opportunities to do that. Perhaps there would be a revolution in some country or other and I would be the only one who could reach the airport to save a Pan Am airplane. It could easily be flown by one pilot. The flight engineer's station could have been set up for automatic operation during take off, and all the necessary controls could be reached from either pilot seat. In flight the autopilot could take over while the pilot went back to make changes at the engineer's station, to change the fuel or the pressurization systems, but that would be a minor problem.

Minimum Load

The closest I ever was to flying a 747 solo was once out of Honolulu when, with eleven crew members, we had only one passenger. Our one passenger may have been a record low, although I expect there have been empty flights on one airline or another.

Maximum Height

On a Boeing 747SP nonstop from Honolulu to Dallas-Fort Worth we had a light load, so that toward the end of that flight we flew at 45,000 feet, which is the highest I ever went. This altitude, in fact, was then the legal limit for civilian aircraft.

Three-Engined 747

On another occasion, we had left Guatemala after dark and were on our way to Venezuela. Just as we leveled off at cruising altitude, No. 1 engine seized up with a bang. Jet engines can seize up with a 'quiet stall' or a 'noisy stall' but this one quit with a very loud bang, and flames shot forward past the cockpit as well as many feet aft of the engine. My crew and I at first pulled the classic "What did we hit?" but then realized that it was an engine failure. We shut it down and turned back for a landing at Guatemala City.

After arrival I walked back through the cabin and there sat one of our flight instructors, Vic McHenry, then retired and on a vacation trip with his wife. I had not known that he was on board. He was grinning at me as I walked down the aisle.

I said, "Vic, if I had known that you were on board I would have known that we were going to have trouble. Whenever you sat behind me all kinds of things happened; engines quit or caught fire, gears would not go down, the pressurization system failed, or all of the above."

He laughed and said that his wife had been concerned about how the airplane would land with three engines and he had assured her it would land just the same as with four.

As soon as I was checked out on the 747, I started giving landings to our third pilots, those who were aboard for relief on long flights. After I had been flying the airplane for six months I received a letter from the chief pilot. It said in part: "Our records show that you have six months on the 747. You may *now* give take offs and landings to second officers."

The Long Stretch

The only criticism I had of the 747 was that it would fly for so long. Fifteen and one-half hours from Sydney, Australia, to Los Angeles is a long and tiring flight, even though we had bunks in the cockpit, or could use a first-class seat in the cabin. Sometimes, when I tried to catch a few winks, my muscles would twitch, causing my legs to jerk, and wake me up. If there were any problems anticipated at the destination, such as fuel usage or weather, I found it difficult to rest properly. The very best time out of the cockpit was to sit in first-class and have a good meal.

I know that some have said that foreign airlines serve the best meals, but I would never want anything better than Pan Am's first-class service. Hors d'oeuvres, prime rib sliced at your table, well-cooked vegetables, choices of desserts, and all the trimmings. Maybe the fact that I was raised on a ranch where a bowl of beans and cornbread was a scrumptious meal had something to do with my opinion.

Two Hours to Learn

On a Boeing 747 trip from New Delhi to Hong Kong we stopped at Bangkok, and learned that a Boeing 707 was in Singapore with a mechanical delay, and, some one hundred and eighty passengers were stranded. We were asked if we would extend our flight time enough to land in Singapore and pick up these passengers. My crew was willing to do so and eager to help, but two hours elapsed while working through the approval of our New York office and obtaining the Thai government's permission. When all that was done I was informed that there would be yet another two hours' delay. I wanted to know why and was told that Singapore had never handled a 747 and provisioning would have to be done in Bangkok.

I said we were ready to go and were leaving now, either to Singapore or Hong Kong, but were not extending our day another two hours. "But how will the airplane be provisioned?" I said, "Easy, wire Singapore that they have two hours (our flight time) to learn how to put food on a 747."

When we arrived they had huge trays of sandwiches and fruit and nearly everybody was content. All our passengers were happy except for one man, who thought we had deviated from our route only to sell more tickets. One of our stewardesses had to spend an hour explaining how those passengers in Singapore would have been stuck for an extra day if we had not picked them up.

Light on her feet

The Boeing 747 was never meant to be aerobatic but, like a plump lady who is light on her feet, it could be agile. On one occasion, I was a bit high on a landing approach on a cargo flight into Los Angeles and the first officer gave me his opinion: I should go around.

"No, I am going to slip it."

A firm pressure on the control wheel to the left along with positive right rudder and the gentle giant obediently rolled into a beautiful side slip. Having lost some hundred feet or so, she straightened out to kiss the runway with a soft touch-down.

The tower operator, who was undoubtedly a pilot, exclaimed, "Very impressive, Clipper."

Back To Texas

In January 1973, Helen died of a sudden stroke. I had two young daughters at home in San Francisco, but the rest of my family were in Texas. I flew for some months leaving two young girls at home alone while I was away for eight or more days. Then I decided to move back to Denton, Texas, where Nancy, the elder one still with me at home, could go to college and help take care of Joanne, the youngest. My eldest daughter, Alice, already lived and worked in Denton, so that was extra comfort. I ended up commuting from Texas to Los Angeles.

Pan Am had many commuter pilots living in faraway places. Some lived in Mexico, Alaska, Tahiti, Sydney, and even in Spain. If you were senior enough to bid for long trips with long times off between them it was not too bad. I really preferred to live closer to my work, but this move seemed necessary for family reasons.

I suppose you would say that I am nothing if not a loyal Pan Am person because in April 1974, I married again, and again to another fellow employee. Dolle had been employed by Pan Am for some seventeen years and was now a crew scheduler. Some said that she had been telling me where to go for years, so she might as well continue to do so at home. She could often tell me after I had flown if my copilot was good or not. We seldom disagreed on that, and she said she could tell because of how he acted in the office.

About three years before I retired we moved to a small town in West Texas. Fort Davis is a small country town of ranchers with a few retired people from other areas. When I first moved there I was often asked where I worked. When I said, "Los Angeles," there were some strange reactions. I would have to explain that I only went to work about twice a month and that I could leave Fort Davis and be in Los Angeles about four hours later. I flew my Cessna to El Paso (an hour and twenty minutes) and caught an airliner to LAX (two hours). So I commuted a total of about sixteen hours per month, at the most. Many suburban dwellers commute many more hours to their jobs in the city, and some as many in a week.

Leaving London one morning for Los Angeles, my son, Ken, was a passenger with us. At the crew briefing with flight service I mentioned that there would be four people in the cockpit. The purser, an English girl, said, "Oh, is the F.A.A. aboard?" I told her that she could call him F.A.A., but that he had a bushy beard and if he happened to call me "Dad" to think nothing of it, it was just the way he talked.

When we reached Los Angeles I turned in toward the runway too soon and could not comfortably get down on the first approach. This was the only time I remember when I had to go around in good weather for a second approach with a Boeing 747. A.T.C. being what is at Los Angeles, this took fifteen minutes. After we shut down at the blocks, and were coming down the spiral staircase, and in front of all the passengers, this purser turned to me and said, "Captain, I'm sure glad you didn't let your son make that second approach!"

Farewell To Boeing

My last trip for Pan American Airways was in April 1981, piloting a Boeing 747. The trip was scheduled over a period of several days and everywhere we went the hotels put on a special spread for me and my wife and our crew. Dolle had been a crew scheduler for Pan Am for so many years that she knew more of the flight service personnel than I did. One of the crew, Nelda Jane Van Tour, had managed to bid for this trip just so that she could be with us for the last goodbye. There were flowers in our room and cakes in the dining room. Nelda Jane had arranged much of that.

The last leg was one of those backbreakers—non-stop from Sydney to Los Angeles. I really hated to walk off that last airplane knowing that I could never fly one of those magnificent flying machines again or, legally, even enter the cockpit in flight.

It seems strange that an airline pilot, in contrast to nearly all other jobs, is expected to be up to speed to the very end, flying, as I did, a long demanding flight to the last day, and then abruptly be deemed to be unsuitable for further use.

Perhaps the Lord will give me a 747 instead of wings.

Unions

No book about airlines would be complete without mentioning something about unions. They seem to be an integral part of the aviation industry. Yet the subject is extremely sensitive. Strong opinions can be found for and against unionism, and some persons involved can find little scope for compromise. In an airline some system had to be found to prevent favoritism in promotions, schedules, or other factors affecting a pilot's life. In spite of its drawbacks, a union seems to be the best answer.

Pan American was a non-union airline when I was first employed in 1942. A year or so later, we voted for the Air Line Pilot's Association (ALPA) to represent us. I joined at that time and, while not a strong union man, I have been, over the years, quite proud of ALPA.

I thought it was good for the industry in improving safety of airplanes and of flights. It was in the forefront of accident investigations, often bringing out facts and causes that might otherwise have been overlooked. In the early days, an accident could only too easily be blamed on the pilot. The true facts were often not readily apparent.

During the early years we often worked between twenty to twenty-five days per month; and with Pan American, that meant being away from home a great deal because most of our trips could last from several days to more than a week; a month on overseas flights. At the same time, some rest intervals at an overnight stop were short, occasionally less than eight hours.

Through our representatives at ALPA we succeeded in negotiating a minimum layover time of nine hours and thirty minutes. Our contract eventually gave us half a month off from flying. We could still go to school or take training on those days off, but we were not supposed to be away from the base for more than fifteen days per month.

ALPA negotiated single rooms for us at hotels—no more having to share a room with someone who wanted to read with the light on when you needed your sleep. Probably the best thing they did for pilots was to initiate a bidding system which allowed pilots to have some control over home life, at least those senior enough to benefit from the bidding system. We had some chance, at least, to be home for the wife's birthday, wedding anniversary, the birth of a child, or Christmas.

My starting pay as a copilot was $200 per month and as a starting captain was $604 per month. Pay today depends upon flight time, equipment flown, seniority, and individual airline. Suffice it to say that it is many times as much, though in recent years some contracts have resulted in reductions in both pay and work rules.

The news media makes much of how few hours a pilot works, but they only refer to actual flight hours, time on the ground is not counted. A better criteria is how much duty time a pilot puts in away from home or at the airport involved in activities such as training.

Pan Am pilots would usually exceed the contractual hours to take a flight to its scheduled destination, because of unforeseeable delays due to weather, minor maintenance problems, or sequential connection snags. I have put in many periods of eighteen to twenty hours on duty. We always had the right to stop a flight for rest if necessary, but most of us would stay with it as long as we thought it safe to do so.

My main disagreement with union members was with those individuals who abuse the rules, who would delay others for no reason other than to

During a stop at Guatemala City (Flight 502 from Panama to Houston), Ned Wilson (left), C.J. Dodge (center, second pilot), and Ed Swenson (chief pilot, Houston base), pose for the camera during a period when the Air Line Pilots Association (ALPA) was engaged in a dispute with the Flight Engineers International Association (F.E.I.A.). The DC-8s at this time had a crew of four, including three pilots.

Ned Wilson meets Charles Willard, veteran member of the American Aviation Pioneers, in 1974 in the flight deck of a Boeing 747. Willard's pilot's license was No. 4. He flew in the Dole Race in 1927—and was one of the fortunate survivors of that ill-fated enterprise.

exercise their 'contractual rights'. One afternoon I was on a flight from Los Angeles to New York. We were already about an hour late but finally ready to go, or so I thought. With all the passengers on board and all ten doors shut, I called on the interphone for the tractor driver to push us off the gate. Nobody answered. Finally I called PANOP (Pan American Operations) on the radio, "There seems to be nobody on the ground to push us back from the gate." "Captain, they are off on a coffee break."

Coffee break! Delaying three hundred passengers who are already late, so that the ground crew can have coffee! I waited another fifteen minutes while passengers sat in the airplane—hot, angry and disturbed—and I didn't blame them. I was so mad that I resolved to try and have someone fired when I returned the next day.

Fat chance! It seems that these ground workers had a contract that guaranteed them two coffee breaks per eight-hour shift. They had been on duty seven hours and thirty minutes and had taken only one coffee break. Their shop foreman insisted that they take the second one because, "If they didn't take it, they lost it."

One night in New York we were delayed because, for some reason or another, no cleaners were there to sweep up and clean the airplane. They had been called, but were not on the scene and we were delaying the flight until they arrived. I thought that a run-through with a broom would be acceptable, if not the very best. My cockpit crew and I had done our work and were ready to go. I suggested that we each be given a broom and that we would sweep out the cabin. Some ground crew union members on board said, "Captain, if you so much as touch a broom, we will all walk off the airplane."

At times when a contract had expired and we were trying to renew it a few real 'union-types' would try to persuade us to 'slow-down'. Such tactics could have added several minutes to a flight, flying through a complete instrument approach at every stop, for example, a matter of about fifteen minutes. Or we could simply pull back on the throttles in cruise.

My response to this was that if they felt we should stop work and go out on strike that I would reluctantly join them, but I was not about to slow down. If the majority was willing to forego their pay to make a point, that was one thing, but I was not about to turn in less than a full day's work for a day's pay, to the best of my ability. That was the way my father had taught me.

Once out of Maiquetía, Venezuela, we were one person short of the required flight service personnel. A 747 had ten doors and a certain number of these must be manned on each take off by persons trained to open the doors and operate the escape slides. The number depended on the number of passengers, and on this flight we needed eight flight service people but only had seven.

Our flight service crew did not want to leave the hotel, but I told them that the company was undoubtedly searching but it did not know where this person might come from. I suggested that they should come on to the airport. I knew I had trouble when I arrived at the airport and found that they were still at the hotel. I called the purser by telephone and told her that she might possibly refuse the flight, but she had no right to refuse to come to the airport.

While waiting for them to show up, I talked with our flight engineer, Jack Grimshaw. He was a check engineer and had a student who, as far as I could tell, was doing fine. I asked if he was agreeable to approving the student for certification as the flight engineer. He said that he was.

"Fine; then, as that makes you an extra cockpit crew member, will you sit in the back on take off and operate the over-the-wing emergency exit?" This particular exit was the most complicated to operate, and Jack knew more about those doors, in my opinion, than did any member of the flight service crew. He said that he would do it.

When the cabin crew arrived at the airport I explained what I intended to do. The purser told me that they were not going because she did not consider it legal. I said, "Fine, but before you tell me that you won't go, let me tell you that I do consider it legal. Now, tell me if you are going to refuse to fly."

They decided to go, but told me that when we arrived in San Francisco they would turn me in to both the F.A.A. and the company. The station manager asked me if I wanted to request approval from our offices in New York to do this. I told him, "No, I am going to do it in any case. I want to get these passengers out of here." I said that he could just advise New York of my actions if he wanted to do so, to clear his own skirts.

Just after take off the station manager relayed a message to us from New York, "We concur in the captain's actions, and tell him 'thank you'."

I participated in only one strike. I was caught in London when everyone throughout the Pan Am system stopped work. The company agreed to continue to pay our expenses and to pay for our hotel rooms if we would stay in place; they would need us there when the strike was settled. Most of us stayed for at least several days. One pilot was F.I.Jacobs, who had hired me. He was not a union member, and was on his last flight as he would be sixty years old in just a few days. The company asked him if he would operate a flight back to New York.

He told them that he would sure like to fly that last flight home, but would not do so unless the union approved. He remained in London until his birthday, hoping each day that the strike would be over. Then he went home on another airline's flight. We gave him a big party before he left. I admired his attitude, and was not sure that I could have done the same thing.

Because of the time difference, it was about two am each day before we found out if there had been any progress toward settlement. We would gather together at that time and make a telephone call to ALPA headquarters to catch up on the day's proceedings.

After five days I decided that I was not going to stay there any longer and made contact with T.W.A. for a ticket home. I found that it would not take me because I did not have a valid passport. At the time I was using an International Crew Card to cross national frontiers, and I was no longer a crew member.

One more day's delay to visit the American Embassy for a passport, which was issued in about four hours. The next morning I showed up at British Immigration. The officer took a long look at my passport, which had no stamp of any kind on it, and said, "Oh, I say, how did you get into Britain?"

While I was still considering the proper answer, he continued, "Oh, yes, you are unemployed, aren't you?" I agreed that I was, indeed, unemployed. And he promptly stamped my passport. I love the British. In some countries that could have occasioned several hours of hassle.

I did not always agree with ALPA's actions but I am proud of many of the stands that it took in the industry, and we would have been in bad shape without it. I have acted as a local council chairman and as membership chairman for all of Pan Am. There was a rule that, if a member ever dropped out, he had to pay all back dues before he would be accepted back as a member. If a person was out for several years that could amount to such a huge sum that it prohibited a return. I managed to reach an agreement that would permit those back dues to be repaid at $15 per month and a substantial number of members were able to return.

Look Ma, No Engine

Perhaps you think that because I was an airline pilot that I oppose smaller airplanes flying around. Nothing could be further from the truth. About ninety-eight percent of all airplanes flying through our skies are privately owned and operated. A mere two percent belong to the airlines. And the safety records of private fliers are good and have been improving each year for a long time. The air traffic rules apply to all aircraft in the sky. An airliner is not supposed to receive preferential treatment.

Recently the press made a big deal over what it called a 'near miss' at an airport near my home. In the wee hours of the morning the tower at this airport was closed. An arriving airliner found ahead of him a small airplane already in the traffic pattern and the airliner circled the field once before he landed. The newspaper made a fuss over the fact that the airliner had to make a '360-degree turn to miss the smaller craft'. Well, that is exactly what would have happened if the tower *had* been operating. The first airplane had the right-of-way, the second had to give way to him, and the tower would have issued instructions accordingly. In this case, the two pilots followed the regulations and handled the situation on their own. Only ignorance caused the press to build up the situation into something sinister.

In a year when deaths in airline accidents amounted to one hundred and fifty-one the press and radio reported "a bad year for safety of the airlines," ignoring the fact that there were more than 45,000 deaths on our highways during the same period.

Airline traffic is separated from smaller craft by altitude. Airliners invariably operate at very high levels far above every-one else; and all flights above 18,000 feet (about three and a half miles) (Positive Control Area) are controlled by Air Traffic Control (A.T.C.) in all weather conditions. Only when close to major airports do the airliners mix with private and other smaller aircraft. The F.A.A. has addressed this by promoting rules that attempt to keep the non-airline traffic out of the immediate vicinity of the major airports by directing the smaller aircraft to 'satellite airports'. The separate flight patterns can often come into conflict and this can be more dangerous than allowing aircraft to land at the same airports with certain controlled conditions.

All that is necessary, in my opinion, and the opinion of a fine air traffic controller I know, is a separate runway at the major airport that need not be very long, perhaps 4,000 to 6,000 feet, and located so that the approach will not interfere with airline approaches. Height can then be used to separate them further, with the big ships coming toward the airport at above 2,000 feet and the smaller ones at under 1,000 feet. They could also have separate control towers if desired.

Mayan Airstrips

Some of my most memorable flights have been in light airplanes. One summer, along with three family members, we flew two Cessna 170s to southern Mexico, into Bonampak, site of some beautiful Mayan ruins. The short, narrow runway was just being cleared and was flanked on either side by still smoldering tree-stumps. An approach had been cleared through the tall trees at only one end, and burning stumps were still in place there, too.

As we approached the runway, it was like flying down a canyon into an inferno. There was no way to go around, as the trees on the far end were at least one hundred and fifty feet high, too tall to climb over. It was land or else. My nephew and I went in first, but there was no place to turn off the runway to clear the way for the second plane. So we sat there on the far end, watching my two brothers land straight into us. They were distracted by our presence and bounced the airplane. It turned sideways and we could see the numbers painted on the side, but they straightened it out and stopped on the dirt strip just before they hit us.

Another time my two sons and I flew into Yaxchilán, Mayan ruins right on the border of Mexico and Guatemala. The grass strip there followed the bank of the Usumacinta River, and it was necessary to fly below the tops of the trees on both sides of the river, and to follow a curve until the strip came into sight. There was no other way to see these ruins unless you wanted to come many miles by boat, as there was no road. After we visited the ruins and were ready to leave, we discovered that the engine would not start. I envisioned waiting there for days until someone could fly in to help. Fortunately it was a minor problem and we soon fixed it.

I like small airplanes and have owned five of them, as well as three gliders. Many airline pilots will not even consider getting into a single-engined airplane. They don't know what they're missing. When he was a check pilot, Roger Sherron said that he could always tell if a man also flew light airplanes just by the way he handled an airliner. To some he would simply say, "What kind of light 'plane do you fly?" The difference is a subtle one, that perhaps can best be described as that between a 'pilot' and an airplane 'driver'.

If I have a trip of more than half a day's drive, I would rather fly my Cessna 180. It's easier than driving, more relaxing, and safer.

Thermals and Waves

I had wanted to fly gliders ever since I learned to fly, but had never got around to it. Houston was not an ideal location, but now (1964) I was in San Francisco and had a chance, at a glider airport near Fremont on the east side of the Bay. I could spare time from 707 training and went to the gliderport to meet Les Arnold, who owned the place. He assigned me to a flight instructor named Ruth, as I remember, and she was the only female flight instructor I ever had. She flew with me twice, mostly showing me what to do on tow behind the tow-plane. She was nice enough to say that she liked to have airline pilots as students because they were usually smoother on the controls.

On my first solo glider flight I did not realize that the light aircraft was not going to roll very far after I touched down because it did not have enough kinetic energy. When I landed, it came to a stop about a hundred yards from where I was supposed to be, where even the novice pilots managed to stop. They helped me roll it to the line that time, but told me I would be granted that courtesy only once. If I landed short after that I had to roll it up my myself.

I had planned to obtain my 707 rating and the glider rating the same day, but the 707 flight was delayed until too late in the day to fly the glider flight. So the next day Les Arnold, who was also a flight examiner for the F.A.A., gave me a commercial pilot rating for gliders.

Ten Hours Flight Time

I could fly gliders, but I did not know how to soar them;I had to learn to climb in thermals and find other kinds of lift. One day one of Les's flight instructors, John Slingerland, told me he would tow me to where a mountain wave was working and let me try staying up in that. He towed me over the hills from Fremont and I could see several gliders far above us. John waggled his rudder at me, which was a sign that I should release from the tow. There seemed to be a little lift, but I was not climbing fast enough until I spotted a small single-place glider of the same type I was flying (a Schweizer 1-26) far above me. It had a red tail and seemed to be higher than everybody else, so I flew right under it and followed its every move. Sure enough, I was gaining altitude and eventually climbed to the same height. As we passed back and forth we would dip wings to each other.

I tired of it all and returned to the gliderport. I waited until the other 1-26 came in for a landing and walked out to meet the pilot, who turned out to be a young man about twenty years old. I told him that I had been following him around to learn how to fly a wave, and he said pleasantly that I seemed to be doing all right. I asked him how much flight time he had. "Ten hours," he said. "You mean ten hours in gliders?" "Yes." So I asked him how much power time he had, and he said that he had never been in a powered airplane. Then he asked me how much flight time I had, whereupon I thought I was wanted on the 'phone and I'd see him later. I was not about to tell him that I had about 25,000 hours.

No Way to Fall

John Slingerland was an ex-Marine and he had only one foot, but he was an excellent glider instructor and one of Les Arnold's best salesmen. If you called on the telephone to ask how flying was, he would tell you how great everybody was doing. "Everyone is staying up and there is no way you could fall down today!" The truth might be that there was no lift and all flights were landing right back, soon after take off, but John was always optimistic.

One day a pilot called John from his car telephone. The weather was awful; drizzle and rain with low clouds. Absolutely no day to fly gliders, but John was giving his usual spiel about how great it was. The car pulled up in front of John's office, and the door was open; the caller said, "John! Turn around." John looked out the door, saw the car telephone and never missed a beat. He said, "Come on in, if you've got enough nerve to fly today, I've got enough nerve to tow you."

Outlanding

My son Ken came to visit and I wanted to give him a ride in a glider, so we went to Fremont. It was an overcast day with a cloud ceiling at about twenty-five hundred feet and with a light drizzle—not a good day to fly gliders. But Ken was going to be there only for the one day, so we prepared to fly anyway. We were lined up behind the tow-plane, ready for take off, when Les Arnold held up his hand to hold the tow-plane. He came over, opened the canopy, and said, "Ned, the area is sure wet today, it would be hard to get you out of some farmer's field, so don't land off the airport." I assured him that I had never landed off field yet and did not intend to start doing so today. He said "Okay" and motioned to the tow-plane to start.

I released near Mission Peak and made a couple of turns in what I thought might be lift, but wasn't. Then I took one look at the airport and immediately recognized that it would be touch-and-go whether or not I could make it back. Still half a mile away from the airport, I had only about two hundred feet of altitude left and had to cross both a busy freeway and a high power line. I did not risk it and instead landed in a very wet plowed field. It had not been more than twenty minutes since we had taken off, and I had Les on the telephone.

"Yes, Ned, where are you?"

I told him I was just across the freeway from where he was. He flew over in a tow-plane to take a look, but waved his hand to indicate that he could not tow me out, but soon showed up with a trailer and crew to disassemble the glider. It took more than half an hour and we all were muddy and cold before the glider was on the trailer.

So much for my first landing off airport in a glider. Les was a good sport, and charged me only $25 total. This was in spite of the fact that he had signs in the office saying that any off-field landing would be charged for the glider rental by the hour until it was back on the field, plus a fee of $25.

My friend Roger Sherron owned a Schweizer 1-26 and allowed me to fly it several times. He even let me fly it on an attempt to earn my 'Silver Badge' from the Soaring Society of America. That required a flight of only fifty kilometers (thirty-two miles) cross-country. I tried it several times with his glider, but never made it, and finally bought my own glider, a Laister LP-49 manufactured by Jack Laister in Los Angeles.

Diamond Goal

Much later, in 1967, Roger and I were flying on a summer day at Truckee, California, and I was now up to trying to make a 'Diamond Goal' flight which required a distance of 300 kilometers (187 miles). I had tried several times to the east from Truckee and had failed every time. My brother, Pat, who was also there, had towed me home using his Cessna 182.

Roger suggested that I try to the north. The country appeared awfully rough to me if I had to land out, but Roger said there were landing places in the small valleys between the mountain ranges. And so began one of the most interesting flights I ever made.

I was off tow about eleven-thirty in the morning, but could not make myself cut the apron strings and leave the field area until about twelve-thirty. Then I started slowly to the north. I had declared Ravendale, California, for my turn point, one hundred and four miles out. I worked every little scrap of lift I could find, a procedure known by glider pilots as 'tiptoeing'. Moving in that way, I finally made it to Ravendale and took a picture of the airport to prove I had been there and looked at my watch. "Good gosh, it's four-thirty!" It had taken four hours to go one hundred miles, and if I expected to get back to Truckee I would have to do it in the next two hours because the lift would die by then.

There was only one thing to do. I would have to fly much more aggressively, that is to say, faster, even though by doing so I rapidly lost altitude. I ignored areas with weak lift and headed towards those that looked better. I actually held out little hope of getting all the way back, but I sighted the airport at Reno, Nevada. However, a big thunderstorm was raging over the field, and lightning was striking the runways. I headed in that direction under the side of the storm, but not in it. I found good lift there and climbed to 12,000 feet. The air from there to Truckee looked very stable, with no lift, and Truckee itself was at 7,000 feet above sea level. I set out, conserving every foot. The prospects looked very questionable.

I called Roger on the radio and told him where I was, how high, and asked him if he thought I could make it to Truckee, as there were few places in between to land. He advised me to detour by a certain mountain, and said that there was often some lift in that area, even late in the day. I followed his advice, found no lift, but at least I did not lose altitude for more than a mile ('zero sink') and, with that slender advantage, I reached the airport with only three hundred feet of altitude left.

My Truckee—Ravendale round trip, more than six hours to fly two hundred and eight miles, was not the greatest flight in the world. I have made longer ones since, but none from which I derived such satisfaction. It was an exhilarating experience, as was the champagne celebration that followed, including steaks at a 'cook-your-own' place.

I sometimes thought that I should write an article called, 'Confessions of a Slow Learner'. When I started flying gliders I was always sure that the thermal that I found at the edge of the airport was the only one in the sky. If I did venture out of gliding range back to the airport and by chance found another thermal, I was sure that it would quit before I climbed high enough to make it home. I would waste time working each one for the very last foot because I just knew there were no others.

With time I learned to be some judge of the sky so that I could tell when the lift was reliable enough to move out on a cross-country flight. And, having moved out, to tell when conditions were weakening and that I had better start for home while there was still a chance of reaching the field. The secret is to know when to 'shift gears'.

Sawmill Landing

In 1975, on a soaring adventure at Taos, New Mexico, some of us were trying to fly more than three hundred miles along the Sangre de Cristo mountain range. Together with another glider flown by a pilot named Bill, I became trapped in a valley near Amalia, a small lumber mill town. We could both stay aloft, but were having trouble achieving enough altitude to climb out over the mountains that hedged the valleys, and there were only a few possible landing sites. Over the radio we discussed our options, and decided not to go back to the only landing field within reach, as it was a small dirt strip with a reputation for bad crosswinds. We rejected several roads, and an unfinished housing development with streets but no houses, because there might be utility wires we could not see.

I spotted a fairly large square area that happened to be clear of obstacles and more or less flat, and with what appeared to be a truck road across the middle of it. Not having much choice, we decided to land there. Bill was a little lower than I was and made the first approach. I saw a plume of dust as he touched down, and then he became airborne again, crossed over the road and touched down once again. I asked him if he was all right and he said, "I think so."

"Any damage to your sailplane?"

"No, I think it's okay."

I told him that I would land and try to roll up alongside him. Then he said, "Okay, but watch that road, it is four feet deep!" Actually, it was about eighteen inches deep, but that would have been enough to seriously damage our sailplanes. I landed beyond the road. Then we began to evaluate just where we had landed. There was a six-foot chainlink fence all around the area and a few buildings. We were inside a lumber mill and the area we had selected for landing was where they normally stored logs.

We finally found the night watchman, a big, burly fellow who was quite surprised to see us. We asked to use the telephone, but it was locked up in the office and he had no key. We asked him to open the gate so we could walk the two miles to town for help. He said we were not going anywhere until his boss arrived. "And when will that be?" "Monday morning." It was just about dark on a Friday night, and it was turning cold.

Bill's wife showed up at the gate with his trailer. She had been listening in on our radio conversations and figured out where to look for us. We thought we had it made when we talked the guard into letting her into the yard. We dismantled Bill's ship, loaded it on the trailer and started to the gate, whereupon the guard closed and padlocked the gate, announcing that we were not going anywhere!

After a big ruckus and a shouting match, the guard allowed Bill and his wife to leave with their trailer, but I had to agree to stay there with my sailplane, locked inside the yard. In town they found the manager of the lumber yard, who came to my rescue. As it was dark by then, he located some pickup trucks to provide light, asked how many men would be needed to help, and would I come to spend the night in his home. In every case where I have landed away from an airport I have been welcomed, helped, fed, and treated royally, except by that guard at the lumber yard. The manager, Mr Sedlack, laughed and said that they had had some pilfering and had instructed the guard that if he ever found anyone on the grounds, to hold them until management arrived. He had never dreamed that an aircraft might land there. In fact, he had already been told that there were two aircraft in his lumber mill and had dismissed the report as fiction because he had not heard any airplanes flying over that very quiet valley.

My brother Pat also landed near Amalia a year or so later, but in a small cotton field. He said a man drove up in a pickup almost before he stopped rolling. He said, "Gliders have landed here before. I know you need help. Here is my pickup, here are my kids, and here is my toolbox. I have to get back to the filling station. Just bring them all by the station when you get through." That was a normal reaction, but not as much fun as my lumber yard.

Contests

I found glider contest flying to be the most challenging. With fifty or sixty competing sailplanes, you are usually assigned to fly a route of between one hundred to three hundred miles. With a timed start and a timed finish the winner is the one who can complete the course in the shortest time. You are only allowed a tow to two thousand feet and the rest is up to you. You may not like the route, the terrain, or the weather, but you go. It is called by some 'the sport of kings', but in a contest it sometimes seems more like 'the sport of slaves'. But when you finish the course, no matter if you are first or last, you do feel like a king.

There is no adequate way to describe the feeling of being a hundred or more miles from where you started, possibly over hostile terrain, and the only way to return is to navigate, by skill, by experience, by some kind of sixth sense (and with per-haps a little luck), the complex, invisible currents of air that make up the sky.

I am often perplexed by questions that people ask. Can I go only where the wind blows me? If I am flying for a hundred miles or more, am I towed all the way? When I say I have been above 30,000 feet in a glider, even pilots may ask, "Do you carry oxygen?" Of all people, they should know that you would be dead if you did not. The classic question, though, is when you land away from an airport and the first person to see you asks, "Did the wind quit?" The best answer is, "Yes, the wind quit." Otherwise you will spend the rest of your day trying to explain by what strange manner the motorless airplane can stay aloft and make its way across the country.

If you land in a farmer's field, children will show up, armed with a camera. Never make the mistake of thinking they want a picture of *you* in the glider; they want a picture of *them* in the glider.

Border to Border

Why would anyone want to fly a sailplane from the Mexican border to the Canadian border? I suppose the correct answer is like that of the mountain climber; because it is there. There was no prize to be won, no record to be set, and in fact it would not even be a first. Three of the pilots on this trip had done it in 1980. In my case it was because I was asked. I was flattered by being included in a flight with pilots for whom I had the highest regard.

For whatever reason, this flight was one of the most memorable that I ever made. For personal identification, glider pilots use the numbers assigned to their gliders. The group who made this trip went like this: a Janus two-place ship—Zulu 9 (Z9), flown by Dr Jim Crisp and Terry Blankenship; Me Too (M2) flown by Darrel Watson; Whiskey Four (W4) flown by Werner Berkelbach, and I was November Whiskey (NW). We were accompanied by Bill Shurley, flying a Cessna Agwagon, who furnished tows each morning.

The border to border flight got under way on June, 10, 1990. The objective was to make an enjoyable trip of it; no competition, no record flights. We were determined to fly as a group, helping each other along, over a reasonable distance each day. The challenge would come from flying over different territories and with different conditions on each flight.

Towing off from Marfa, Texas (close to where I now live) we touched the Rio Grande River, the Mexican border, south of Sierra Blanca, Texas, and turned north, passing east of El Paso to enter a narrow corridor between restricted areas on the route from El Paso to Alamogordo, New Mexico. As we approached the corridor, cloud cover increased until it was totally overcast and, in fact, began to rain in the corridor. Near the town of Orogrande, we spotted a long, wide, dirt strip that none of us had known was there. Zulu Nine asked if we should return to it and land, but the consensus was to continue. In the rain there were areas of zero sink which enabled us to reach Alamogordo with adequate altitude.

After two or three hours on the ground we spotted the welcome sight of four trailers coming down the highway. Shirley Crisp and Shay Blankenship crewed for Z9; Wally Watson and his daughter Renee for M2; Dorothy Birkelbach for W4; and my wife Dolle and our dog Spunky for me. The crews were an essential part of this trek and did an excellent job, convoying down the road while keeping in touch with each other and their pilots on the radio. They drove almost twice the distance that we flew.

Bill Shurley not only towed every day but also acted as contact between us and our crews when we were beyond radio range. He also stopped quite often along the way to call ahead to our intended landing spot and make hotel reservations. A congenial, helpful, competent pilot, he deserves much credit for the success of this trip.

Our first attempt from Alamogordo to Taos, New Mexico, ended with all of us towing off and being unable to sustain, so we waited a day. This flight was one of the longest, but caused very little anxiety. Me Too seemed to be slow getting under way (Dolle said they could see him low in the foothills of Sierra Blanca peak as they drove down the highway). But once up, he settled into the lead showing the way past Santa Fe and into the Taos valley.

At Taos a tradition was born. From the notes of Wally Watson: "When the soaring is over, it's time to EAT! This group was on the search for the perfect dessert. 'Pie' became the battle cry, starting with mud pie at Ogilvie's. Fabulous! The Janus and the LS-6 were equipped with high-tech, whiz-bang computers and, during the first several days there was constant radio chatter asking, "What does your computer say?" "How high do we need to be to make the next airport?", and "How far out are we?". Neither Birkelbach nor I had computers. One night at supper someone asked Werner how his ship was equipped. He said that he had a McCready ring but was not using it. Then he made one of the best comments of the trip, "You need to know only two things about soaring: When you are low, you need to climb, and when you are high, you can fly fast." Werner Birkelbach was the one most people were interested in. He was 70 years old, and had been a glider pilot in two invasions during World War II, everyone wanted to talk to him.

As the days went on, we each had our good days and bad days. Listen to Terry Blankenship:

"On the leg from Taos to Gunnison, Col., Z9 had a hard time getting away from Taos and nearly landed at Questa. We were very low, but not in danger because the landing strip was right under us, but none of us wanted to land out. On that same flight, we had to cross the valley south of Salida and northwest of the Great Sand Dunes. I had flown that same course ten years before and knew to expect trouble. We were on the west slope of the Sangre de Cristo

Ned Wilson, on tow in his Laister LP.15 Nugget, built by Jack Laister, of El Monte, California.

Ned Wilson goes through the checks before a tow in the Laister.

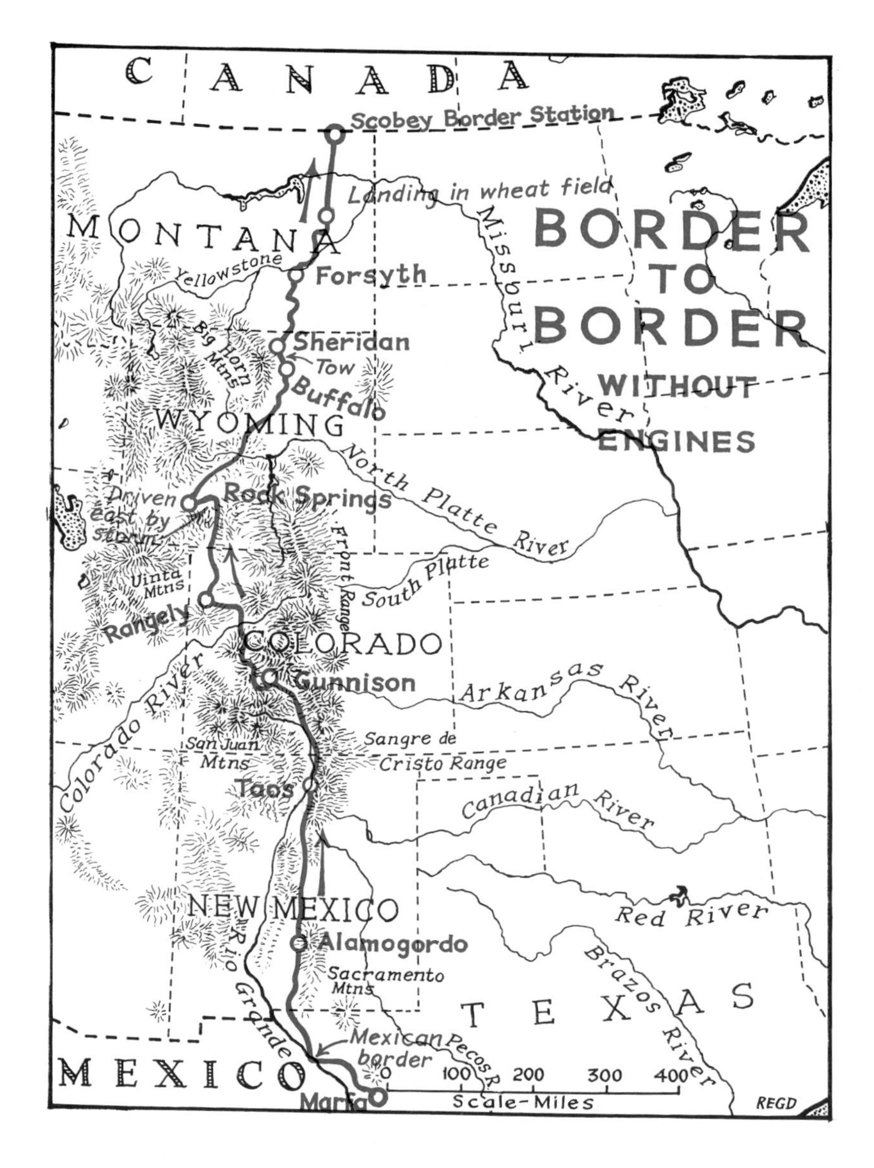

range in the afternoon, just when and where we should be. The wind was from the west and the sun was heating up the western slopes. Great! But the time had come to cross the valley to the west and over the mountains at Saguache—the lowest pass was more than 10,000 feet up—to reach Gunnison. This was not so great. We were now on the eastern slopes of the mountains in the lee wind.

Bad! We made it fine but Jim and I had to work a choppy thermal on the eastern slope to climb high enough to get over the top of the ridge. We thought we had enough altitude but, as we penetrated the western lee wind we lost more height than we expected, and had to dive for the ridgetop, hoping to find lift on the other side. If we made it we would have to trust our mountain-flying experience and find ridge lift on the west side. At fifty feet above the trees, almost to the crest, our instincts told us to turn back and land safely at Saguache but our experience told us to keep going, there would be ridge lift on the other side. Experience won out and we worked the ridge until we found a thermal which had worked its way up the valley. Then up we went. The final glide to Gunnison was great fun at one hundred knots."

Ironically, as opposed to Terry's flight, that had been one of my best days. Off behind Z9 I had found good lift and worked up the sides of the Sangre de Cristos, never low. I had flown slowly, waiting for the others to come along, but they never did. I crossed the Alamosa valley without incident and went easily over the crest of Terry's ridge into a long glide to Gunnison. What beautiful country! Bill Shurley's comment was, "I thought I was in Tibet and the Himalayas, it was breathtaking." I called in to the Unicom to report my approach and to advise them that there were three more gliders a few minutes behind me. They immediately wanted to know what services we would need. I told them that we would not be needing any fuel. Gunnison Valley Aviation was very helpful and furnished a large hangar to accommodate all of our sailplanes and the tow plane.

From Gunnison our planned stop was Rifle, Colorado, but in flight over some of the most beautiful snow-capped mountains with peaks well above 12,000 feet, real 'postcard' country, we elected to continue to Meeker and then on to Rangely, still in Colorado. Geographically, Rangely did not have the best of accommodations, but the people were nice and we were able to hangar the ships.

We checked into a hotel where the lady clerk, who must have had emphysema, was attached by a mask and very long hose to an oxygen tank somewhere out of sight: some fifty feet of hose coiled and strung out through the check-in, office, and home area. It took an hour and a half check-in and she smoked cigarettes the entire time. We were all afraid we would be blown up before we got out of there. One of us accidentally stepped on the hose but she never seemed to notice.

The crews had had a tough day. One vehicle overheated on the mountain roads and this had held their speed down at times to as little as 20mph. However, there were other comments as to the beauty of the area; the fields of columbines, and the mountain streams and valleys were a feast for the eyes.

We had trouble leaving Rangely. I towed first, ahead of W4, from a runway with a strong crosswind. Bill wisely made the decision to change runways for the other two tows. With the help of some local pilots, they pushed their ships about two miles, to be in position on a safer runway. Whisky Four and I were flying around for an hour and twenty minutes while watching a storm front come in from the west, and we were anxious to be under way. After everybody was in the air, the front, which was a dry sandstorm, drove us off course to the east. We ended up about twenty miles east of Rock Springs where we saw a gap in the storm and could see the airport. We ducked through the hole and landed at about three-thirty to find that the winds had torn down buildings and highway signs. The newspaper reported that the storm had hit at three p.m.

We awoke the next morning to drizzle and light hail. The ships were safely in the hangar, so we left the trailers and took off by road to Jackson Hole. We had intended to fly there, but drove the two hundred miles each way instead, stopping in Pinedale for lunch and finding 'pie heaven' at The Wrangler Cafe, with every kind a mouth-watering delight. We crowned our tow pilot, Bill Shurley, 'Pie King'.

Back at Rock Springs the following day our goal was now Sheridan, Wyoming, a 'fur piece' away. My story of this day should properly be written up in the 'Safety Corner'.

We had allowed the ground crews to depart before we towed. Off first and easing out on course, I was joined half an hour later by the rest of the group. Unfortunately, I was having trouble keeping up with them and soon lost visual contact. We were cruising well above 12,000 feet, often at 15,000 or 16,000 feet. I noticed that I was not making sense of things. Terry, who was invaluable as a navigator, not only for Z9 but also for the rest of us, was giving me explicit directions on how to follow them, but I seemed to have trouble doing so. I saw an airport that seemed to agree with his description of one near them, but the roads did not radiate in the right directions. I was confident that I was going in the correct direction, but my compass showed that I was heading at least forty-five degrees off course. I would not believe the compass and, in fact, told the others that there must be something wrong with it. Dr Crisp later said he wanted to ask if I was on oxygen because I "didn't sound right." Dolle said she knew I was not on course because she could hear me on the radio and not the others. The crews were well to the east of our course, and I was closer to them than the others.

Terry kept on asking me for my position until I finally told him, irritably, to quit asking me, and that when I knew where I was I would let him know. He then asked if I could see any snow-capped peaks from where I was. I could. Terry said, "Ned, Sheridan is just to the north of those peaks". I had enough sense left to head toward the snow and disregard all else. On the way to the mountains I sank lower and reached a range of mountains—the Bighorns—about forty miles east of Thermopolis, Wyoming. I was down to about 8,500 feet, had turned my oxygen off, and was taking a close look at a dirt road as a possible landing site. The other pilots were talking about a possibility of having to land at Thermopolis.

Flashback: Preparing to take off, back at Rock Springs, I had found the tube to my cannula pulled out and knew that if I tried to put it on in flight that I would probably pull it loose. So, I put it on while standing outside the airplane and rolled up the tube and put it into my shirt pocket, thinking that when I needed oxygen I would plug it in.

Finding lift, I climbed back to 12,000 feet where I tried to put the cannula on and pulled the tube loose. My pocket knife was handy so I cut the tube off and put it directly into my mouth only to find there was no oxygen flow. Tracing the tube, I found it just where I had placed it—in my pocket. I was later told by my crew that, had she been present at the time I took off, she would have seen to it that my oxygen tube was plugged in.

Now that things were more or less normal and I had located myself, I started up the highway which led through Buffalo to Sheridan, Wyoming. I was now on the best side of the Bighorns and the others were on the wrong side, where there was no lift. I arrived at Buffalo at 3,000 feet above the airport in the late afternoon. Though it was late in the day I might have been able to reach Sheridan, thirty-five miles away, but did not want to 'land out', so I landed at Buffalo.

Calling our contact phone in Lubbock, I found that the others had flown a few more miles after Thermopolis but had landed at Worland. After all that hassle, I was further along than they were. Dolle met me in Buffalo where we left the sailplane and trailer and drove on to Sheridan. Bill towed the others out of Worland that afternoon and supplied me a tow the next morning for the flight to Sheridan. Quite a day! One unexpected pleasure, for me, was landing at Buffalo on a runway that had once been part of a ranch belonging to a beloved uncle, Texas Grey Burleson.

We had wonderful help from the glider club in Sheridan, under the leadership of its president, Joe Burris, who again furnished hangars and support of all kinds.

Leaving Sheridan we headed north, across Montana, not really sure how far we would go. The further we went, the tougher it became. On this day, we were all low at one time or another. I was low only twenty miles out but climbed up to a reasonable altitude just as the others came along. Then, while I had no further trouble, Z9 and W4 were low over an airport at Ashland, Montana. Me Too went back to help and also ended low. Even though Z9 had his gear down to land, they all climbed out. But a thunderstorm approaching Forsyth determined that we had to land there. The storm arrived just as we secured the ships on the ramp. Jim Crisp reported that time as being his worst—he stood beside the Janus in the wind and rain, with his hand in the canopy vent holding the stick forward to keep the ship on the ground.

The next morning was still wet. Around the breakfast table there was some discussion about this being the last day. If we did not reach the Canadian border this day, M2 and Z9 felt they had to quit. It was Friday and they had to be at work on Monday. Someone turned to W4 and asked how much longer he could give to the project and Werner gave us another gem: "I don't know, what month is this?"

About ten a.m. the sky began to clear and we decided to make the attempt. We had also smugly commented that we appeared to be all set to go the distance without a single off-airport landing; however, I was to correct that situation.

Off first again and struggling to stay up, I drifted toward the town of Miles City, Montana. As conditions improved, the others got away and cut across on me a little so that I was twelve or fifteen miles behind when they reached the town of Brockway, near Circle, Montana. I assured them that I was okay and did not need help. Conditions were fair except for some rain showers. But I was running too low and pushing too hard. Suddenly finding myself very low and in heavy sink, I had to land in a wheat field just ten miles away from Circle. Fortunately, our guardian tow pilot was close enough to watch my landing. With the sailplane back on a runway at Circle and a new start the next morning I, too, arrived at the Scobey border station, north of the town of Scobey where the others had landed the evening before. The runway was a grass strip laying exactly on the border with customs stations of each country on either side. I was only sorry to have missed their celebration in Scobey, but I had some compensations for my late arrival. I was a day late, but far from being a dollar short, if measured in personal satisfaction.

I was able to wait in the air until Dolle was at the runway to see the landing, and I had my own welcoming committee. Two men, who had missed the excitement the day before, followed Dolle's trailer out of the town of Scobey, determined not to miss the last landing. Our little dog, Spunky, who did not like riding in the car, seemed to be glad the ordeal was over for her, too. She celebrated the occasion by going straight to the monument on the border at the end of the runway and decorating it in the approved canine tradition.

We had a wonderful trip, and a great experience which is hard to describe; but I think Wally Watson said it best, "Thank you Lord, for friends such as these."

Operation Dignity

The Pan American people were always family to me, as close in many ways as the family I grew up with. I was never more proud of this connection than when Ned Avary started an organization called 'Operation Dignity'.

Its purpose was to seek and find members of our Pan Am family who, for one reason or another, were unable to provide adequately for their own needs. Many of the early pilots did not have the benefit of a retirement plan that would cover the necessities of their later years; or, because of illness or poor planning, they (or their widows) had ended up nearly destitute.

Operation Dignity takes aggressive, affirmative action in identifying these cases and ensures that they receive a monthly stipend to provide for their essential requirements. Active and retired pilots alike contribute to this cause, and a fund is well in hand to accomplish and perpetuate this worthy goal.

Contributing to this cause gives me a very good feeling. Pan Am people taking care of their own, as a family should.

Captain Ned Wilson, not long before he retired, an older and wiser, not to say canny, captain of his ship. The picture was taken almost 40 years after the one used for the frontispiece of this book.

Postscript

To select appropriate events from over fifty years of flying was no easy task. I hope I have chosen those that will be of general interest, but I feel somewhat like the little boy who lost his chewing gum in the chicken coop and was not sure which pieces to pick up.

Pilots have sometimes been considered (at least by themselves) as a different breed from lesser mortals on the ground. One early Pan Am pilot was told so many times by his associates that he was crazy, that on his vacation he checked himself into a psychiatric hospital for an examination. Given a clean bill of health, he obtained a statement in writing and thereafter, when anyone called him 'crazy', he would pull out the statement, saying, "Here is my certificate saying I am sane. Where is yours?"

It seems to me that, in the last decade or so, airline pilots have been squeezed by regulations and standard procedures into a common mold. They think alike, act alike, and generally, even look alike. They have very little freedom for independent actions of their own. This may be a good thing, but I can not help but wonder what they are going to do when they are confronted with situations not covered by the manual.

It is a different world today. I read in an aviation magazine that a certain modern airplane was not designed to be flown manually. It still has that capability, but is expected to be flown entirely on the autopilot. The pilot is there, but is effectively no more than a systems manager. How long will it be before automation takes over completely?

These changes were inevitable but, as the old cowboy said when barbed-wire and pickup trucks came into this world, "I might accept it, but I don't have to like it."

I preferred the days when a pilot was in charge, and when there was the opportunity to try different ways of doing things, many of which became the standard procedures of today, evolved by pilots who had little or no written manual to go by.

Today I think it is more fun to fly a light airplane or a glider. I sympathize with the airline pilot flying his trip under the relentless microscope of regulation and media attention; having to submit to random drug testing of his blood and urine; and having almost every action of his working life dictated to him. I am glad that most of my flying was in another era.

I am sure that I would have enjoyed other careers had I not been an airline pilot. I could have been engaged in any profession performed out-of-doors, such as archeology, oceanography, or exploring, or even being a cowboy, and would probably have liked any of them. But I have enjoyed to the full the career that I did have, and I still enthusiastically ride on airliners 'with my head hanging out the window.'

Epilogue

Why has Pan American Airways, once the premier international airline, become only history today? There are many factors, economic and political, but I can only speak of what I have observed and learned through almost fifty years of association with Pan American. What I say may be colored by loyalty to the company which was my lifetime's source of bread and butter: the opinion of one person based largely on his association with fellow workers and on how he was treated as an employee.

During my entire career I never came face-to-face with Juan Trippe, but I was present at his funeral. I treasure a note sent to me afterwards by his wife, Betty, in which she said, "The pilots were, and are, the heart of the company."

In building Pan American's route system around the world Juan Trippe used very aggressive tactics. He bypassed governmental agencies and dealt directly, in many instances, with foreign governments, to obtain routes and landing rights. Air highways across both the Pacific and Atlantic were pioneered in this way. In doing this, in the formative years of the company, he certainly stepped on many toes, and later on earned the enmity of many who had long memories.

Having said this, I ask, in what other way could he have built his airline? To put such an empire together he had to act independently and in what might be considered a forthright, even ruthless manner. Pan American Airways could not have built its ocean-spanning network, from the Pacific Rim in the west to the countries of Europe in the east, if every decision had to be submitted to a committee.

Few people today understand how difficult it was to develop air routes over the remote areas of the world, especially over the vast ocean expanses during the early years. Thousands of operational problems had to be solved: navigation systems developed, fuel made available, radio stations put into place, landing fields constructed, accommodations arranged for passengers at remote sites (such as Wake Island or Midway) and above all, airplanes obtained that could negotiate the long over-water flights—no easy task in the 1930s.

So Pan American, under Juan Trippe, built itself into a worldwide enterprise which was, at that time, the finest air transport system available. And it was all accomplished in a single decade. In so doing it developed what must be called a monopoly among U.S. airline companies for international flying. It had no routes within the continental United States, at least not until more than forty years later. Back in the pioneering days there was no great clamor by other U.S. airlines for overseas routes. These airlines became interested only when it became easier to fly those routes that Pan Am had pioneered; when land-planes were able to replace the cumbersome flying boats, when communications, airfields, hotels, and myriads of other necessary items were in place. Pan Am was a major contributor to the war effort in airfield construction and technical support. But after Pan American led the way and the flying of these routes had become a normal operation, then, and only then, did the others want to be international airlines. Envy, too, played its part.

While Pan American had its monopoly among U.S. airlines, it still had to compete against the airlines of all the other countries into whose territories it carried the U.S. flag. Pan Am received a subsidy in the form of mail payments which at times reached as high as $2.00 per mile. For that, Pan American represented the Stars and Stripes around the world, and secured an entrée into many places that would otherwise have been difficult to obtain.

In many countries, for much of its lifetime, Pan American's local office offered more support and often represented its government more effectively than did the local U.S. consulate or embassy.

This situation did not last for ever. By the time I was flying for Pan Am, in the 1940s, other U.S. airlines were making inroads into international flying, and these continued and expanded over the years. Juan Trippe tried to have his 'Chosen Instrument' policy accepted, without success. He wanted a single airline to represent the United States overseas—a policy that was common in other countries. He was willing for this to be a consortium of all U.S. airlines, with each owning shares, but it was not to be—quite the contrary.

After World War II, the airlines of the United States continued to expand overseas; and Pan Am's monopoly was fast disappearing. At this stage it would have been only fair to allow Pan American to have some domestic routes to cross-feed with its international flights. And, when U.S. domestic airlines went overseas, they wanted to serve only the highly traveled destinations such as London, Tokyo, Frankfurt, or Rome; not Rangoon, Calcutta, Istanbul or Lisbon: places that Pan Am had faithfully served for years, but where the traffic potential was not too substantial.

Other countries too began to push Pan American out in favor of their own developing airlines. These countries reduced the number of schedules that Pan Am had earlier been permitted, required flights at inopportune hours, and used other, more subtle, tactics. In many places we were made to park in some obscure place on the airport where our insignia would not be visible from the terminal building. And still Pan American could not obtain routes within the United States. At about this time, I think, Pan Am began its slide.

Pan American was the first U.S. airline to order jet aircraft. The initial order of twenty-five Douglas DC-8s and twenty Boeing 707s launched the United States into the jet age and gave Pan Am an edge for a while. The jets were outstandingly successful. Perhaps encouraged by this, Juan Trippe put in an order for some forty-five Boeing 747s. Many have said that was his downfall. Perhaps it was too many and too early, but it was a reasonable decision at the time. He did not foresee the fuel shortage and consequent high fuel prices. Boeing 747s do burn quite a lot of fuel and newer aircraft flying the Atlantic do so far more economically. In general, longer flights and larger aircraft make more money than shorter flights. However, that is with the critical provision that the flight is carrying a sufficient number of paying customers. At times, such as during the recession following the so-called fuel crisis, many flights were flying with fewer than break-even numbers. At such times the large 747 became a liability.

With the arrival of turbine-powered aircraft the F.A.A. required, in contrast to piston-engined airplanes, an extra ten percent of the fuel required to fly from departure to destination. On a long flight such as Los Angeles to London this can amount to many thousands of pounds of fuel. Many pilots, of the older school, liked to carry even more, for 'Mama and the kids'. One such pilot told me, "The only time you can have too much fuel is when you are on fire."

During the fuel crisis of the seventies we were discouraged from carrying 'stored' fuel because on the long flights we would burn as much as one third of it just to carry it. It takes the same amount of fuel to carry a given weight whether that weight is composed of passengers, freight, or jet fuel. One captain who customarily liked to have extra fuel, once asked, in London, to have ten thousand pounds of stored fuel put on. The dispatcher said, "Captain, remember that you will burn three thousand of that in order to carry it to Los Angeles." The intent was to discourage the loading of the extra fuel, but the captain's reply was, "Oh yes, that is so; put on thirteen thousand pounds." He was not to be thwarted.

The Boeing 747 is one of the most reliable aircraft built, but even so it is occasionally grounded for needed mechanical repairs. If that happens in Pago Pago or Rangoon it takes much longer to bring in a replacement; not the same as in Chicago or Boston. During such delays Pan American has incurred many expenses, including accommodations and re-routing for passengers. To bring in and replace an engine, which sometimes has had to be done, was a major expense.

International flying is just not as simple as domestic flying. The Civil Aeronautics Board did make the right decision in the case of PANAGRA, owned equally by Pan American and by the W.R. Grace Corporation. The government determined that Grace must sell its half and the C.A.B. recommended that Pan American be allowed to buy it. However, Lyndon Johnson, as president, overrode that decision and granted the entire airline (including Pan Am's portion) to Braniff. Where is Braniff today? Trying to expand overseas at too rapid a rate was a major reason for its downfall.

Over the years, many who worked for Pan Am were distressed at the injustices we observed. QANTAS, flying into Los Angeles, paid only a small landing fee of a few hundred dollars while Pan Am paid $5,000 to land at Sydney. Flying over the same routes with Pan Am, Japan Air Lines was operating 747s purchased through the Export Import Bank at very low interest rates; while Pan Am, at the same time, was paying interest rates of eleven to fifteen percent. High debt was another factor in Pan Am's troubles.

Who Needed National?

I think the management of Pan Am had become so obsessed with obtaining domestic routes that they jumped unnecessarily at the opportunity to buy National Airlines. National was on its way to bankruptcy, its aircraft types, primarily Douglas, did not match Pan Am's, primarily Boeing. Its route structure was a doubtful fit, and deregulation was on the way. Yet Pan Am, already in trouble itself, took on National. This resulted in tremendous problems of integrating aircraft, pilot groups and other personnel, changing route structures, and so on. Sadly, Pan Am did not wait just a few short months for deregulation.

I remember well having a copilot with me on a flight from San Francisco who told me, "I may be blue on the outside, but I'm still orange (National's color) on the inside." Management may think that a pilot is a pilot, but when people do not work well together they do not bring out their best for their employer.

Management

In the early days Pan American invariably developed its management from inside the company. When Juan Trippe stepped down from the presidency, Harold Gray, who had come up from the pilot ranks, took over. But he died prematurely from cancer and Najeeb Halaby succeeded him. Many in the company thought that Halaby had been lured away from the position of administrator of the F.A.A. in the hope that he could have some influence in obtaining domestic routes and perhaps other concessions from Washington. It did not happen. Managements followed managements but ill-judged decisions continued to be made with horrendous results, and worse, decisions were not followed through. It seemed that we were on a train that kept changing tracks. Pan Am began to be sold off, piece by piece. The Pacific routes went for little more than the cost of a few 747s, and this at a time when Pacific Rim prosperity was in the ascendancy—and still is. Interests in the Intercontinental Hotels and the Pan Am Building were sold. In every case we were told that these sales were necessary to obtain cash for operating expenses, and that these specific assets were sold because they were the parts that would bring in the most money. Perhaps that is correct, but it seems to me that some way should have been found to retain those assets. It reminded me of a coyote gnawing off his own leg to escape a trap.

The Pan Am Spirit

All the while talent inside the company was being wasted. My friend and fellow pilot, Jim Waugh, is a case in point. In 1977, when Jim was senior vice president, maintenance and engineering, Guatemala experienced a severe earthquake. A friend in Houston had gathered a large quantity of medical and similar supplies donated for victims of the 'quake. He called to ask me if I could persuade Pan Am to haul them to Guatemala at no cost to him. I approached the Houston station manager who told me that it was impossible. I then called Jim Waugh in New York and left a message for him to call me at home. He returned the call the next day and said, "Ned, I did not return your call yesterday because I was sure of what you wanted. I know you are concerned about Guatemala. I have arranged for Pan Am to let you put supplies on for three days. After the normal load is determined for the day, your people can load the airplane up to full gross weight with relief supplies for Guatemala."

Jim's proudest accomplishment was his part in the development of the crew concept, known as 'Cockpit Resource Management', which has been adopted, world-wide, throughout the industry. He retired as senior vice president operations.

After he and I had both retired I received a telephone call from Washington, D.C. It was Mr Justin Dart, commissioner of the Rehabilitation Services Administration (RSA), who is also a friend and neighbor of mine. He was attempting to have a physically handicapped person, wheelchair-bound, brought to the United States from Japan, and Pan Am's staff in Tokyo was refusing to board him. I called Jim Waugh who, though retired, managed to arrange for this passenger to be boarded the next day and to be accompanied and looked after by a Pan Am employee who was traveling on vacation.

I recite those two instances because Jim Waugh was typical of those who had the 'Pan Am heart' and was also talented enough to hold any position in top management.

Hopes and Fears

Did Pan Am fail because of Juan Trippe's earlier actions? Was it government regulation? Was it poor management? Was it heavy debt? Was it a loss of spirit among employees? Most likely it was a combination of all of these. Yet, until the bitter end we still had hope.

The last flight that my wife and I made with Pan Am revealed both the good and the bad. We arrived in New York, tickets in hand for travel to Tel Aviv, only to find that in the time since we had left Texas the flight had been reduced from twice a day to a single flight. Instead of a 747 there was a much smaller Airbus. The flight went through Paris and tickets were being sold at bargain prices, so the flights were oversold. It reminded me of the fellow selling peanuts below cost. He said that he was losing money on every bag, but made it up on volume.

We checked in, on standby, but could not board. Our bags, however, were marked 'standby' and away they went, in violation of regulations, to Tel Aviv. I was assured that the bags would be returned on the next flight but, when I went to the lost baggage department, two days later, to claim them, I encountered a rude and unpleasant employee who did not care in the least if I found my luggage or not. Though I had received a wire informing me that they were arriving that day, she refused to call customs to check on them and informed me that, even if they had arrived, it would be three days before they would be in the baggage room. I could not resist telling her that she was part of the reason Pan Am was in such a bad way.

We were rescued by a stewardess, coming off duty from a long night flight who, on her own time, stopped to be of help. Recognizing our distress, and without knowing that we were retirees, she led us to another office where a young man named Green made a quick phone call, verified that the luggage had arrived, and said he would have them in his office in twenty minutes. He was as good as his word and we boarded a flight to an alternate destination, Zürich, an hour later. These two restored my faith in at least some Pan Am employees.

I am proud to have worked for Pan American. Many of the pilots with whom I flew had operated the flying boats, such as the Boeing 314, in other areas before coming to what became the Western Division of Pan American. These pilots had pioneered the procedures of ocean flying which later arrivals were able to use to their advantage. We had a shared pride in Pan American and in ourselves. The management treated us with respect and gave us a latitude to make decisions and to fly the airplane as we thought best. Do you remember what I said about the instructions I was given by the chief pilot when I checked out as captain? The emphasis was on safety. I was lucky to have known, and flown with, such a fine group of people.

"A prophet is not without honour, save in his own country" (Matthew 13:57). Having done its most outstanding work outside the United States, Pan American never became a recognized name inside the States, except to knowledgeable people in the industry; it was far better-known and respected around the world. In its prime, it was the world's only megacarrier—to us a contemporary fashionable term, and the world may never see its like again.

The Family Breaks Up

Corporations are supposed to be inanimate. So, who but the shareholders care if they go under? But it is not like that. We who have been with Pan Am, which supplied us a good livelihood, a way to raise our families, and above all, gave us a marvelous way of life, consider it a family. I have known many who left Pan Am to work elsewhere and gained better titles and more pay. When you talk to them Pan Am always shows in their hearts.

So, though we had hope right to the end, the show is over. I cry for those employees left without jobs, pensions, health care, or insurance.

Goodbye Pan Am, it was fun while it lasted.

The Last Clipper

by Mark S. Pyle

I once subscribed to a publication by the name of *Aviation Quarterly*. It was remarkable in its quality, its appreciation of aviation, and its unrelenting pursuit of excellence. It was hardbound and worthy of your favorite lounge chair and a snifter of choice brandy. I was a *life time* charter member of this *now defunct* relic. It belongs to history. NOTHING IS FOREVER! My airline now belongs to the past as surely as my aging lot of forgotten magazines. Pan American World Airways is lost...lost to corporate ineptitude, governmental indifference, and an inability to change with the world it helped bring together.

"It looks like a beautiful day to go flying," First Officer Robert Knox of Greensboro N.C., stated. We began our ritual of checking the weather along our route of flight. Flight 219, bound for Bridgetown, Barbados, was one hour from departure. We completed the necessary paperwork that ensured the trip would meet all legal requirements of performance and weight and balance. We were more than businesslike, because CNN had reported the night before that Delta Air Lines had withdrawn its support for our newly-proposed company. On most occasions, a comment or two about sports or hobbies would be mentioned at a pre-departure briefing. Individuals who had not flown together before used such small talk to break the ice of unfamiliarity. This morning was certainly different...an air of finality hung about everyone at our counter. The fact that it was six a.m. further depressed the atmosphere. The engineer, Chuck Freeman of Washington, D.C., was pouring over the fuel figures. He had just returned to the Boeing 727 from its much larger cousin the 747 and was having difficulty rationalizing the reduced fuel load. It was only his second trip on the 727 since his removal from the larger equipment. Many pilots were downgraded. A result of the Delta purchase of our remaining European routes.

We walked briskly to our aircraft...Ship #368, one of the newest 727s in the fleet and quite a pleasure to fly with its more powerful engines and spirited performance. Pan Am had many 727s but most were older. The engines were always adequate but would not produce the kick in the seat of this newer model. It was with a feeling of quiet pride, generated by command of such a machine that I stowed my gear in the cockpit. I then walked aft to greet the flight attendants that would complete our ship's company on this beautiful New York morning.

Immediately the purser questioned the Delta withdrawal and my answer was the same as it would be to my cockpit crew members, "Whatever the day held, we would make it a good trip." All agreed that it would be, whether as the *first* of many, as the promised 'Born Again' Pan Am with roots in Miami, or the *last* of many.

We acknowledged the pushback clearance from our ground team, or what had been our ground team. Now attired in their Delta uniforms there was a sense of unreality as we left the gate. Our aircraft responded in its usual marvelous manner: the engines whined to life as though longing to push onward into the promise of this cloudless morning. A salute was given from the ground team and we were off. Navigational computer engaged, we took our place on the runway as the final check list items, routine with years of repetition, were completed.

As we gathered speed, I marveled at what fine engines the wonderful folks at Pratt and Whitney had provided for us. Gently, I eased the nose of this beautiful airplane skyward, the sound of rushing wind, and whirring instruments added to what is always a magic moment in every pilot's life. The ground fell rapidly away and the sky above beckoned. Both man and machine were happy to oblige. We turned away from the familiar Manhattan skyline and pointed the nose of *Clipper Goodwill* south—toward the Island of Barbados.

After leveling at 31,000 feet, the routine of monitoring engine and navigational instruments settled in. The conversation once again turned, to what felt to be, the betrayal of our airline by what we had all thought was a corporate good guy. My wife and I had discussed this abandonment only the night before, as no doubt thousands of Pan American employees had done. Not a visionary by any means, I had detailed my fears along these same lines from the day the agreement was finalized. "The Delta promises were necessary to cement the agreement and nothing more," I had said, and all along I had hoped to be wrong! Like many of my friends, I was not fortunate enough to transfer, or more correctly, was not qualified on the right airplane, the Airbus A310. (Delta only wanted certain groups of pilots based primarily on airplane qualification.) We could only count on the good faith of Delta. After all, wasn't the company known for its corporate integrity?

Bermuda passed behind us, that incredible twenty-one square miles-piece of volcanic rock, where I had spent my last Christmas on layover. There were many happy memories there and other places, all associated with destinations of what had been a world carrier. Tokyo, Seoul, Bangkok, Manila, and Beijing; Berlin, Frankfurt, London, Venice, Oslo, and Istanbul. All held memories as did so many more cities. Destinations pioneered largely by previous Pan Am employees.

Only a few puffy cumulus clouds, airborne cotton balls, blocked our way to Bridgetown as we began our descent. The approach along the western coast of Barbados is so surreal, a truly multicolored jewel set in a background of turquoise sea. We landed to the east, as the winds of trade nearly always dictate, touching down four hours and thirty minutes after our departure from Kennedy. Taxi to the gate and shutdown of our engines occurred as they had hundreds of times before, this time there would be a difference. A notable difference! In the two hundred and seventy minutes of our flight, tragic history had been made.

The station manager approached as he always did and greeted the inbound passengers. He then stepped into our office (the cockpit) and greeted us cordially, explaining he had bad news. I quickly responded that I thought we could guess the nature of his grim tidings. He produced a message from New York operations in a very familiar format, however, with content *never* before inscribed on any Pan American document in its sixty-four-year history. Pan Am, as of 0900 on 4 December 1991, had ceased operations. None of our flight attendants could restrain their emotions, or their tears. All were at least twenty-year veterans with Pan American or National Airlines. Disbelief and resentment of the Delta betrayal were vented and consoling them prevented those of us in the cockpit from showing our own pent-up feelings.

Our station manager asked us if we would operate the trip to Miami. He would find a way to buy fuel. There were many stranded passengers and some Pan Am employees were packing to leave their station and their jobs.

We informed the station manager that we would delay as long as possible. This would ensure that all those wishing to return to Miami had time to board. We waited over two hours in mostly silent thought while the passengers gathered from their hotels and employees packed their belongings.

At one point the local airport employees who had served Pan Am so well, and whom Pan Am had so well served, came to the aircraft. A tearful ceremony followed. Flowers and good wishes were exchanged. The local television station requested interviews. Airport employees barraged the *Clipper Goodwill* for last pictures which would adorn family scrapbooks.

At two p.m. E.S.T., the wheels came up on Clipper 436, hailing from Bridgetown, Barbados, and bound for the city of Pan Am's birth. Few words were exchanged as time passed with silent thought. San Juan Center cleared our flight direct to Miami and I punched in the navigational coordinates for

Miami International a final time. There is little to be said when faced with a solemn reality. Our reality was the certain knowledge of dead-end careers. It can best be summed up as a death in your immediate family. Pan American was my family in every sense. It was the corporate family to thousands.

My thoughts are interrupted by the engineer as we began our descent into Miami. "Should I call in range?" "Yes," I said, "Someone will surely still be there. The planes must be put to bed." He spoke again in my direction very softly, so softly I could not understand, "Pardon me?" I said. This veteran engineer of over twenty-five years choked back tears through clouded eyes. He said, "Mark, we're the last flight—the final flight." That circumstance had never occurred to me. He continued, "They want us to make a low pass over the field." I said, "Your kidding, right—they're joking!" Privately, I thought it might be a friend who had landed before me, now pulling my leg. "No joke," said Chuck. "They are going to be there to meet us, some kind of ceremony."

Miami lay before us, a cold front had just passed and fog followed the coast line. It extended out to sea almost to the Bahamas. Miami sat on the other side of the fog bank, eerie and beautiful at the same time. Dinner Key lay nestled in the fog. My mind raced at the finality of what I was doing. This was not just the end of my career! Careers of individuals were far surpassed, by the passing into history of this airline. Franklin Roosevelt had left from that same Dinner Key. Aboard the *Dixie Clipper* he was bound for Casablanca in 1943, the first American president to fly while in office. Pan Am had not just been a part of history, it had made history for all of its sixty-four years. It was always there when the government needed it. Indeed Pan American Clippers had many scars as mementos from encounters with enemies of the United States. From Japanese bullet holes, received (as a lumbering Clipper evacuated key military personnel from Wake Island) during the early stages of World War II, to the terrorist bombing of Clipper 103. More recently, Pan Am pilots and planes had aided in *Operation Desert Storm.* It was a Pan American Clipper that had brought me home from Vietnam. Now there was only *Clipper Goodwill* and this last crew. This final flight.

With the passengers briefed carefully as to our intentions, I called for flaps fifteen. We descended on the electronic glideslope that had so often guided me to Miami. We now executed the requested low pass, my first since I left the Navy many years ago. As we flew down the centerline of Runway 12, I noted the line up of American Airlines aircraft that would soon take our place. At the completion of the low pass the tower issued a final statement. "Outstanding Clipper!"

Pulling up and turning downwind for our final approach and landing I looked at the beautiful Miami Airport and the city she serves. We all realized it would be the last time. Again the finality of this moment slams my senses. My wheels touch for the concluding time in a Pan American aircraft. The last time for a scheduled revenue flight of *any kind* for this airline of history.

Approaching the taxiway we begin to see the reception that stretches before us. Airport vehicles of every description line the taxiway and video cameras abound. Police and security vehicles, port authority and fire equipment. Lines of individuals in semi-military formation are everywhere. As we taxi past the first formations, men and women come to brisk attention and render military salute to 'The Last of the Clippers'. My eyes then tear for the first time. Many rows of men and machines, all smartly formed, all make salute. I return the salute just as crisply, fully knowing that their salutes are to this Machine and all the Machines that have borne the title Clipper for sixty-four years. Their salute is to the history that this ship represents and all that has gone before.

We pass the line of fire equipment. The water cannon is fired over the aircraft. (My emotions reel under the weight of this tribute to Pan Am's last flight.) I engage the windshield wiper to clear water that is on the windscreen, but that does little good for the water in my eyes. My first officer fights back his tears. For twenty-three years he has worn Pan Am blue.

One final formation of men, all Pan American ground personnel, tender their last salute. We approach the gate and set the brakes for the last time. We shut down systems for the last time and secure the faithful engines. Sadly, gathering our belongings, we shake hands. Our final flight is over. There were no dry eyes in the cockpit. Many of the departing passengers shared our moment of grief. The tears for Pan Am will continue.

Upon return to my home, our thirteen-year-old son presented me with a letter. Through his own tears, he named me Pan Am's greatest pilot. For one brief moment, on one tearful occasion, ...I was.